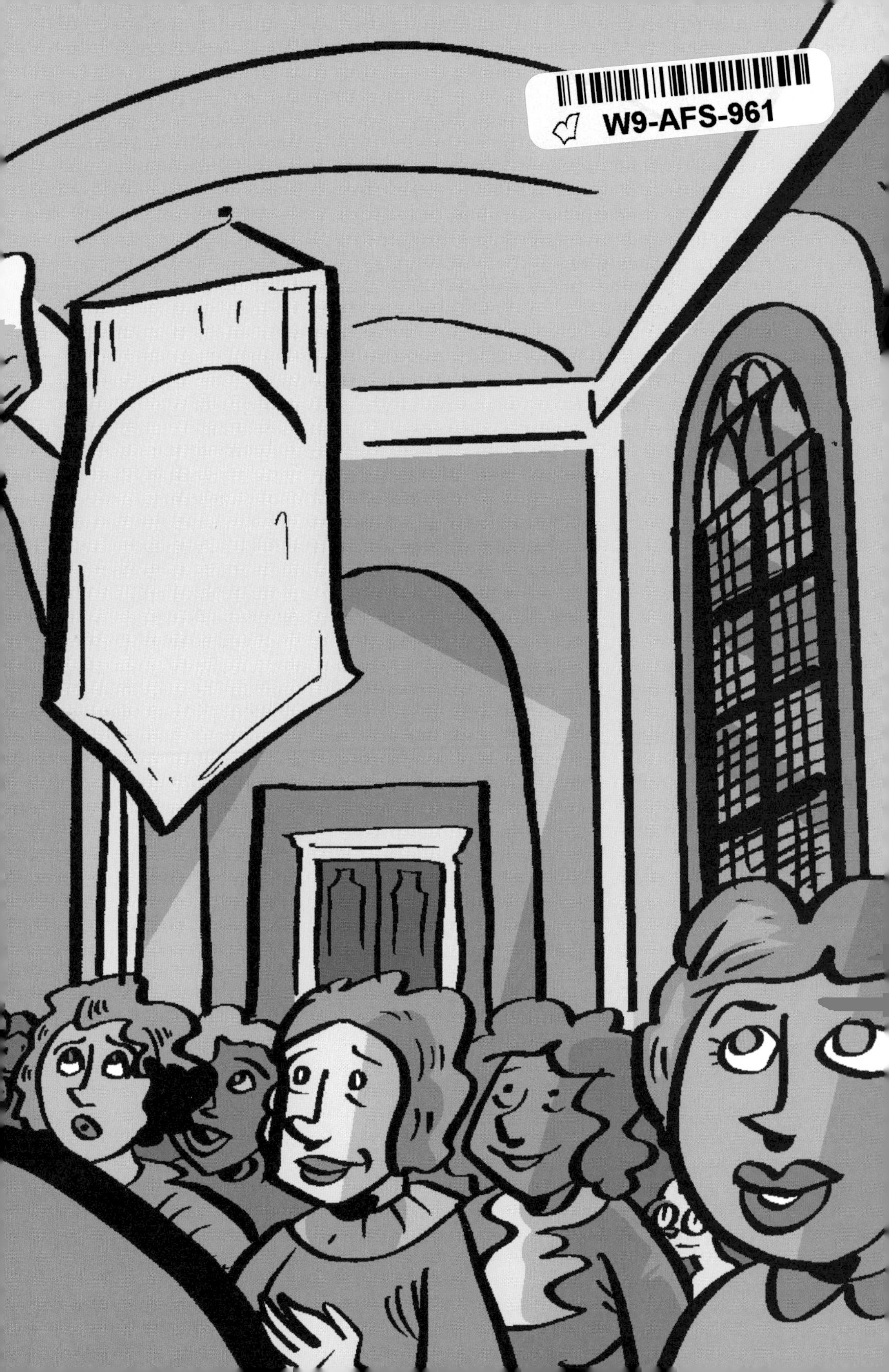

# SHOW ME HISTORY!

# SUSAN B. ANTHONY

## CHAMPION for VOTING RIGHTS!

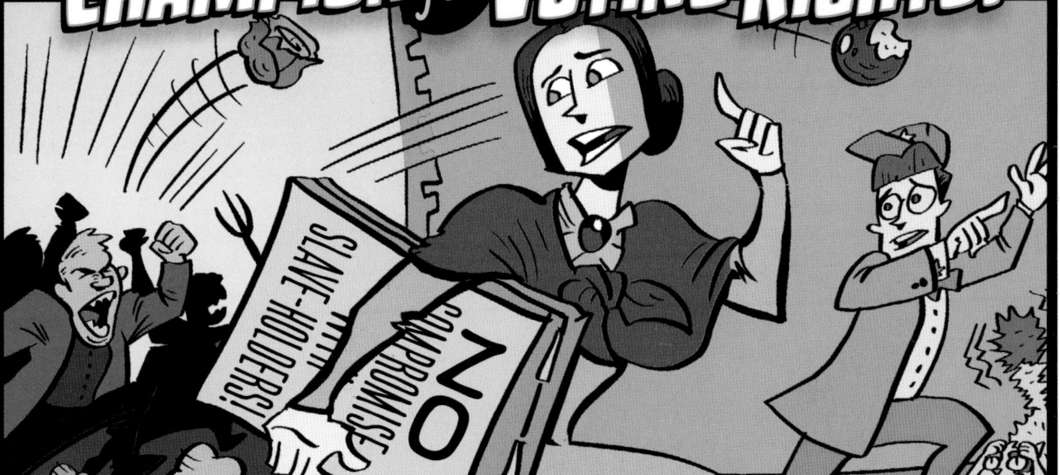
SLAVE-HOLDERS!
NO COMPROMISE

BY
MARK SHULMAN

ILLUSTRATED BY
KELLY TINDALL

LETTERING & DESIGN BY
COMICRAFT

COVER ART BY
IAN CHURCHILL

PORTABLE PRESS
SAN DIEGO, CALIFORNIA

## Portable Press

An imprint of Printers Row Publishing Group
10350 Barnes Canyon Road, Suite 100, San Diego, CA 92121
www.portablepress.com • mail@portablepress.com

Printers Row Publishing Group is a division of Readerlink Distribution Services, LLC. Portable Press is a registered trademark of Readerlink Distribution Services, LLC.

Correspondence regarding the content of this book should be addressed to Portable Press, Editorial Department, at the above address. Author or illustrator inquiries should be addressed to Oomf, Inc., www.oomf.com.

Publisher: Peter Norton
Associate Publisher: Ana Parker
Developmental Editor: Vicki Jaeger
Senior Product Manager: Kathryn C. Dalby
Production Team: Jonathan Lopes, Rusty von Dyl

**O•MF** Created at Oomf, Inc., www.Oomf.com
Director: Mark Shulman
Producer: James Buckley Jr.

Author: Mark Shulman
Illustrator: Kelly Tindall
Inker: Chris Peterson
Colorist: Shane Corn
Lettering & design by Comicraft: John Roshell,
    Forest Dempsey, & Sarah Jacobs
Cover illustrator: Ian Churchill

Library of Congress Cataloging-in-Publication Data

Names: Shulman, Mark, 1962- author. | Tindall, Kelly, illustrator. |
  Churchill, Ian, illustrator. | Comicraft (Firm), letterer, book
  designer.
Title: Susan B. Anthony: champion for voting rights! / by Mark Shulman;
  illustrated by Kelly Tindall; lettering & design by Comicraft; cover
  art by Ian Churchill.
Description: San Diego, CA: Printers Row Publishing Group, [2019] |
  Audience: Ages 8-12. | Summary: "Learn about the amazing Susan B.
  Anthony as she fought for social equality and women's suffrage"--
  Provided by publisher.
Identifiers: LCCN 2019021310 | ISBN 9781645170747 (hardcover) |
  ISBN 9781645173724 (ebook)
Subjects: LCSH: Anthony, Susan B. (Susan Brownell), 1820-1906--Juvenile
  literature. | Anthony, Susan B. (Susan Brownell), 1820-1906--Comic
  books, strips, etc. | Women social reformers--United
  States--Biography--Juvenile literature. | Suffragists--United
  States--Biography--Juvenile literature. | Suffragists--United
  States--Biography--Comic books, strips, etc. | Feminists--United
  States--Biography--Juvenile literature. | Feminists--United
  States--Biography--Comic books, strips, etc.
Classification: LCC HQ1413.A55 S487 2019 | DDC 305.42092 [B]--dc23
LC record available at https://lccn.loc.gov/2019021310

Printed in China

24 23 22 21 20   1 2 3 4 5

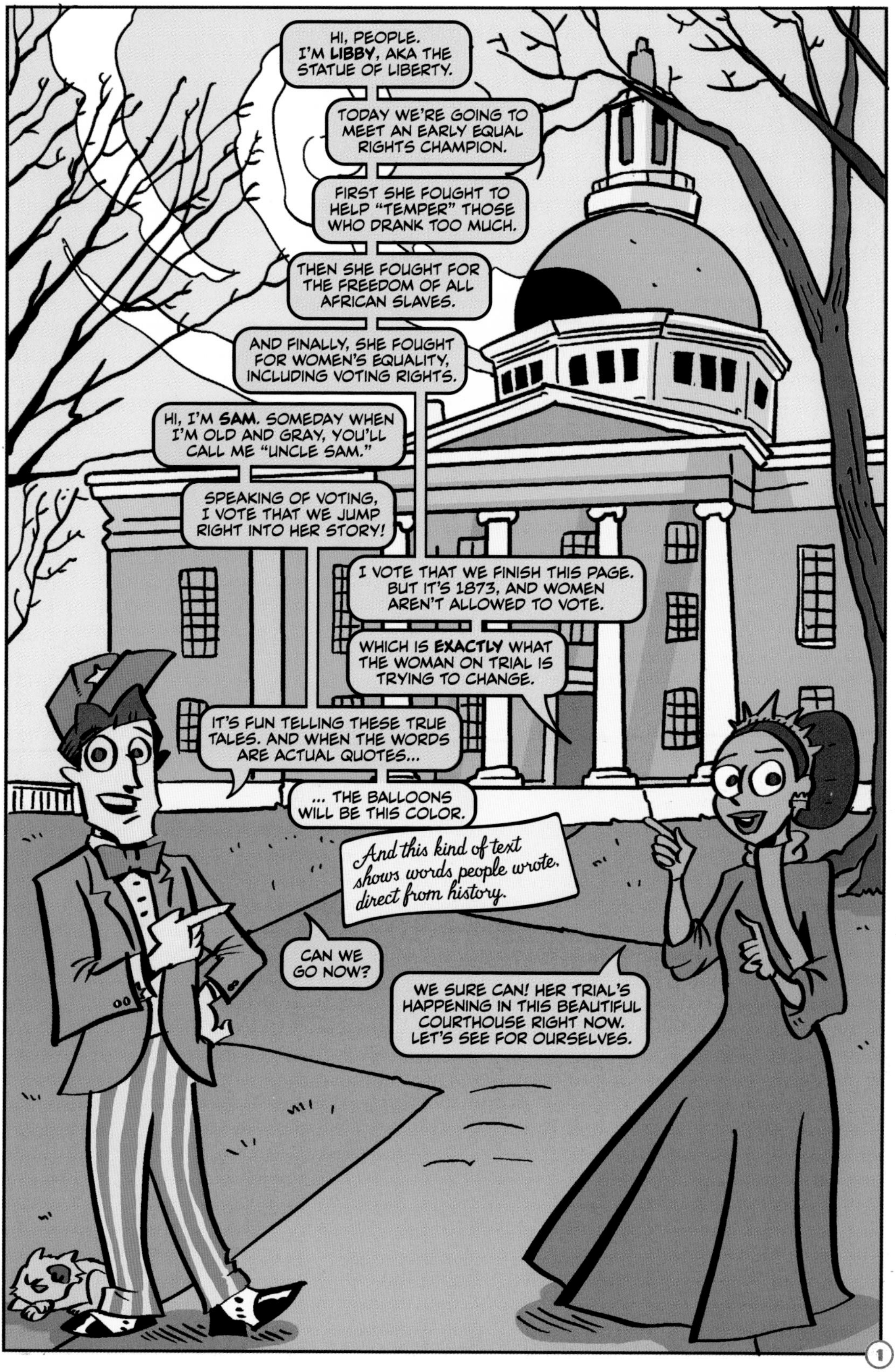
HI, PEOPLE. I'M LIBBY, AKA THE STATUE OF LIBERTY.
TODAY WE'RE GOING TO MEET AN EARLY EQUAL RIGHTS CHAMPION.
FIRST SHE FOUGHT TO HELP "TEMPER" THOSE WHO DRANK TOO MUCH.
THEN SHE FOUGHT FOR THE FREEDOM OF ALL AFRICAN SLAVES.
AND FINALLY, SHE FOUGHT FOR WOMEN'S EQUALITY, INCLUDING VOTING RIGHTS.
HI, I'M SAM. SOMEDAY WHEN I'M OLD AND GRAY, YOU'LL CALL ME "UNCLE SAM."
SPEAKING OF VOTING, I VOTE THAT WE JUMP RIGHT INTO HER STORY!
I VOTE THAT WE FINISH THIS PAGE. BUT IT'S 1873, AND WOMEN AREN'T ALLOWED TO VOTE.
WHICH IS EXACTLY WHAT THE WOMAN ON TRIAL IS TRYING TO CHANGE.
IT'S FUN TELLING THESE TRUE TALES. AND WHEN THE WORDS ARE ACTUAL QUOTES...
... THE BALLOONS WILL BE THIS COLOR.
And this kind of text shows words people wrote, direct from history.
CAN WE GO NOW?
WE SURE CAN! HER TRIAL'S HAPPENING IN THIS BEAUTIFUL COURTHOUSE RIGHT NOW. LET'S SEE FOR OURSELVES.

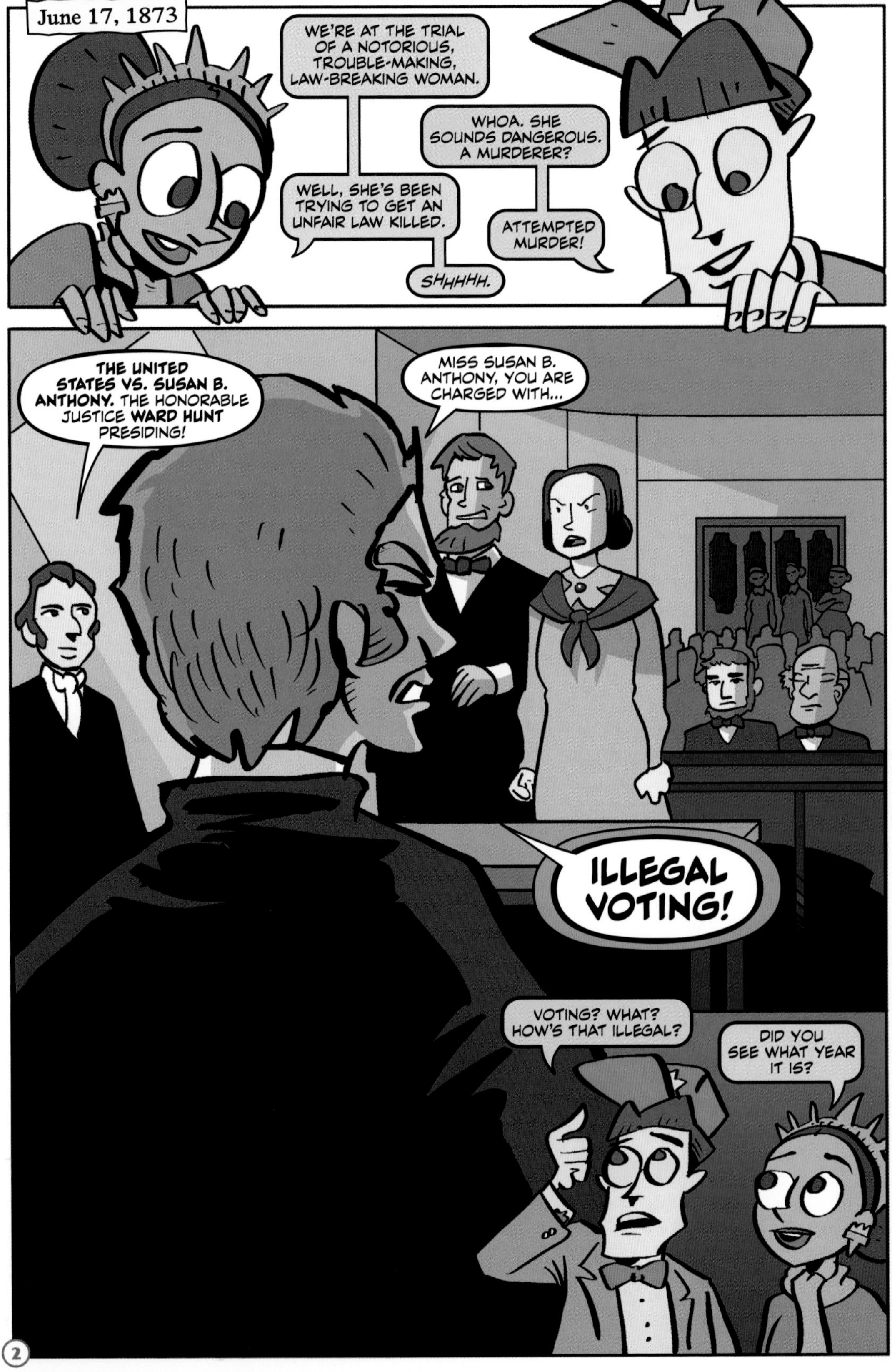

June 17, 1873
WE'RE AT THE TRIAL OF A NOTORIOUS, TROUBLE-MAKING, LAW-BREAKING WOMAN.
WHOA. SHE SOUNDS DANGEROUS. A MURDERER?
WELL, SHE'S BEEN TRYING TO GET AN UNFAIR LAW KILLED.
ATTEMPTED MURDER!
SHHHHH.
THE UNITED STATES VS. SUSAN B. ANTHONY. THE HONORABLE JUSTICE WARD HUNT PRESIDING!
MISS SUSAN B. ANTHONY, YOU ARE CHARGED WITH...
ILLEGAL VOTING!
VOTING? WHAT? HOW'S THAT ILLEGAL?
DID YOU SEE WHAT YEAR IT IS?

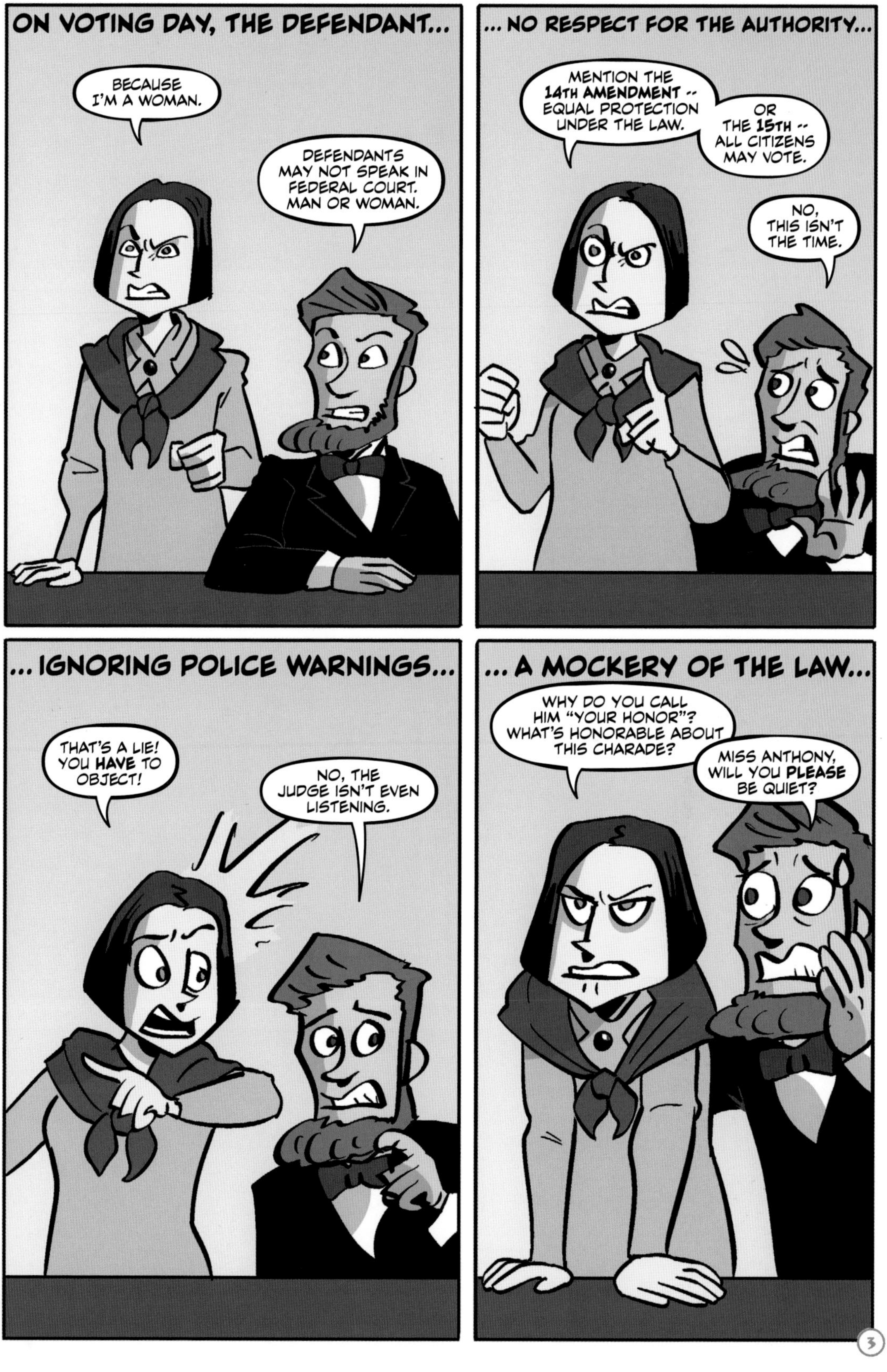
ON VOTING DAY, THE DEFENDANT...
BECAUSE I'M A WOMAN.
DEFENDANTS MAY NOT SPEAK IN FEDERAL COURT. MAN OR WOMAN.
... NO RESPECT FOR THE AUTHORITY...
MENTION THE **14TH AMENDMENT** -- EQUAL PROTECTION UNDER THE LAW.
OR THE **15TH** -- ALL CITIZENS MAY VOTE.
NO, THIS ISN'T THE TIME.
... IGNORING POLICE WARNINGS...
THAT'S A LIE! YOU **HAVE** TO OBJECT!
NO, THE JUDGE ISN'T EVEN LISTENING.
... A MOCKERY OF THE LAW...
WHY DO YOU CALL HIM "YOUR HONOR"? WHAT'S HONORABLE ABOUT THIS CHARADE?
MISS ANTHONY, WILL YOU **PLEASE** BE QUIET?

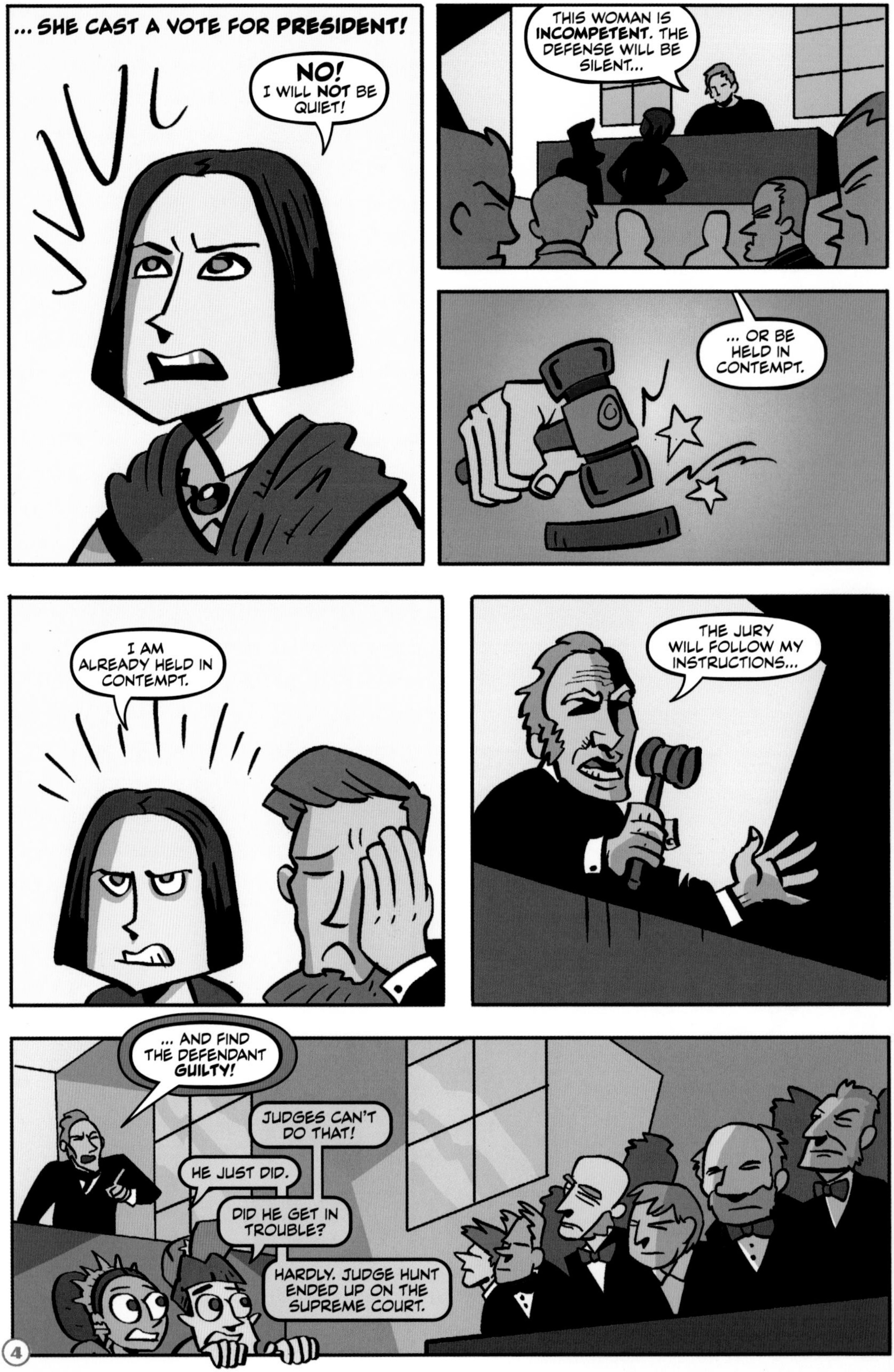
... SHE CAST A VOTE FOR PRESIDENT!
NO! I WILL NOT BE QUIET!
THIS WOMAN IS INCOMPETENT. THE DEFENSE WILL BE SILENT...
... OR BE HELD IN CONTEMPT.
I AM ALREADY HELD IN CONTEMPT.
THE JURY WILL FOLLOW MY INSTRUCTIONS...
... AND FIND THE DEFENDANT GUILTY!
JUDGES CAN'T DO THAT!
HE JUST DID.
DID HE GET IN TROUBLE?
HARDLY. JUDGE HUNT ENDED UP ON THE SUPREME COURT.

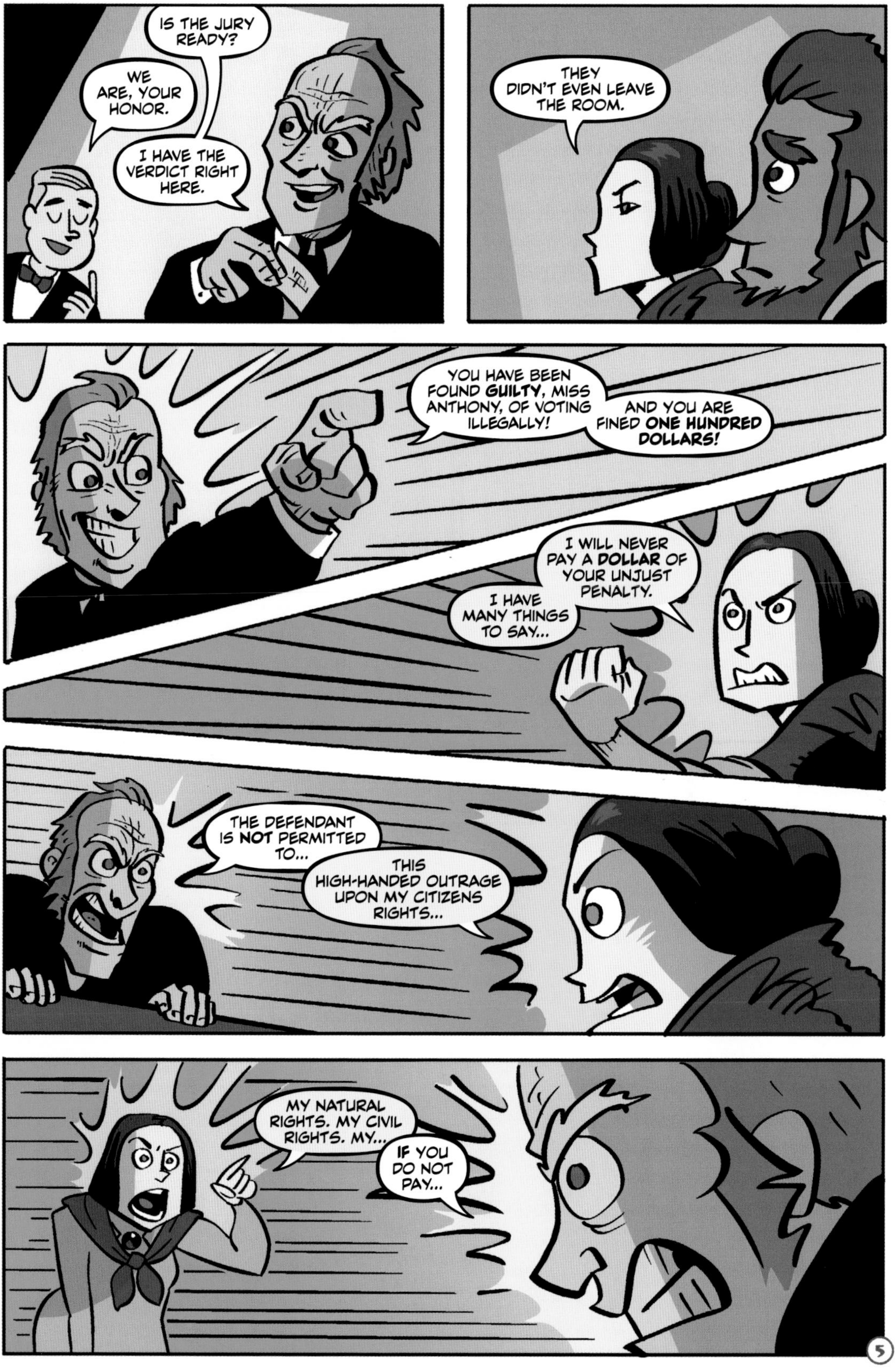
IS THE JURY READY?
WE ARE, YOUR HONOR.
I HAVE THE VERDICT RIGHT HERE.
THEY DIDN'T EVEN LEAVE THE ROOM.
YOU HAVE BEEN FOUND **GUILTY**, MISS ANTHONY, OF VOTING ILLEGALLY!
AND YOU ARE FINED **ONE HUNDRED DOLLARS!**
I WILL NEVER PAY A **DOLLAR** OF YOUR UNJUST PENALTY.
I HAVE MANY THINGS TO SAY...
THE DEFENDANT IS **NOT** PERMITTED TO...
THIS HIGH-HANDED OUTRAGE UPON MY CITIZENS RIGHTS...
MY NATURAL RIGHTS. MY CIVIL RIGHTS. MY...
**IF** YOU DO NOT PAY...

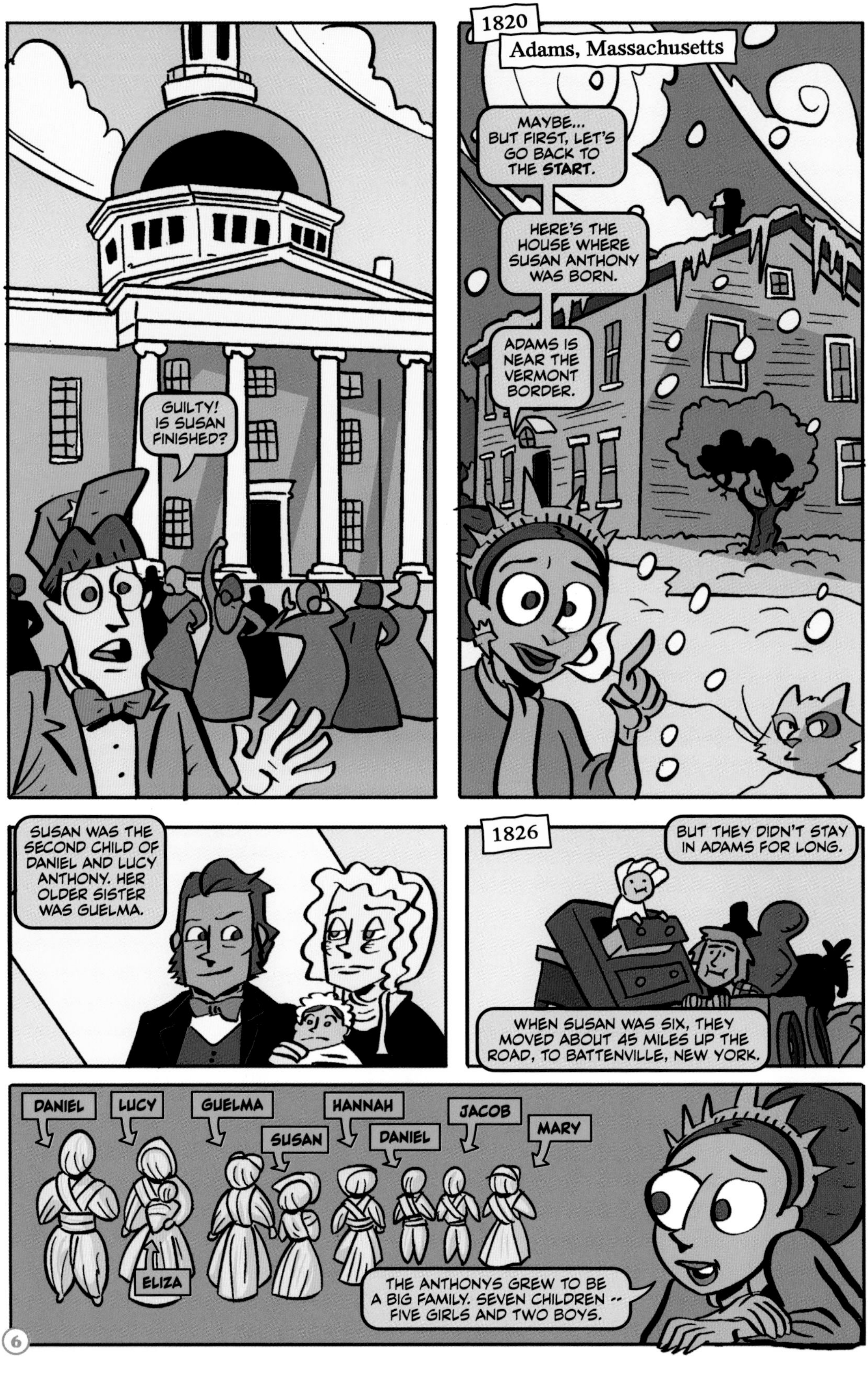
GUILTY! IS SUSAN FINISHED?
1820
Adams, Massachusetts
MAYBE... BUT FIRST, LET'S GO BACK TO THE **START**.
HERE'S THE HOUSE WHERE SUSAN ANTHONY WAS BORN.
ADAMS IS NEAR THE VERMONT BORDER.
SUSAN WAS THE SECOND CHILD OF DANIEL AND LUCY ANTHONY. HER OLDER SISTER WAS GUELMA.
1826
BUT THEY DIDN'T STAY IN ADAMS FOR LONG.
WHEN SUSAN WAS SIX, THEY MOVED ABOUT 45 MILES UP THE ROAD, TO BATTENVILLE, NEW YORK.
DANIEL
LUCY
ELIZA
GUELMA
SUSAN
HANNAH
DANIEL
JACOB
MARY
THE ANTHONYS GREW TO BE A BIG FAMILY. SEVEN CHILDREN -- FIVE GIRLS AND TWO BOYS.

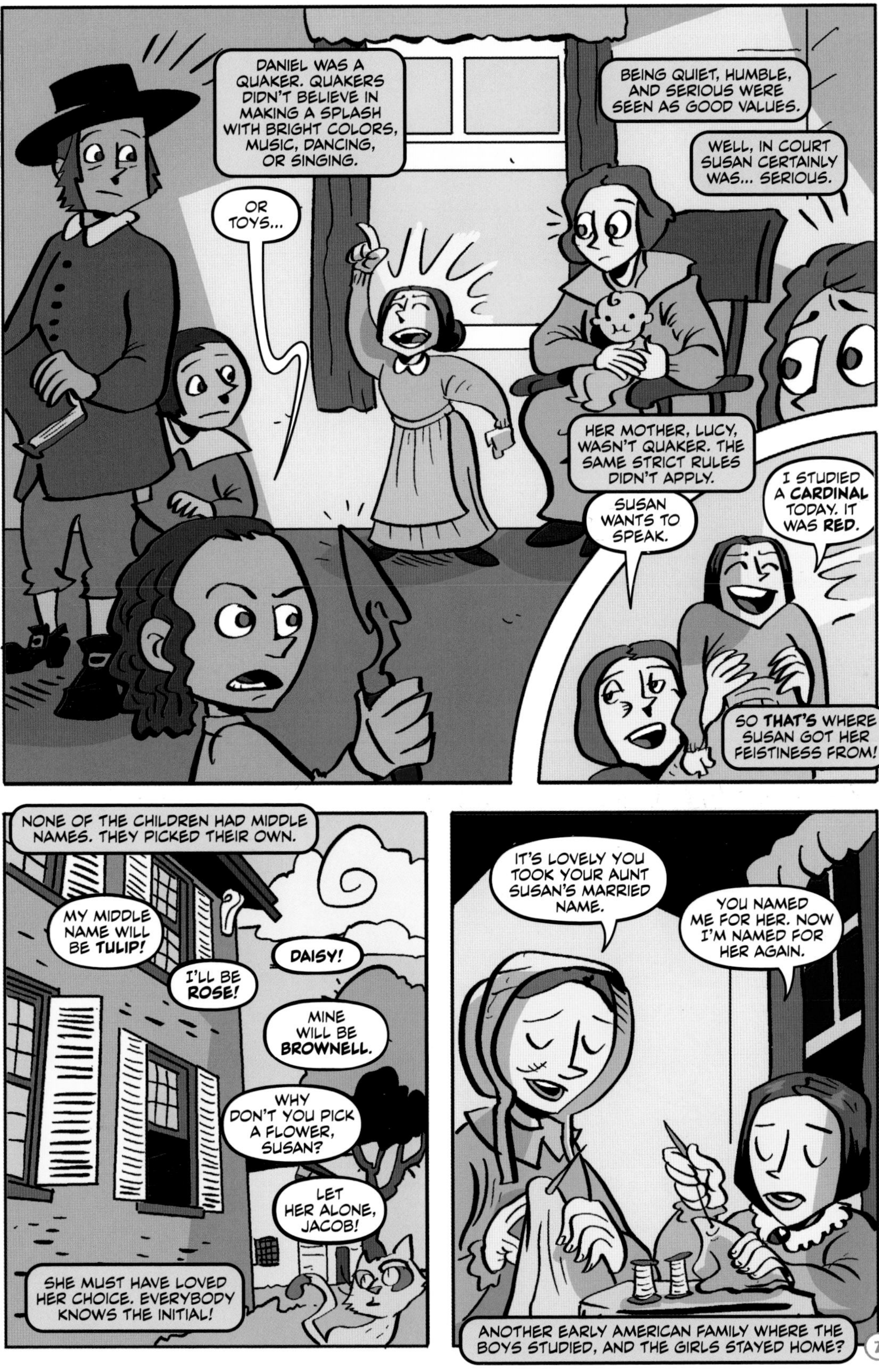
DANIEL WAS A QUAKER. QUAKERS DIDN'T BELIEVE IN MAKING A SPLASH WITH BRIGHT COLORS, MUSIC, DANCING, OR SINGING.
OR TOYS...
BEING QUIET, HUMBLE, AND SERIOUS WERE SEEN AS GOOD VALUES.
WELL, IN COURT SUSAN CERTAINLY WAS... SERIOUS.
HER MOTHER, LUCY, WASN'T QUAKER. THE SAME STRICT RULES DIDN'T APPLY.
SUSAN WANTS TO SPEAK.
I STUDIED A **CARDINAL** TODAY. IT WAS **RED**.
SO **THAT'S** WHERE SUSAN GOT HER FEISTINESS FROM!
NONE OF THE CHILDREN HAD MIDDLE NAMES. THEY PICKED THEIR OWN.
MY MIDDLE NAME WILL BE **TULIP**!
I'LL BE **ROSE**!
**DAISY**!
MINE WILL BE **BROWNELL**.
WHY DON'T YOU PICK A FLOWER, SUSAN?
LET HER ALONE, JACOB!
SHE MUST HAVE LOVED HER CHOICE. EVERYBODY KNOWS THE INITIAL!
IT'S LOVELY YOU TOOK YOUR AUNT SUSAN'S MARRIED NAME.
YOU NAMED ME FOR HER. NOW I'M NAMED FOR HER AGAIN.
ANOTHER EARLY AMERICAN FAMILY WHERE THE BOYS STUDIED, AND THE GIRLS STAYED HOME?

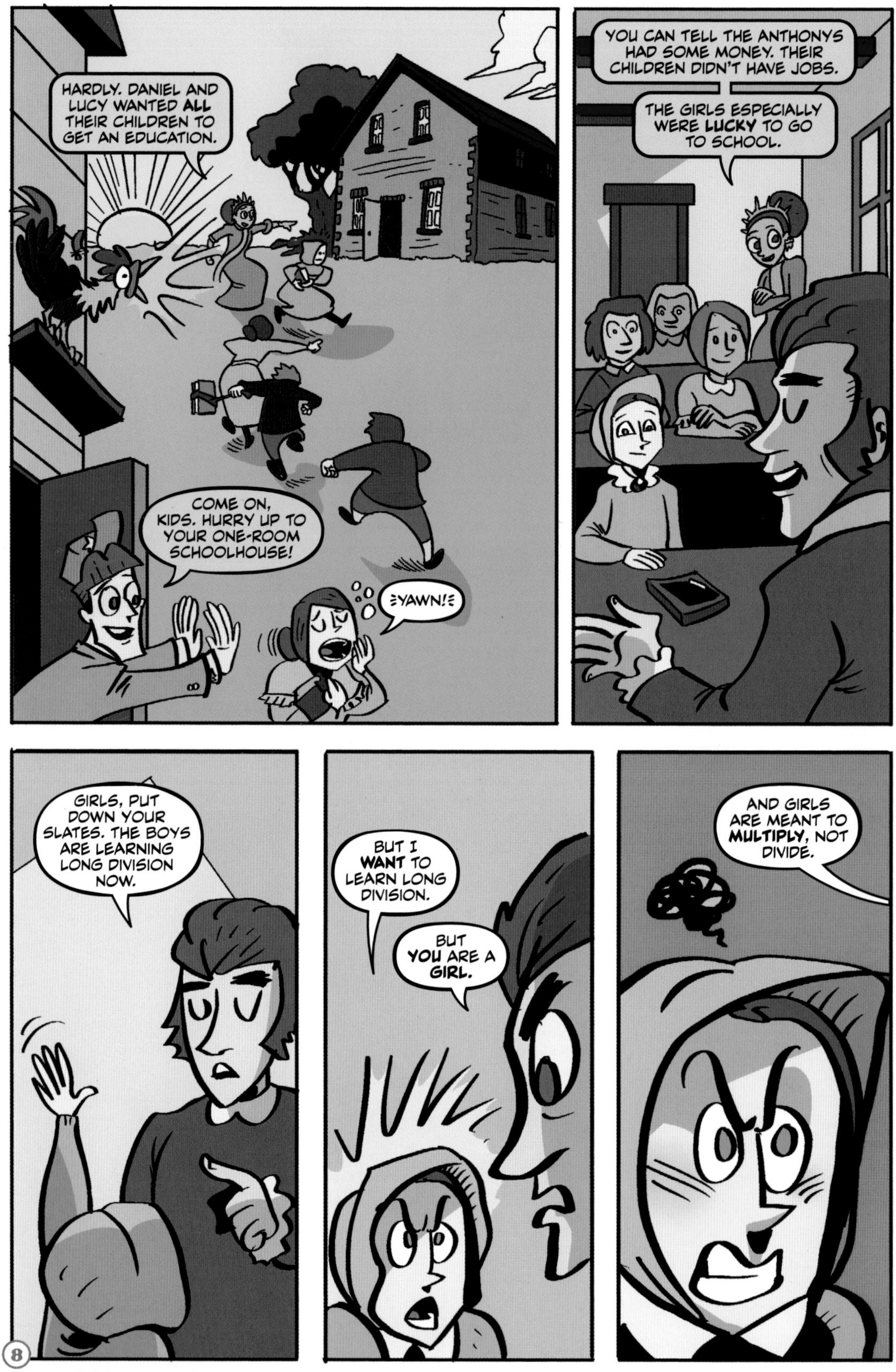
HARDLY. DANIEL AND LUCY WANTED **ALL** THEIR CHILDREN TO GET AN EDUCATION.
COME ON, KIDS. HURRY UP TO YOUR ONE-ROOM SCHOOLHOUSE!
YAWN!
YOU CAN TELL THE ANTHONYS HAD SOME MONEY. THEIR CHILDREN DIDN'T HAVE JOBS.
THE GIRLS ESPECIALLY WERE **LUCKY** TO GO TO SCHOOL.
GIRLS, PUT DOWN YOUR SLATES. THE BOYS ARE LEARNING LONG DIVISION NOW.
BUT I **WANT** TO LEARN LONG DIVISION.
BUT **YOU** ARE A **GIRL.**
AND GIRLS ARE MEANT TO **MULTIPLY**, NOT DIVIDE.

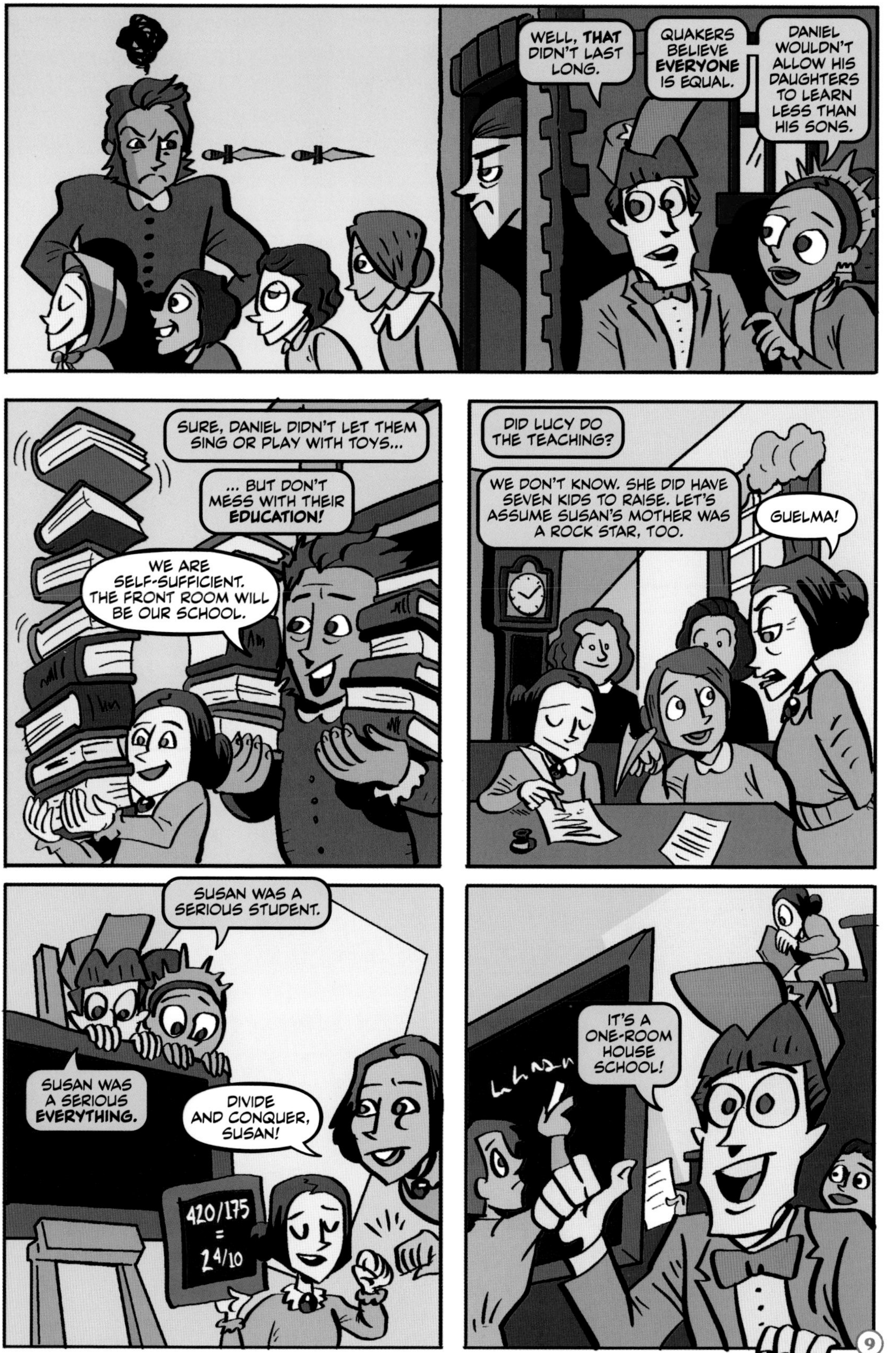
WELL, THAT DIDN'T LAST LONG.
QUAKERS BELIEVE EVERYONE IS EQUAL.
DANIEL WOULDN'T ALLOW HIS DAUGHTERS TO LEARN LESS THAN HIS SONS.
SURE, DANIEL DIDN'T LET THEM SING OR PLAY WITH TOYS...
... BUT DON'T MESS WITH THEIR EDUCATION!
WE ARE SELF-SUFFICIENT. THE FRONT ROOM WILL BE OUR SCHOOL.
DID LUCY DO THE TEACHING?
WE DON'T KNOW. SHE DID HAVE SEVEN KIDS TO RAISE. LET'S ASSUME SUSAN'S MOTHER WAS A ROCK STAR, TOO.
GUELMA!
SUSAN WAS A SERIOUS STUDENT.
SUSAN WAS A SERIOUS EVERYTHING.
DIVIDE AND CONQUER, SUSAN!
420/175 = 2 4/10
IT'S A ONE-ROOM HOUSE SCHOOL!

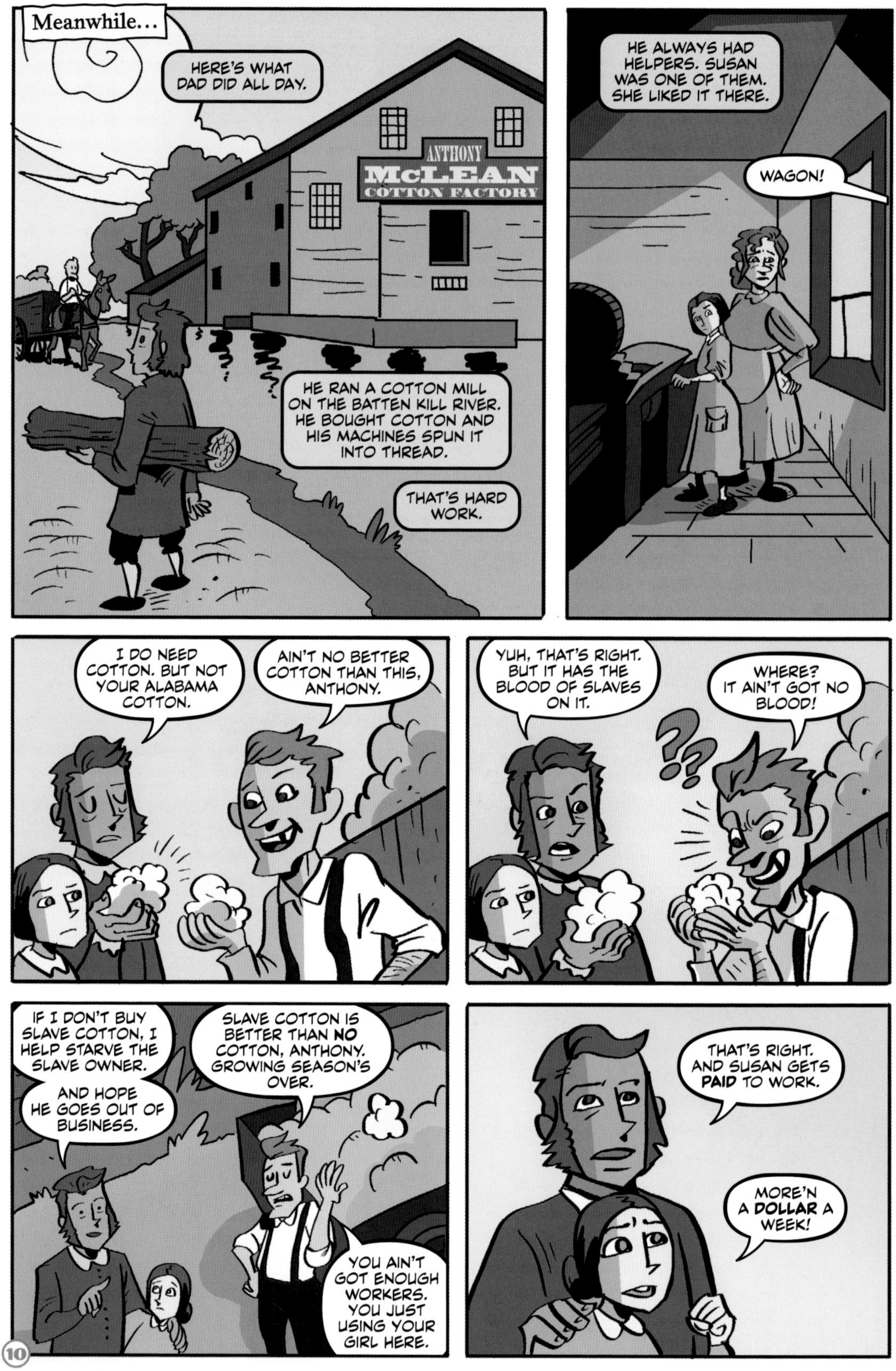
Meanwhile…
HERE'S WHAT DAD DID ALL DAY.
ANTHONY McLEAN COTTON FACTORY
HE RAN A COTTON MILL ON THE BATTEN KILL RIVER. HE BOUGHT COTTON AND HIS MACHINES SPUN IT INTO THREAD.
THAT'S HARD WORK.
HE ALWAYS HAD HELPERS. SUSAN WAS ONE OF THEM. SHE LIKED IT THERE.
WAGON!
I DO NEED COTTON. BUT NOT YOUR ALABAMA COTTON.
AIN'T NO BETTER COTTON THAN THIS, ANTHONY.
YUH, THAT'S RIGHT. BUT IT HAS THE BLOOD OF SLAVES ON IT.
WHERE? IT AIN'T GOT NO BLOOD!
IF I DON'T BUY SLAVE COTTON, I HELP STARVE THE SLAVE OWNER.
AND HOPE HE GOES OUT OF BUSINESS.
SLAVE COTTON IS BETTER THAN NO COTTON, ANTHONY. GROWING SEASON'S OVER.
YOU AIN'T GOT ENOUGH WORKERS. YOU JUST USING YOUR GIRL HERE.
THAT'S RIGHT. AND SUSAN GETS PAID TO WORK.
MORE'N A DOLLAR A WEEK!

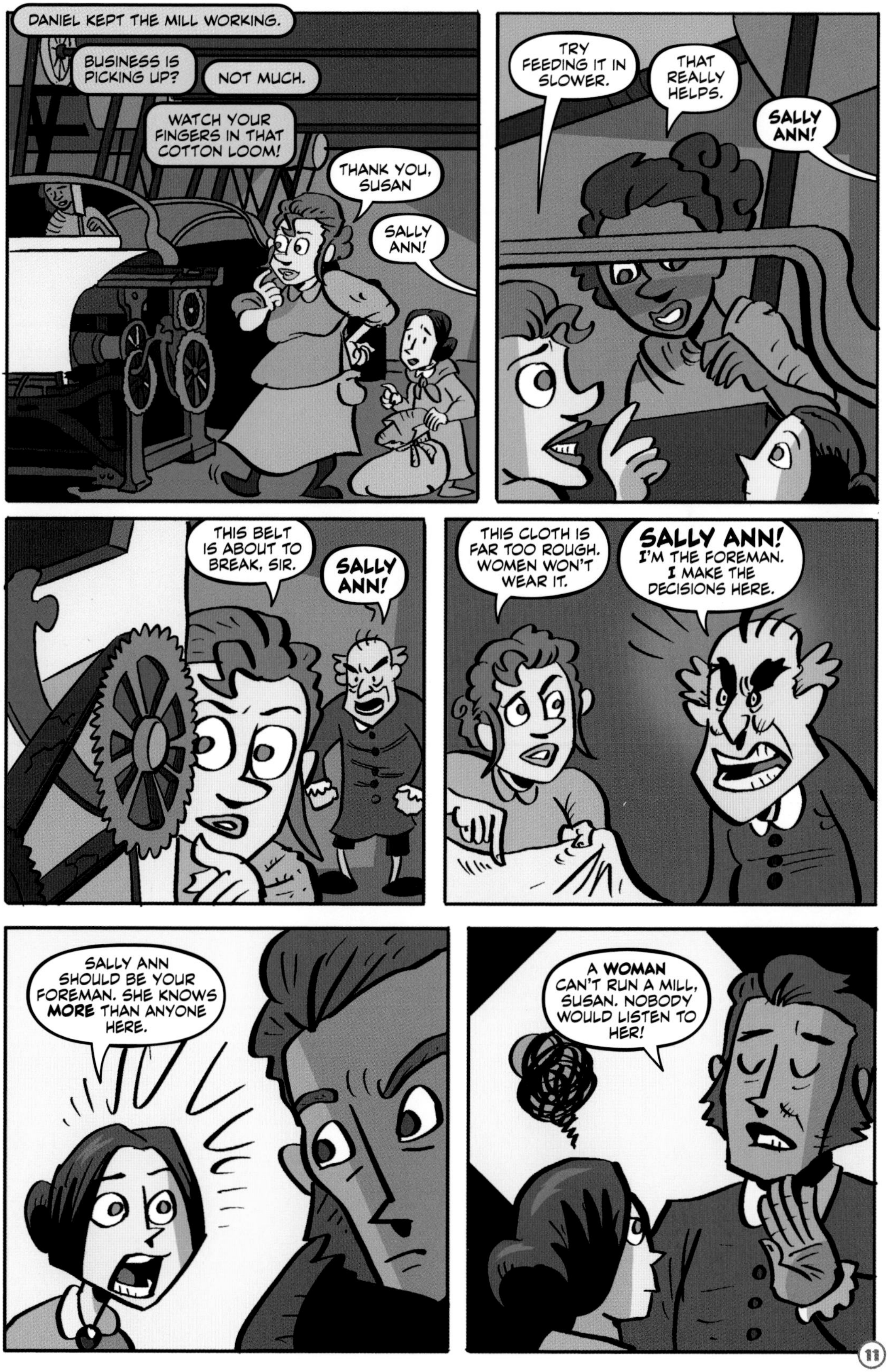
DANIEL KEPT THE MILL WORKING.
BUSINESS IS PICKING UP?
NOT MUCH.
WATCH YOUR FINGERS IN THAT COTTON LOOM!
THANK YOU, SUSAN
SALLY ANN!
TRY FEEDING IT IN SLOWER.
THAT REALLY HELPS.
SALLY ANN!
THIS BELT IS ABOUT TO BREAK, SIR.
SALLY ANN!
THIS CLOTH IS FAR TOO ROUGH. WOMEN WON'T WEAR IT.
SALLY ANN! I'M THE FOREMAN. I MAKE THE DECISIONS HERE.
SALLY ANN SHOULD BE YOUR FOREMAN. SHE KNOWS MORE THAN ANYONE HERE.
A WOMAN CAN'T RUN A MILL, SUSAN. NOBODY WOULD LISTEN TO HER!

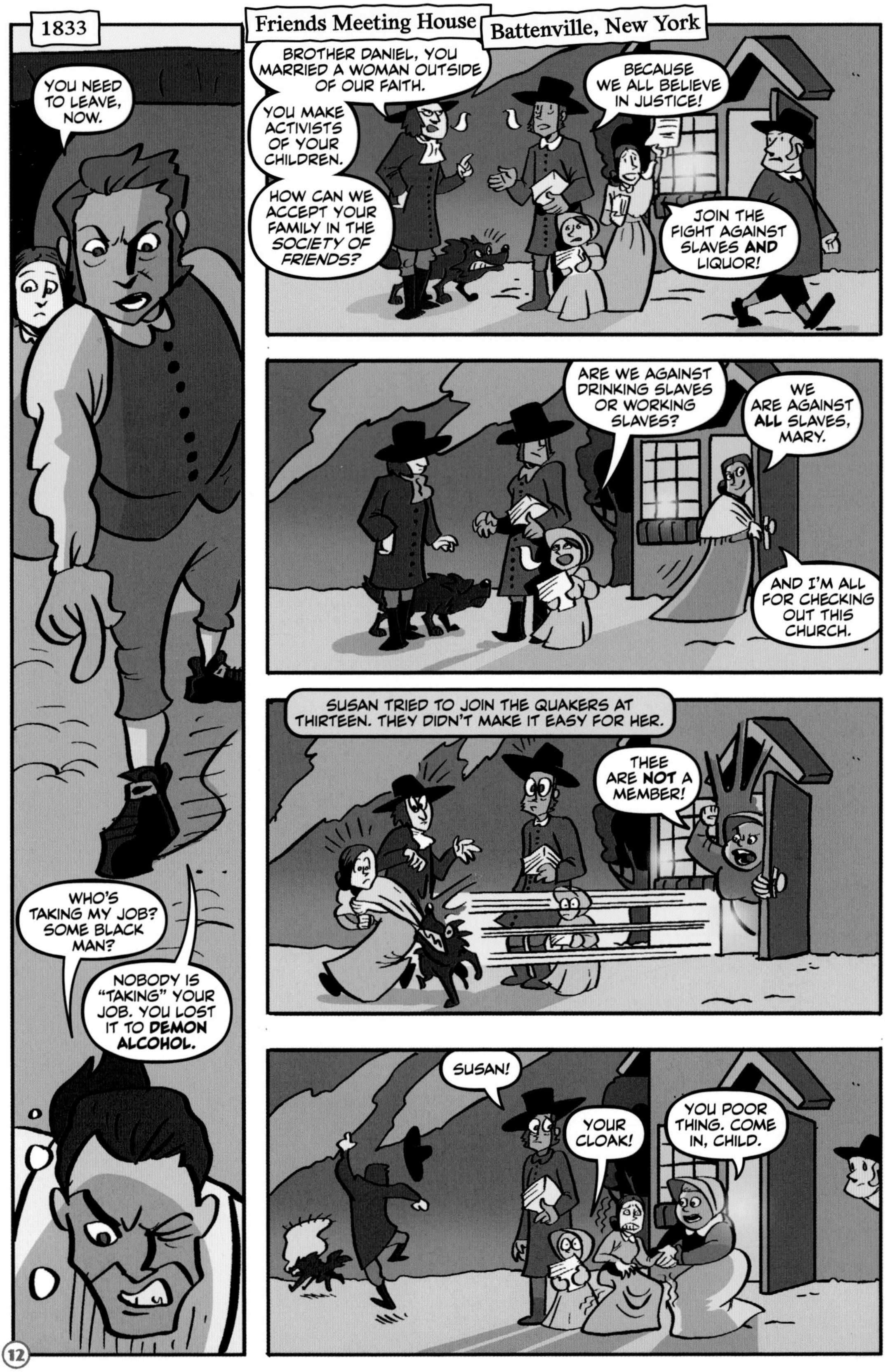
1833
YOU NEED TO LEAVE, NOW.
WHO'S TAKING MY JOB? SOME BLACK MAN?
NOBODY IS "TAKING" YOUR JOB. YOU LOST IT TO **DEMON ALCOHOL.**
Friends Meeting House
Battenville, New York
BROTHER DANIEL, YOU MARRIED A WOMAN OUTSIDE OF OUR FAITH.
YOU MAKE ACTIVISTS OF YOUR CHILDREN.
HOW CAN WE ACCEPT YOUR FAMILY IN THE *SOCIETY OF FRIENDS?*
BECAUSE WE ALL BELIEVE IN JUSTICE!
JOIN THE FIGHT AGAINST SLAVES **AND** LIQUOR!
ARE WE AGAINST DRINKING SLAVES OR WORKING SLAVES?
WE ARE AGAINST **ALL** SLAVES, MARY.
AND I'M ALL FOR CHECKING OUT THIS CHURCH.
SUSAN TRIED TO JOIN THE QUAKERS AT THIRTEEN. THEY DIDN'T MAKE IT EASY FOR HER.
THEE ARE **NOT** A MEMBER!
SUSAN!
YOUR CLOAK!
YOU POOR THING. COME IN, CHILD.

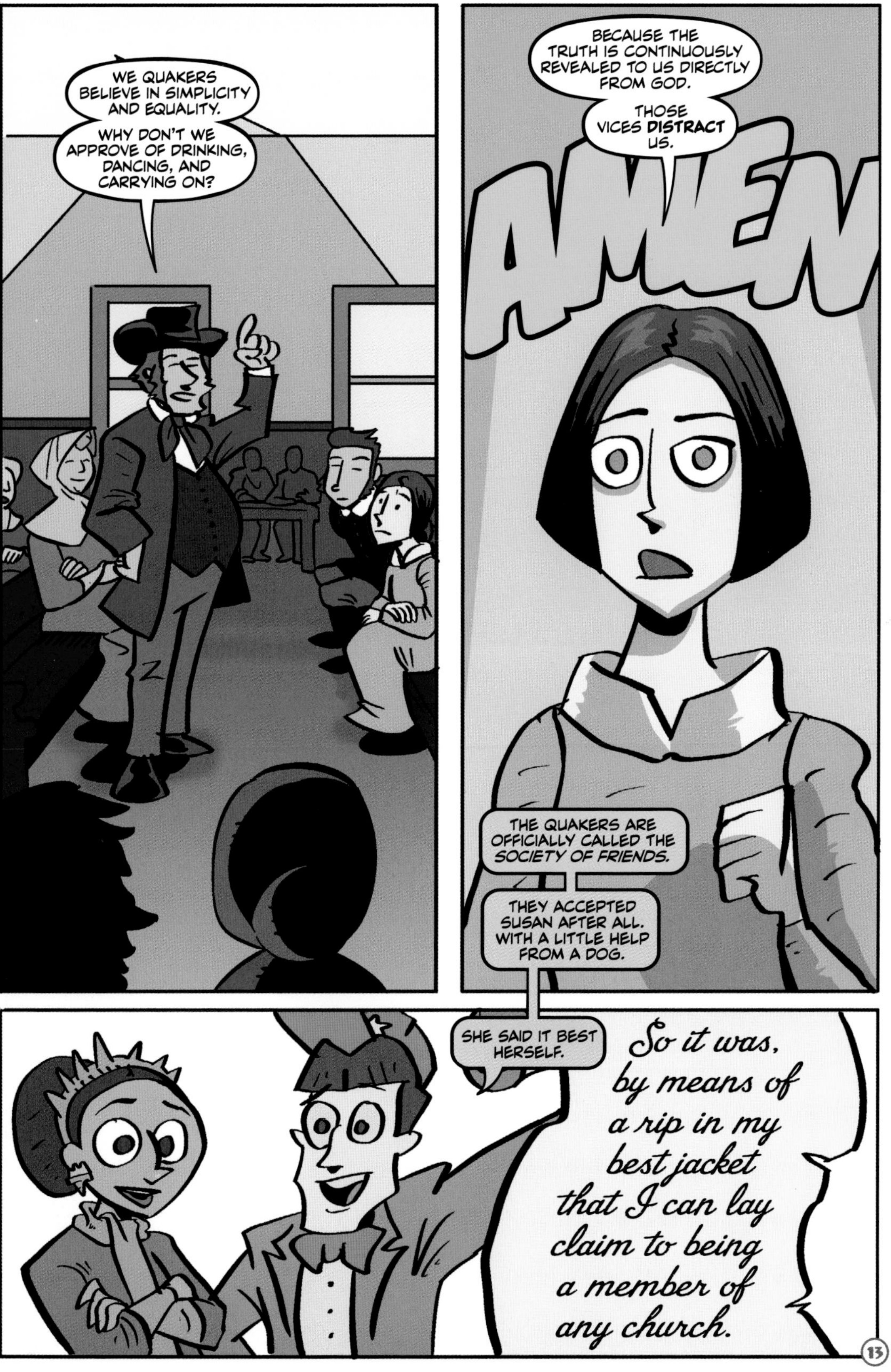

WE QUAKERS BELIEVE IN SIMPLICITY AND EQUALITY.
WHY DON'T WE APPROVE OF DRINKING, DANCING, AND CARRYING ON?
BECAUSE THE TRUTH IS CONTINUOUSLY REVEALED TO US DIRECTLY FROM GOD.
THOSE VICES DISTRACT US.
AMEN
THE QUAKERS ARE OFFICIALLY CALLED THE SOCIETY OF FRIENDS.
THEY ACCEPTED SUSAN AFTER ALL. WITH A LITTLE HELP FROM A DOG.
SHE SAID IT BEST HERSELF.
So it was, by means of a rip in my best jacket that I can lay claim to being a member of any church.

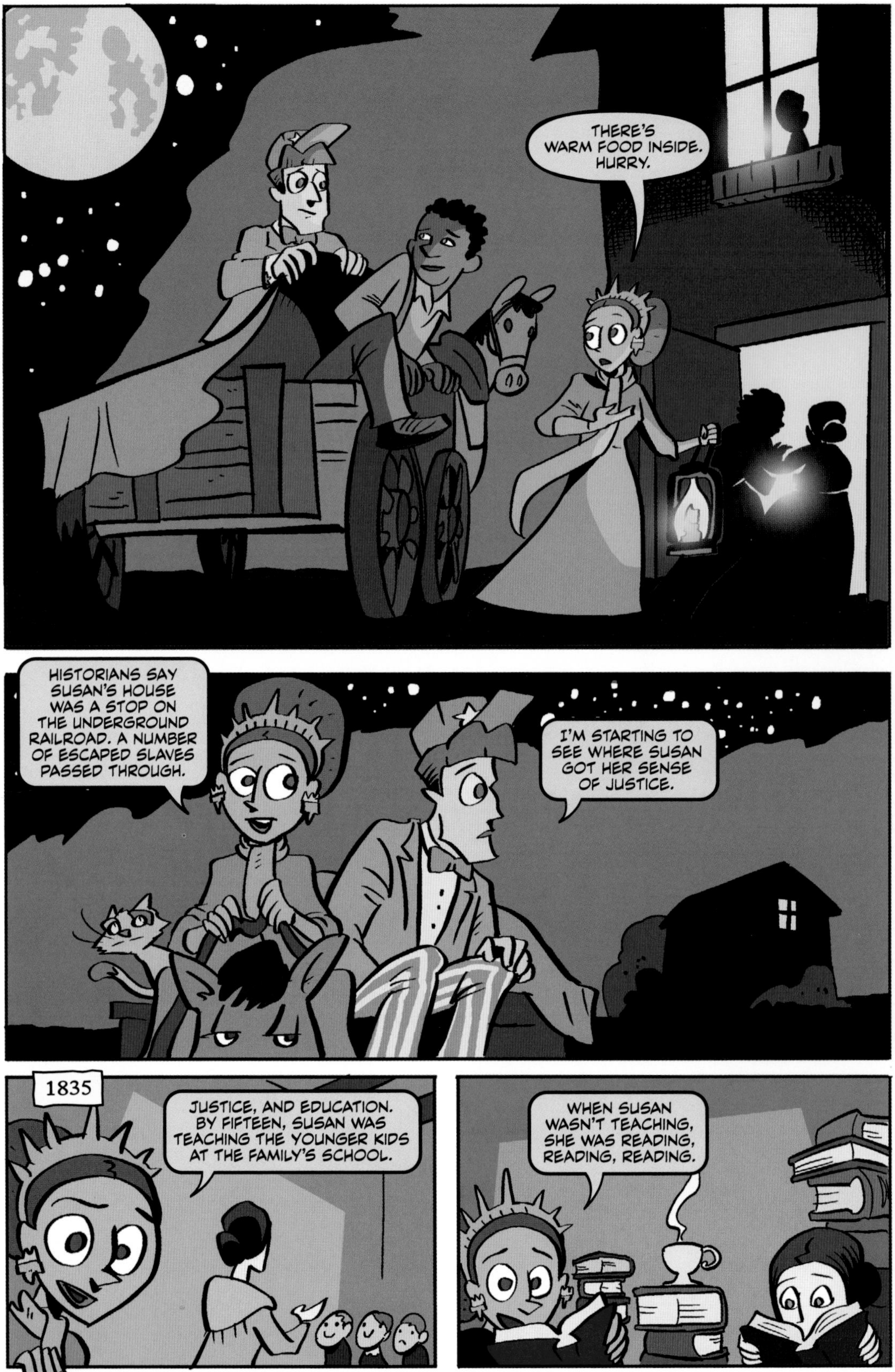
THERE'S WARM FOOD INSIDE. HURRY.
HISTORIANS SAY SUSAN'S HOUSE WAS A STOP ON THE UNDERGROUND RAILROAD. A NUMBER OF ESCAPED SLAVES PASSED THROUGH.
I'M STARTING TO SEE WHERE SUSAN GOT HER SENSE OF JUSTICE.
1835
JUSTICE, AND EDUCATION. BY FIFTEEN, SUSAN WAS TEACHING THE YOUNGER KIDS AT THE FAMILY'S SCHOOL.
WHEN SUSAN WASN'T TEACHING, SHE WAS READING, READING, READING.

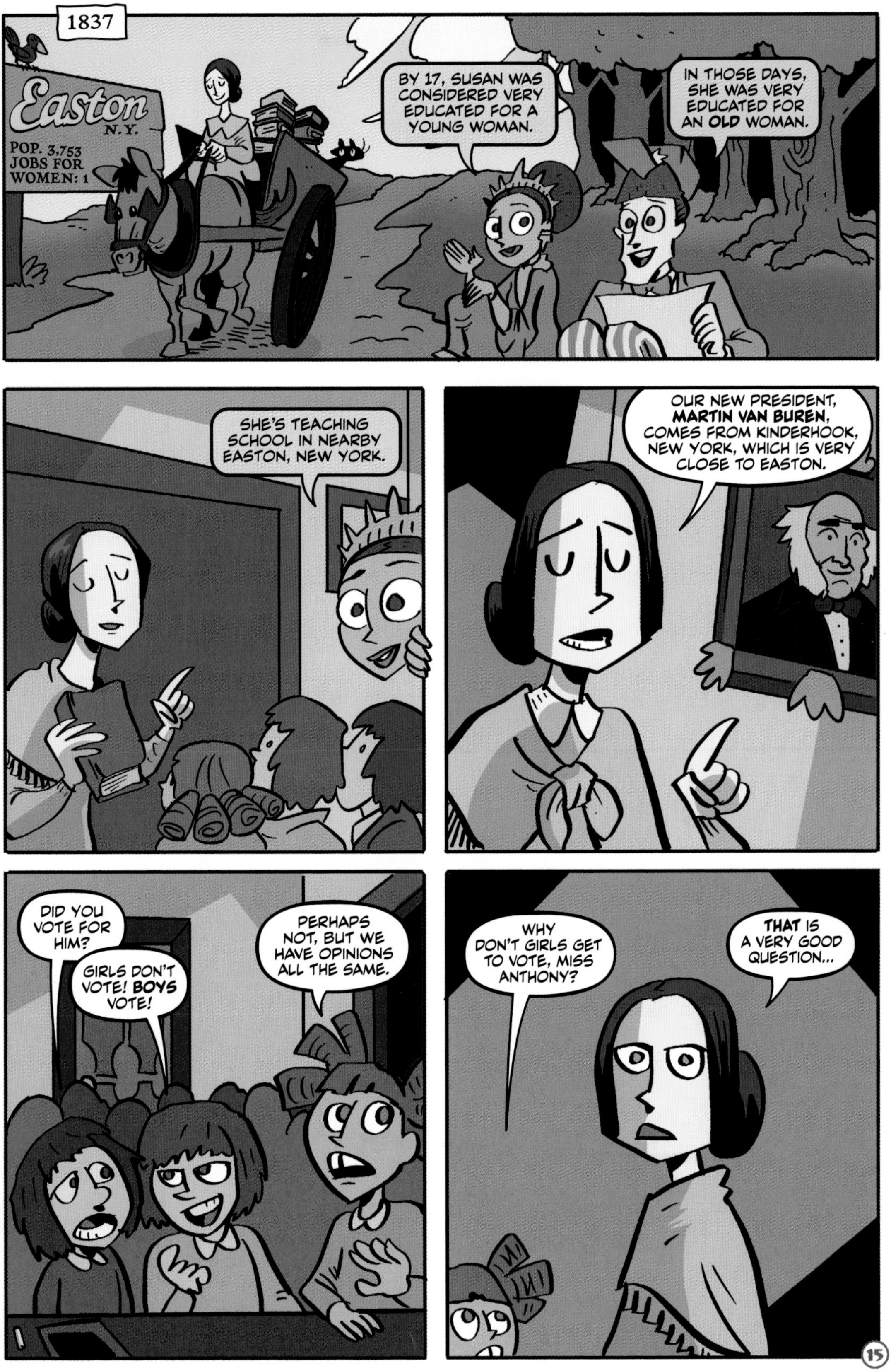
1837
Easton N.Y.
POP. 3,753 JOBS FOR WOMEN: 1
BY 17, SUSAN WAS CONSIDERED VERY EDUCATED FOR A YOUNG WOMAN.
IN THOSE DAYS, SHE WAS VERY EDUCATED FOR AN OLD WOMAN.
SHE'S TEACHING SCHOOL IN NEARBY EASTON, NEW YORK.
OUR NEW PRESIDENT, MARTIN VAN BUREN, COMES FROM KINDERHOOK, NEW YORK, WHICH IS VERY CLOSE TO EASTON.
DID YOU VOTE FOR HIM?
GIRLS DON'T VOTE! BOYS VOTE!
PERHAPS NOT, BUT WE HAVE OPINIONS ALL THE SAME.
WHY DON'T GIRLS GET TO VOTE, MISS ANTHONY?
THAT IS A VERY GOOD QUESTION...

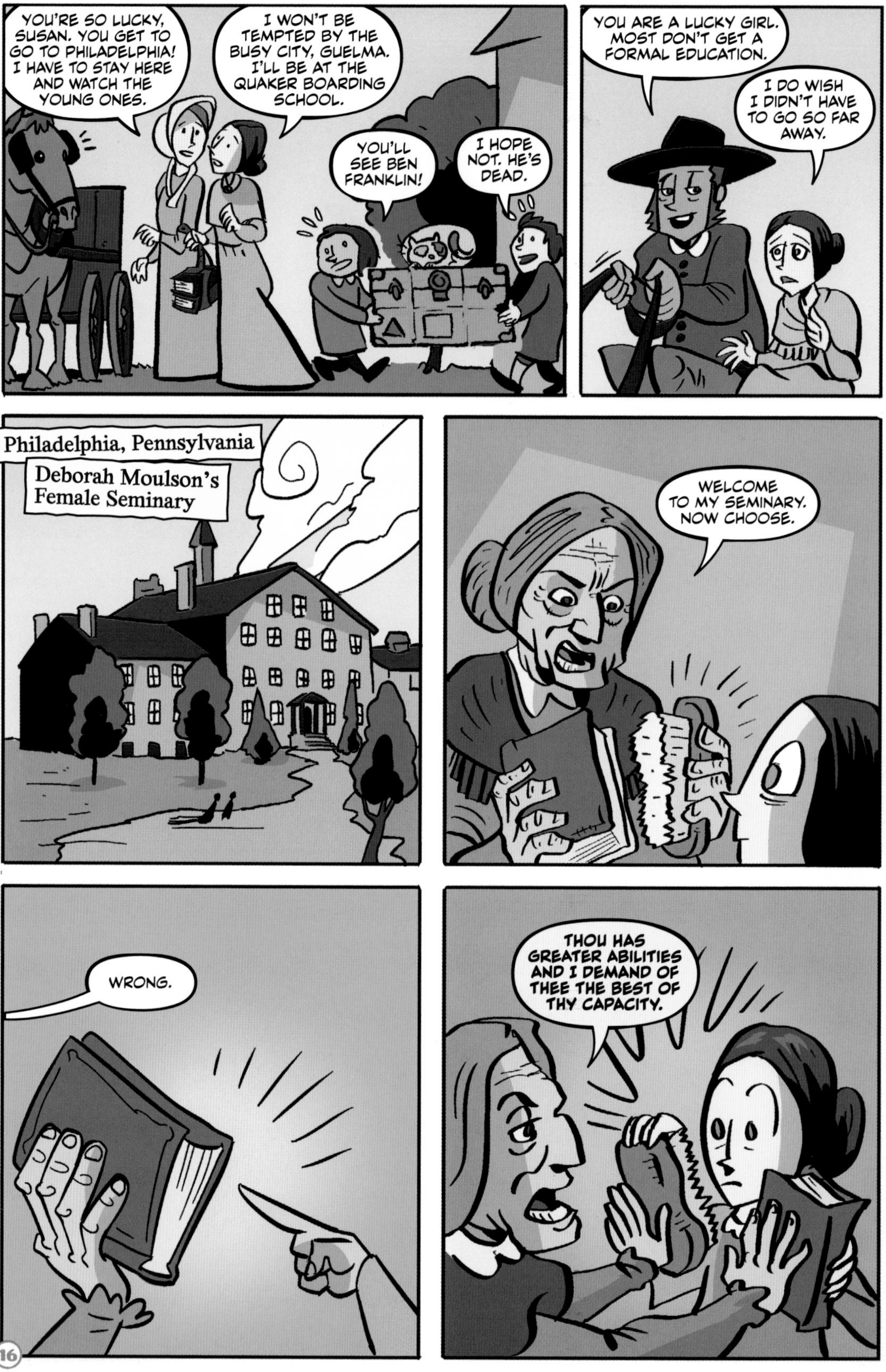
YOU'RE SO LUCKY, SUSAN. YOU GET TO GO TO PHILADELPHIA! I HAVE TO STAY HERE AND WATCH THE YOUNG ONES.
I WON'T BE TEMPTED BY THE BUSY CITY, GUELMA. I'LL BE AT THE QUAKER BOARDING SCHOOL.
YOU'LL SEE BEN FRANKLIN!
I HOPE NOT. HE'S DEAD.
YOU ARE A LUCKY GIRL. MOST DON'T GET A FORMAL EDUCATION.
I DO WISH I DIDN'T HAVE TO GO SO FAR AWAY.
Philadelphia, Pennsylvania
Deborah Moulson's Female Seminary
WELCOME TO MY SEMINARY. NOW CHOOSE.
WRONG.
THOU HAS GREATER ABILITIES AND I DEMAND OF THEE THE BEST OF THY CAPACITY.

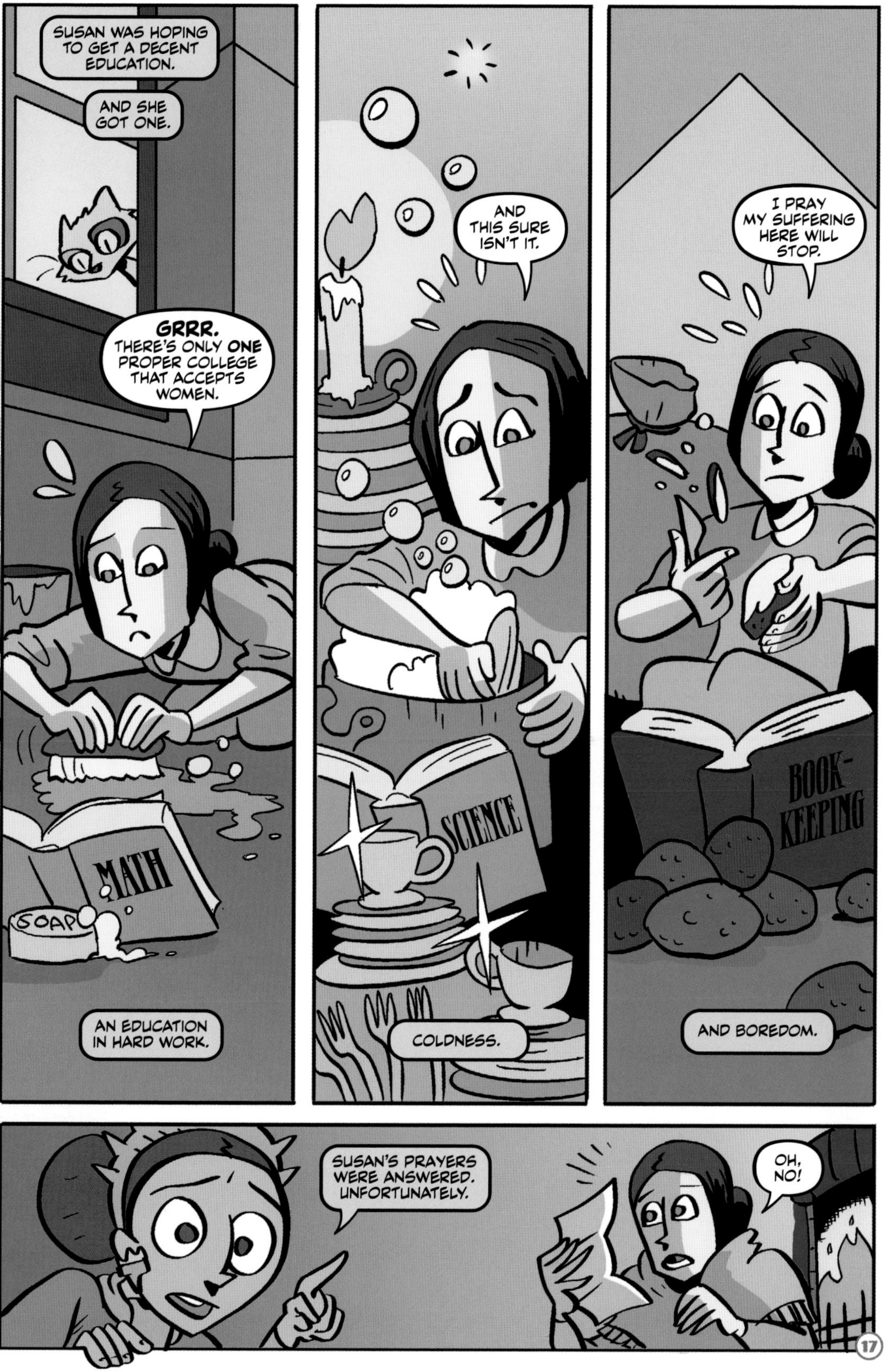
SUSAN WAS HOPING TO GET A DECENT EDUCATION.
AND SHE GOT ONE.
GRRR. THERE'S ONLY ONE PROPER COLLEGE THAT ACCEPTS WOMEN.
MATH
SOAP
AN EDUCATION IN HARD WORK.
AND THIS SURE ISN'T IT.
SCIENCE
COLDNESS.
I PRAY MY SUFFERING HERE WILL STOP.
BOOK-KEEPING
AND BOREDOM.
SUSAN'S PRAYERS WERE ANSWERED. UNFORTUNATELY.
OH, NO!

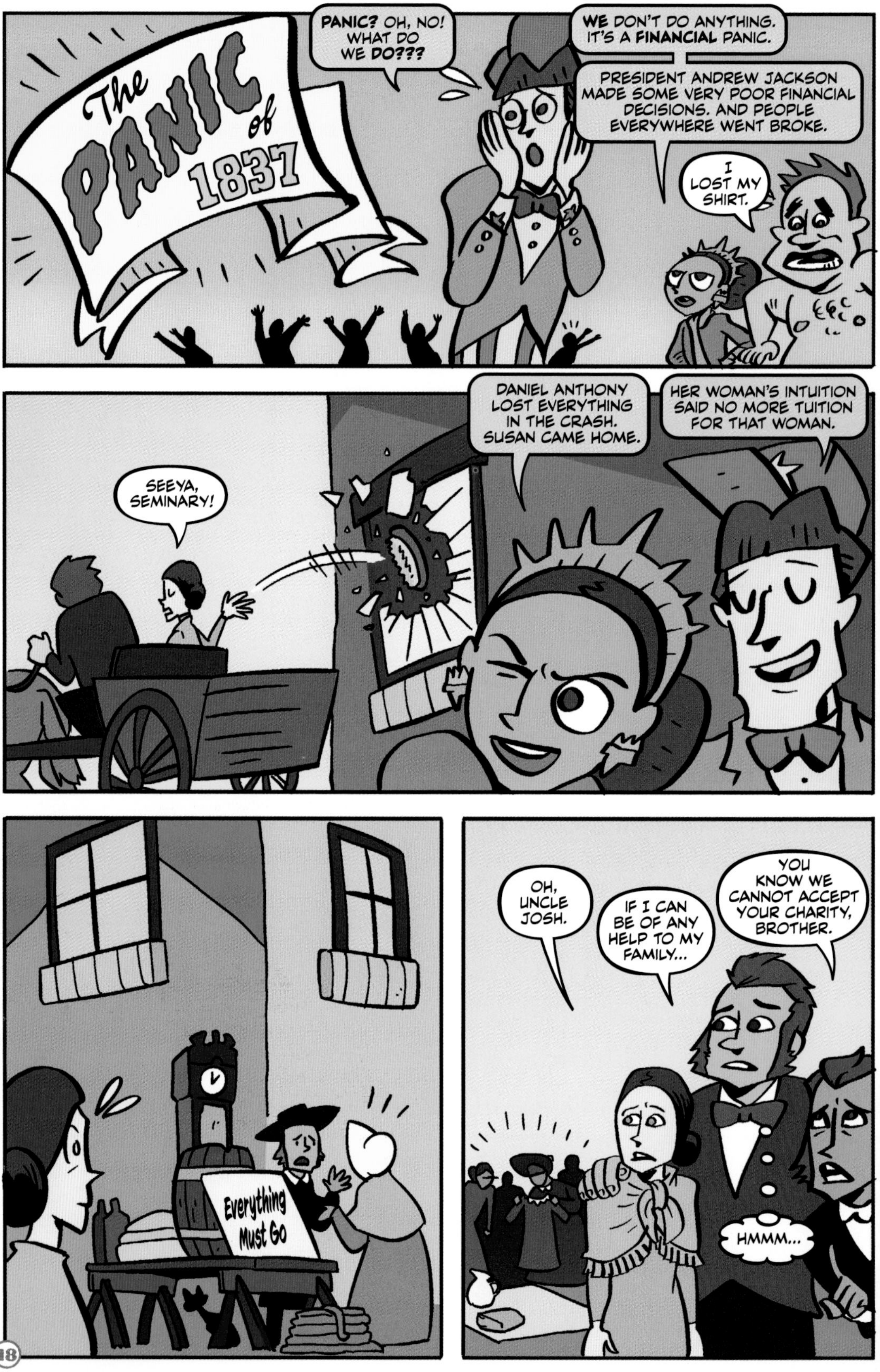
The PANIC of 1837
PANIC? OH, NO! WHAT DO WE DO???
WE DON'T DO ANYTHING. IT'S A FINANCIAL PANIC.
PRESIDENT ANDREW JACKSON MADE SOME VERY POOR FINANCIAL DECISIONS. AND PEOPLE EVERYWHERE WENT BROKE.
I LOST MY SHIRT.
SEEYA, SEMINARY!
DANIEL ANTHONY LOST EVERYTHING IN THE CRASH. SUSAN CAME HOME.
HER WOMAN'S INTUITION SAID NO MORE TUITION FOR THAT WOMAN.
Everything Must Go
OH, UNCLE JOSH.
IF I CAN BE OF ANY HELP TO MY FAMILY...
YOU KNOW WE CANNOT ACCEPT YOUR CHARITY, BROTHER.
HMMM...

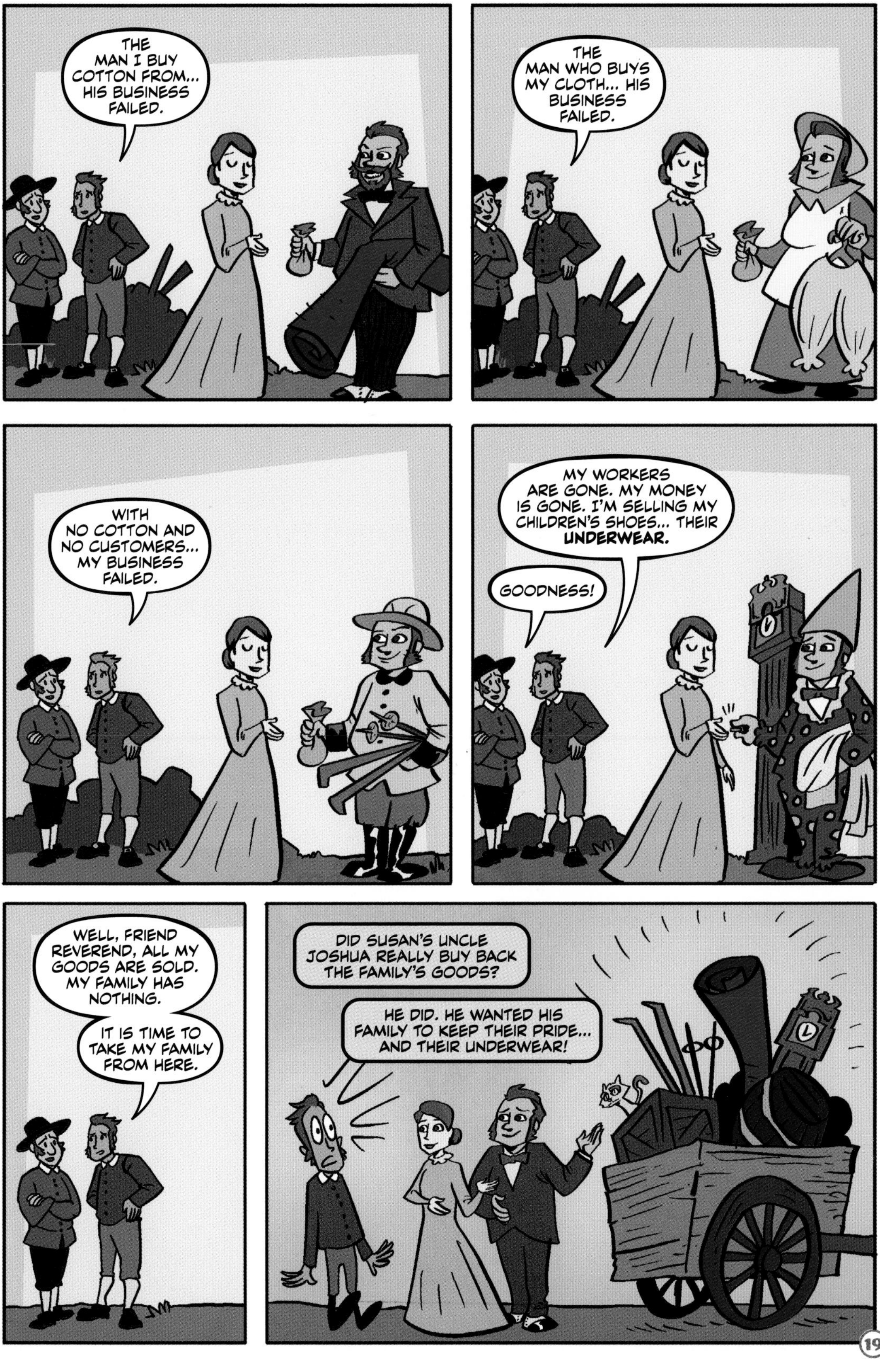
THE MAN I BUY COTTON FROM... HIS BUSINESS FAILED.
THE MAN WHO BUYS MY CLOTH... HIS BUSINESS FAILED.
WITH NO COTTON AND NO CUSTOMERS... MY BUSINESS FAILED.
MY WORKERS ARE GONE. MY MONEY IS GONE. I'M SELLING MY CHILDREN'S SHOES... THEIR **UNDERWEAR.**
GOODNESS!
WELL, FRIEND REVEREND, ALL MY GOODS ARE SOLD. MY FAMILY HAS NOTHING.
IT IS TIME TO TAKE MY FAMILY FROM HERE.
DID SUSAN'S UNCLE JOSHUA REALLY BUY BACK THE FAMILY'S GOODS?
HE DID. HE WANTED HIS FAMILY TO KEEP THEIR PRIDE... AND THEIR UNDERWEAR!

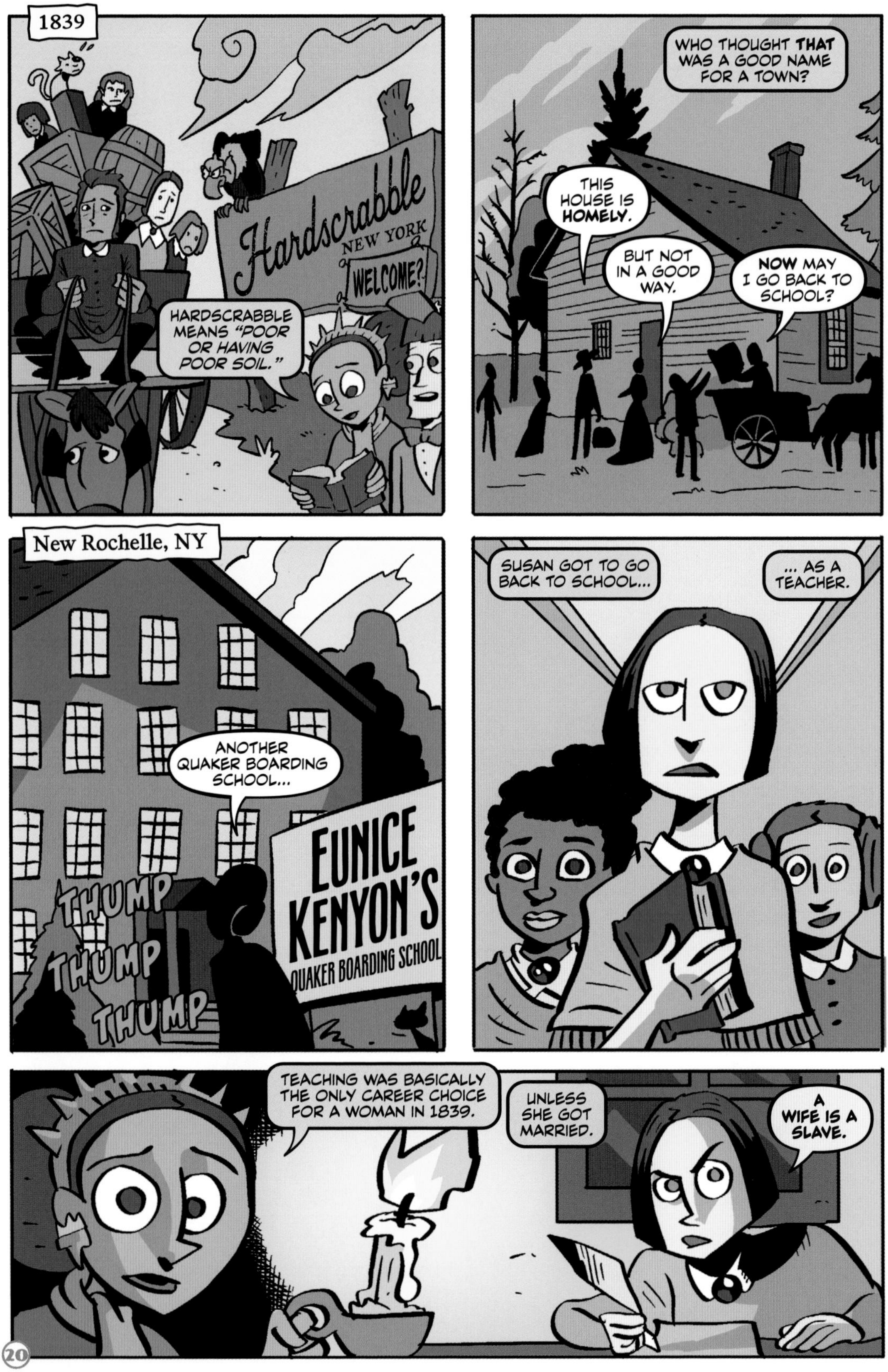
1839
Hardscrabble
NEW YORK
WELCOME?
HARDSCRABBLE MEANS "POOR OR HAVING POOR SOIL."
WHO THOUGHT **THAT** WAS A GOOD NAME FOR A TOWN?
THIS HOUSE IS **HOMELY**.
BUT NOT IN A GOOD WAY.
**NOW** MAY I GO BACK TO SCHOOL?
New Rochelle, NY
ANOTHER QUAKER BOARDING SCHOOL...
EUNICE KENYON'S
QUAKER BOARDING SCHOOL
THUMP
THUMP
THUMP
SUSAN GOT TO GO BACK TO SCHOOL...
... AS A TEACHER.
TEACHING WAS BASICALLY THE ONLY CAREER CHOICE FOR A WOMAN IN 1839.
UNLESS SHE GOT MARRIED.
A WIFE IS A SLAVE.

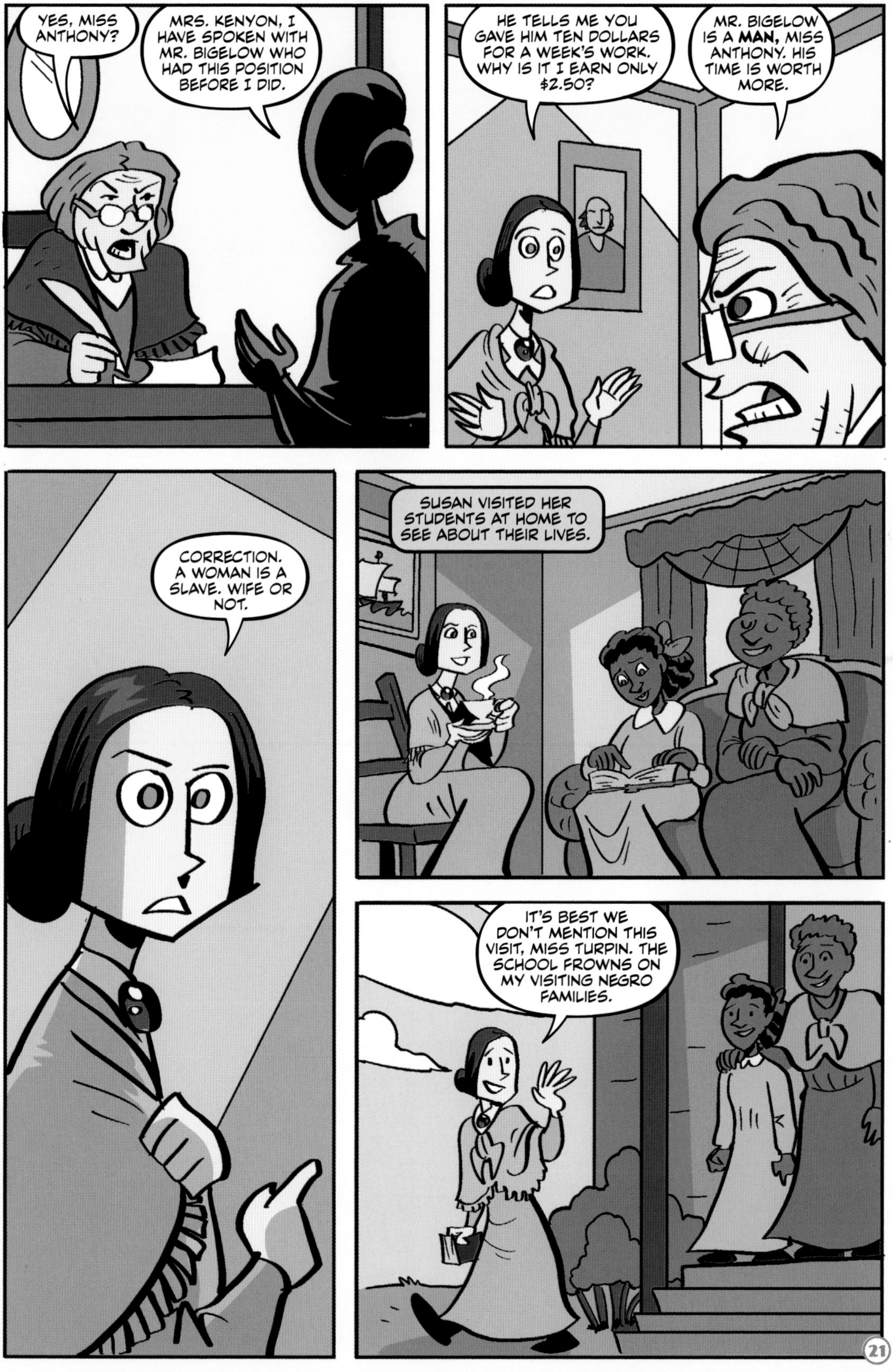
YES, MISS ANTHONY?
MRS. KENYON, I HAVE SPOKEN WITH MR. BIGELOW WHO HAD THIS POSITION BEFORE I DID.
HE TELLS ME YOU GAVE HIM TEN DOLLARS FOR A WEEK'S WORK. WHY IS IT I EARN ONLY $2.50?
MR. BIGELOW IS A **MAN,** MISS ANTHONY. HIS TIME IS WORTH MORE.
CORRECTION. A WOMAN IS A SLAVE. WIFE OR NOT.
SUSAN VISITED HER STUDENTS AT HOME TO SEE ABOUT THEIR LIVES.
IT'S BEST WE DON'T MENTION THIS VISIT, MISS TURPIN. THE SCHOOL FROWNS ON MY VISITING NEGRO FAMILIES.

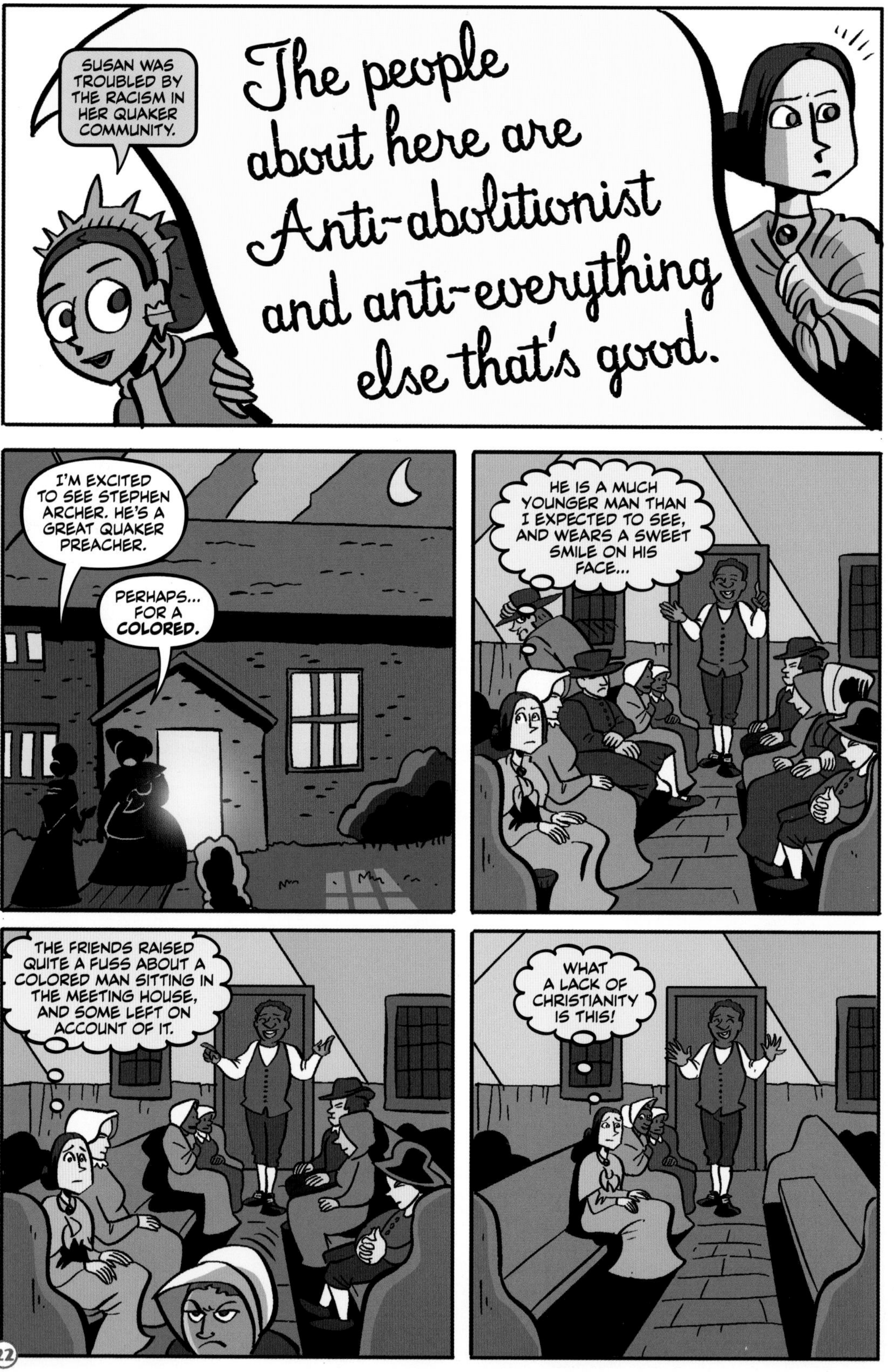

SUSAN WAS TROUBLED BY THE RACISM IN HER QUAKER COMMUNITY.
The people about here are Anti-abolitionist and anti-everything else that's good.
I'M EXCITED TO SEE STEPHEN ARCHER. HE'S A GREAT QUAKER PREACHER.
PERHAPS... FOR A COLORED.
HE IS A MUCH YOUNGER MAN THAN I EXPECTED TO SEE, AND WEARS A SWEET SMILE ON HIS FACE...
THE FRIENDS RAISED QUITE A FUSS ABOUT A COLORED MAN SITTING IN THE MEETING HOUSE, AND SOME LEFT ON ACCOUNT OF IT.
WHAT A LACK OF CHRISTIANITY IS THIS!

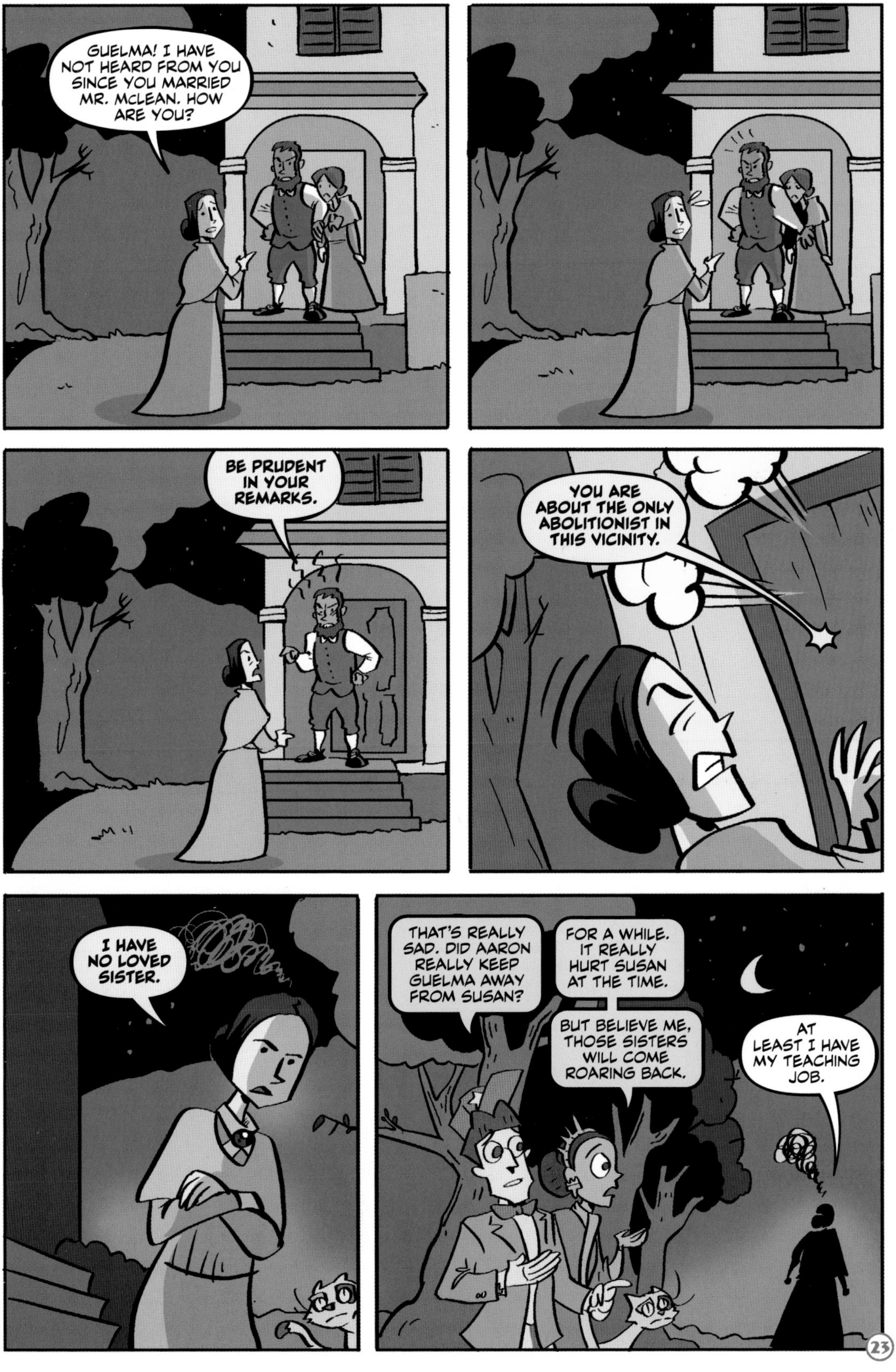
GUELMA! I HAVE NOT HEARD FROM YOU SINCE YOU MARRIED MR. McLEAN. HOW ARE YOU?
BE PRUDENT IN YOUR REMARKS.
YOU ARE ABOUT THE ONLY ABOLITIONIST IN THIS VICINITY.
I HAVE NO LOVED SISTER.
THAT'S REALLY SAD. DID AARON REALLY KEEP GUELMA AWAY FROM SUSAN?
FOR A WHILE. IT REALLY HURT SUSAN AT THE TIME.
BUT BELIEVE ME, THOSE SISTERS WILL COME ROARING BACK.
AT LEAST I HAVE MY TEACHING JOB.

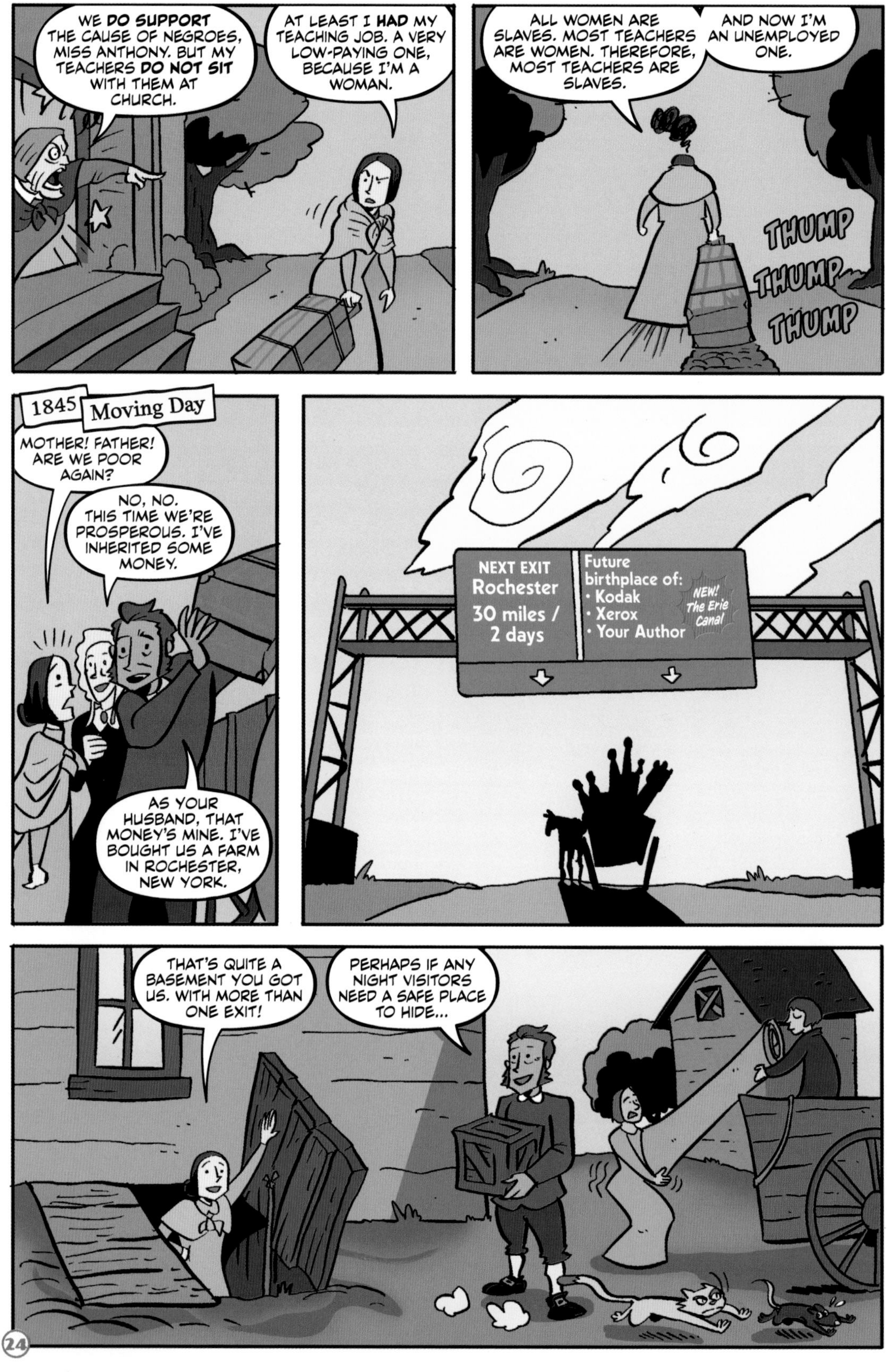

WE **DO SUPPORT** THE CAUSE OF NEGROES, MISS ANTHONY. BUT MY TEACHERS **DO NOT SIT** WITH THEM AT CHURCH.
AT LEAST I **HAD** MY TEACHING JOB. A VERY LOW-PAYING ONE, BECAUSE I'M A WOMAN.
ALL WOMEN ARE SLAVES. MOST TEACHERS ARE WOMEN. THEREFORE, MOST TEACHERS ARE SLAVES.
AND NOW I'M AN UNEMPLOYED ONE.
THUMP
THUMP
THUMP
1845
Moving Day
MOTHER! FATHER! ARE WE POOR AGAIN?
NO, NO. THIS TIME WE'RE PROSPEROUS. I'VE INHERITED SOME MONEY.
AS YOUR HUSBAND, THAT MONEY'S MINE. I'VE BOUGHT US A FARM IN ROCHESTER, NEW YORK.
NEXT EXIT
Rochester
30 miles / 2 days
Future birthplace of:
• Kodak
• Xerox
• Your Author
NEW! The Erie Canal
THAT'S QUITE A BASEMENT YOU GOT US. WITH MORE THAN ONE EXIT!
PERHAPS IF ANY NIGHT VISITORS NEED A SAFE PLACE TO HIDE...

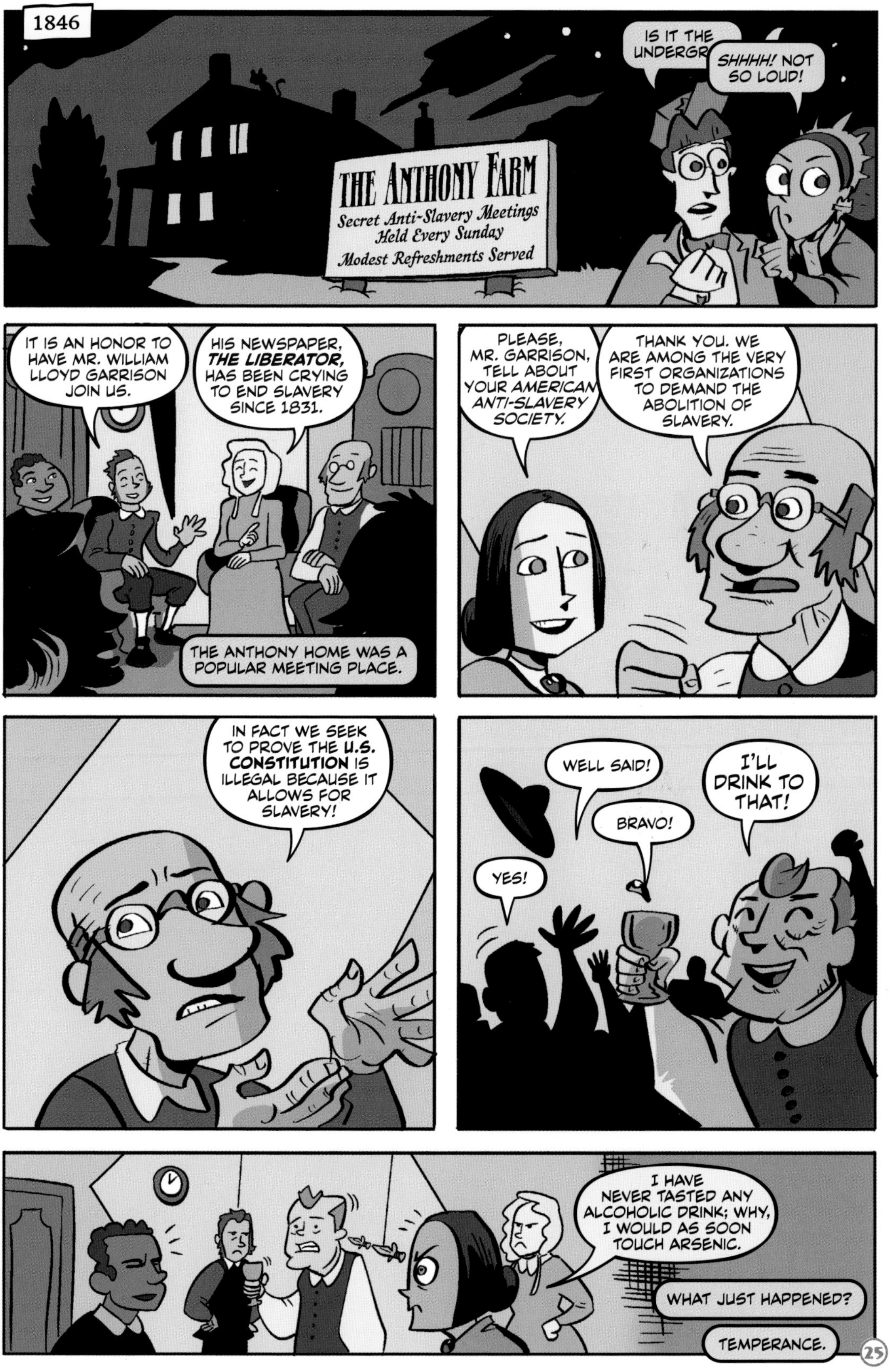
1846
THE ANTHONY FARM
Secret Anti-Slavery Meetings
Held Every Sunday
Modest Refreshments Served
IS IT THE UNDERGR
SHHHH! NOT SO LOUD!
IT IS AN HONOR TO HAVE MR. WILLIAM LLOYD GARRISON JOIN US.
HIS NEWSPAPER, THE LIBERATOR, HAS BEEN CRYING TO END SLAVERY SINCE 1831.
THE ANTHONY HOME WAS A POPULAR MEETING PLACE.
PLEASE, MR. GARRISON, TELL ABOUT YOUR AMERICAN ANTI-SLAVERY SOCIETY.
THANK YOU. WE ARE AMONG THE VERY FIRST ORGANIZATIONS TO DEMAND THE ABOLITION OF SLAVERY.
IN FACT WE SEEK TO PROVE THE U.S. CONSTITUTION IS ILLEGAL BECAUSE IT ALLOWS FOR SLAVERY!
WELL SAID!
I'LL DRINK TO THAT!
BRAVO!
YES!
I HAVE NEVER TASTED ANY ALCOHOLIC DRINK; WHY, I WOULD AS SOON TOUCH ARSENIC.
WHAT JUST HAPPENED?
TEMPERANCE.

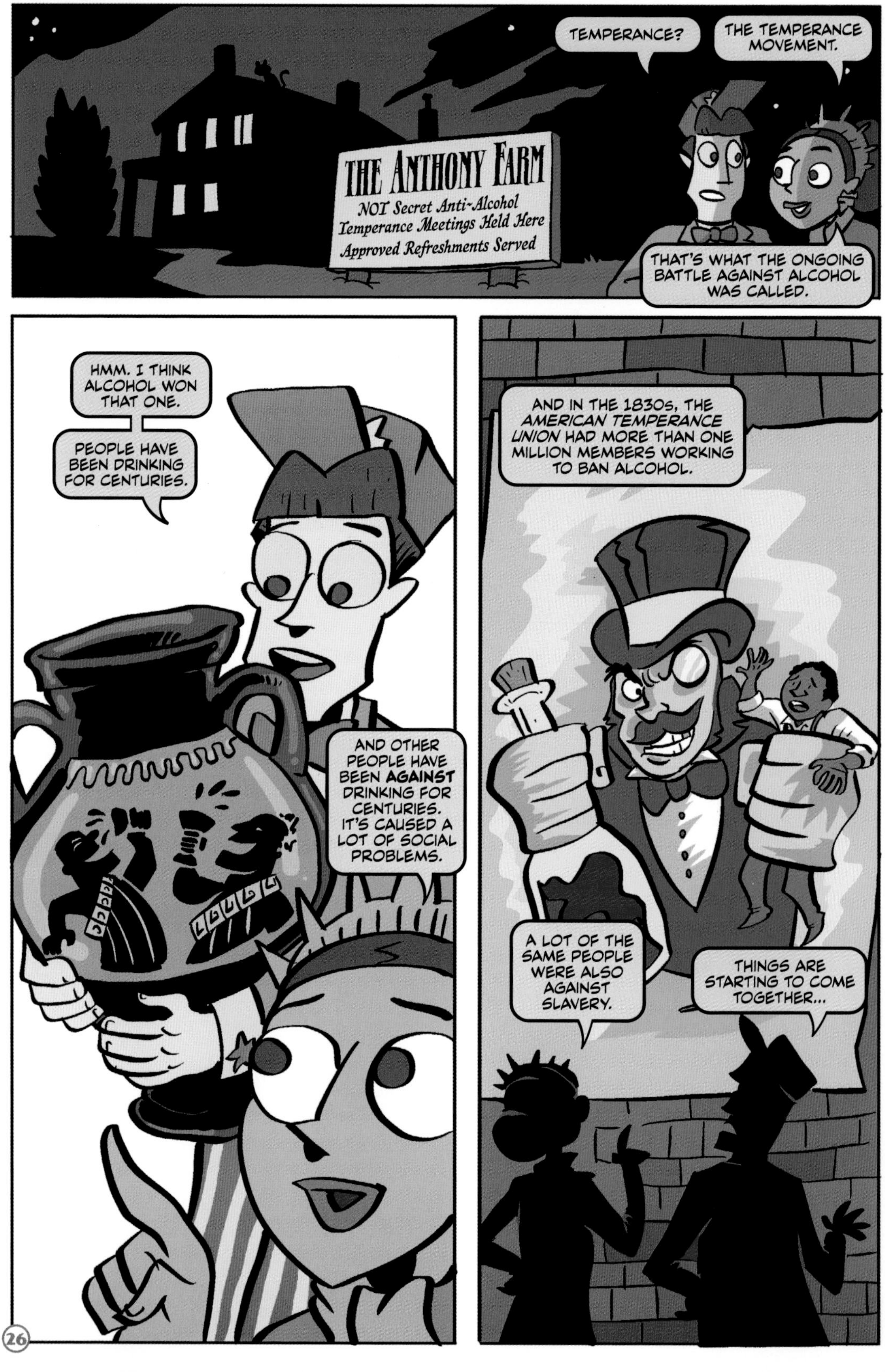
TEMPERANCE?
THE TEMPERANCE MOVEMENT.
THE ANTHONY FARM
NOT Secret Anti-Alcohol Temperance Meetings Held Here
Approved Refreshments Served
THAT'S WHAT THE ONGOING BATTLE AGAINST ALCOHOL WAS CALLED.
HMM. I THINK ALCOHOL WON THAT ONE.
PEOPLE HAVE BEEN DRINKING FOR CENTURIES.
AND OTHER PEOPLE HAVE BEEN **AGAINST** DRINKING FOR CENTURIES. IT'S CAUSED A LOT OF SOCIAL PROBLEMS.
AND IN THE 1830s, THE *AMERICAN TEMPERANCE UNION* HAD MORE THAN ONE MILLION MEMBERS WORKING TO BAN ALCOHOL.
A LOT OF THE SAME PEOPLE WERE ALSO AGAINST SLAVERY.
THINGS ARE STARTING TO COME TOGETHER...

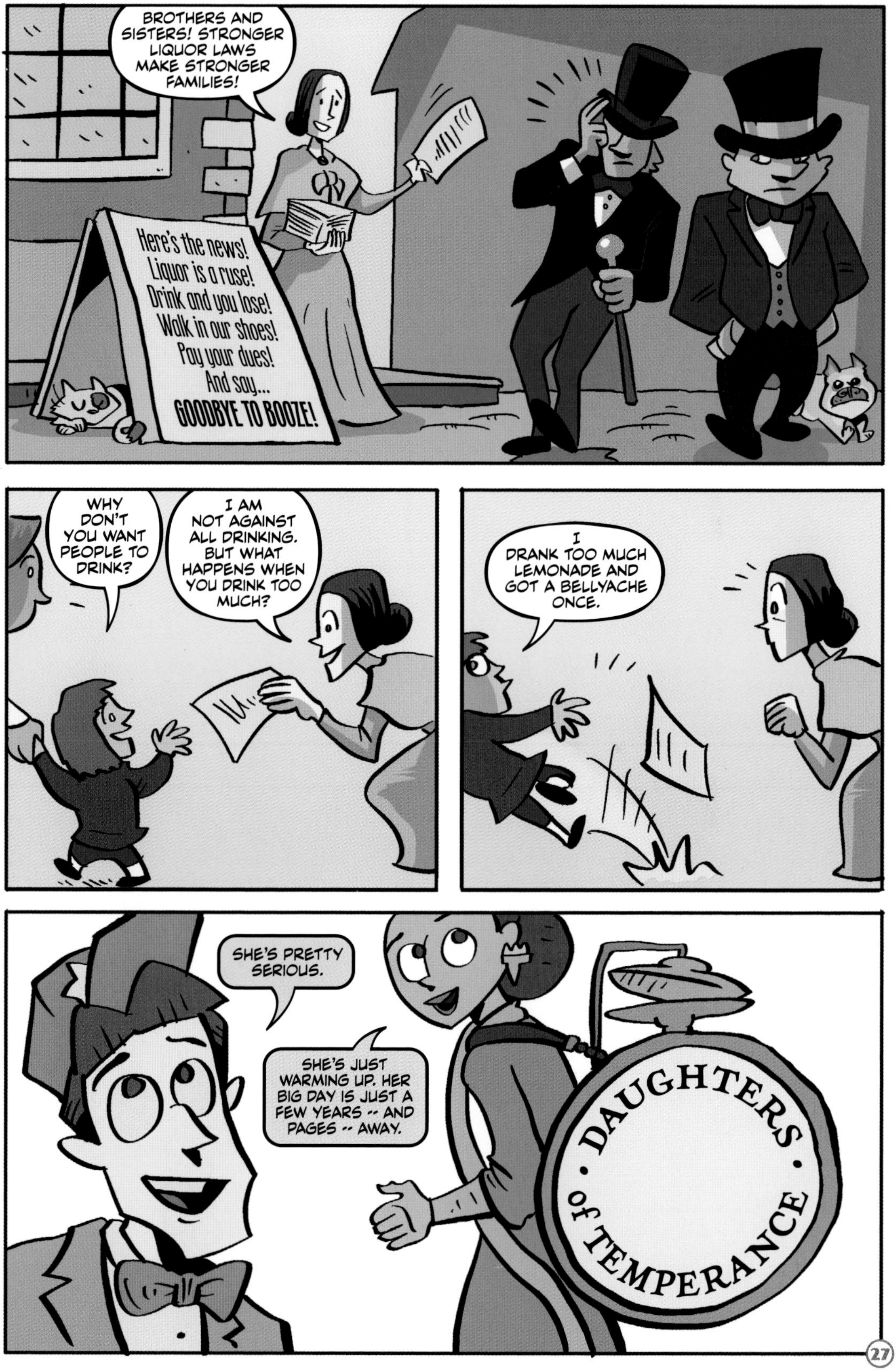
BROTHERS AND SISTERS! STRONGER LIQUOR LAWS MAKE STRONGER FAMILIES!
Here's the news! Liquor is a ruse! Drink and you lose! Walk in our shoes! Pay your dues! And say... GOODBYE TO BOOZE!
WHY DON'T YOU WANT PEOPLE TO DRINK?
I AM NOT AGAINST ALL DRINKING. BUT WHAT HAPPENS WHEN YOU DRINK TOO MUCH?
I DRANK TOO MUCH LEMONADE AND GOT A BELLYACHE ONCE.
SHE'S PRETTY SERIOUS.
SHE'S JUST WARMING UP. HER BIG DAY IS JUST A FEW YEARS -- AND PAGES -- AWAY.
DAUGHTERS of TEMPERANCE

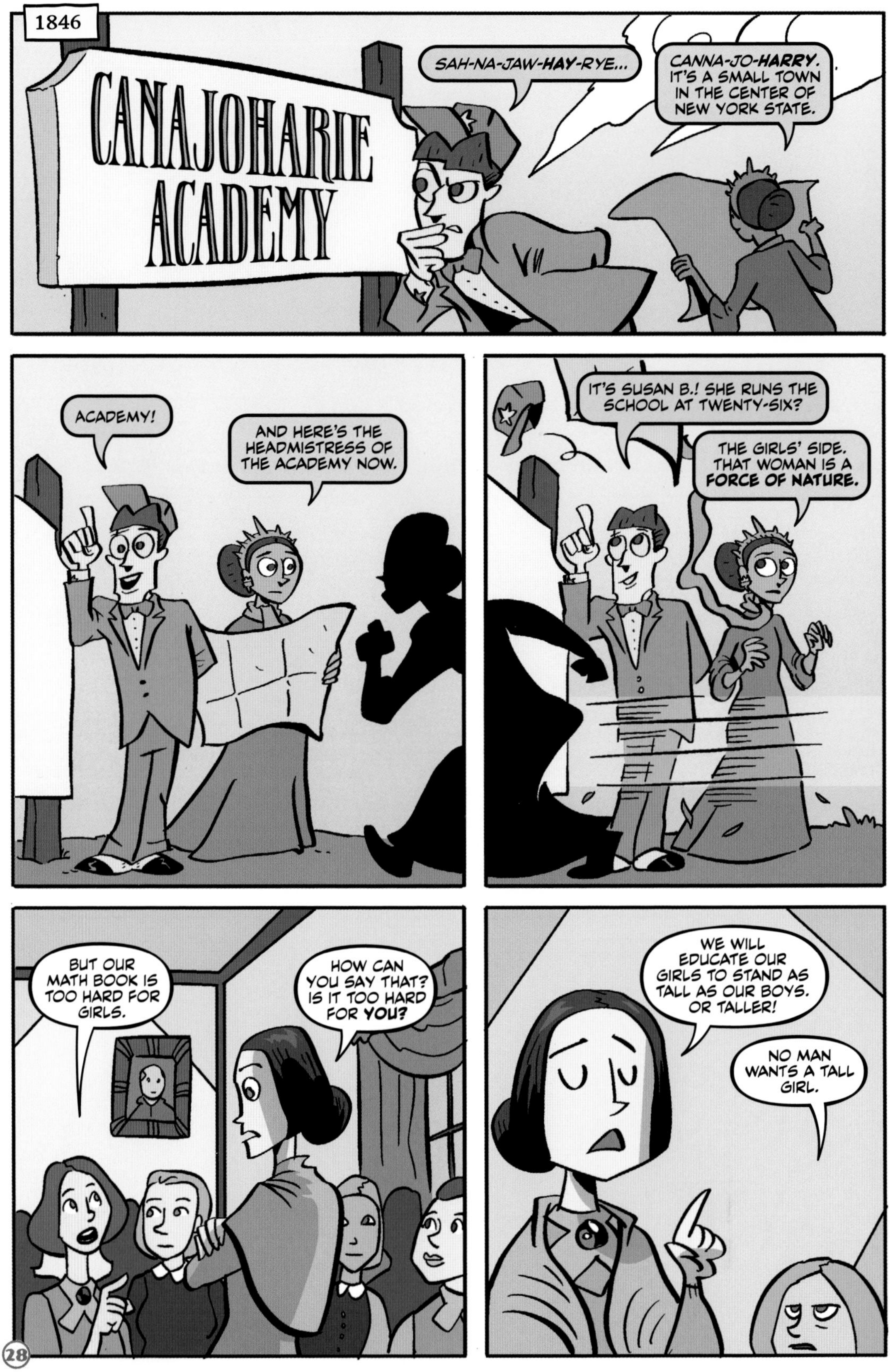
1846
CANAJOHARIE ACADEMY
SAH-NA-JAW-HAY-RYE...
CANNA-JO-HARRY. IT'S A SMALL TOWN IN THE CENTER OF NEW YORK STATE.
ACADEMY!
AND HERE'S THE HEADMISTRESS OF THE ACADEMY NOW.
IT'S SUSAN B.! SHE RUNS THE SCHOOL AT TWENTY-SIX?
THE GIRLS' SIDE. THAT WOMAN IS A FORCE OF NATURE.
BUT OUR MATH BOOK IS TOO HARD FOR GIRLS.
HOW CAN YOU SAY THAT? IS IT TOO HARD FOR YOU?
WE WILL EDUCATE OUR GIRLS TO STAND AS TALL AS OUR BOYS. OR TALLER!
NO MAN WANTS A TALL GIRL.

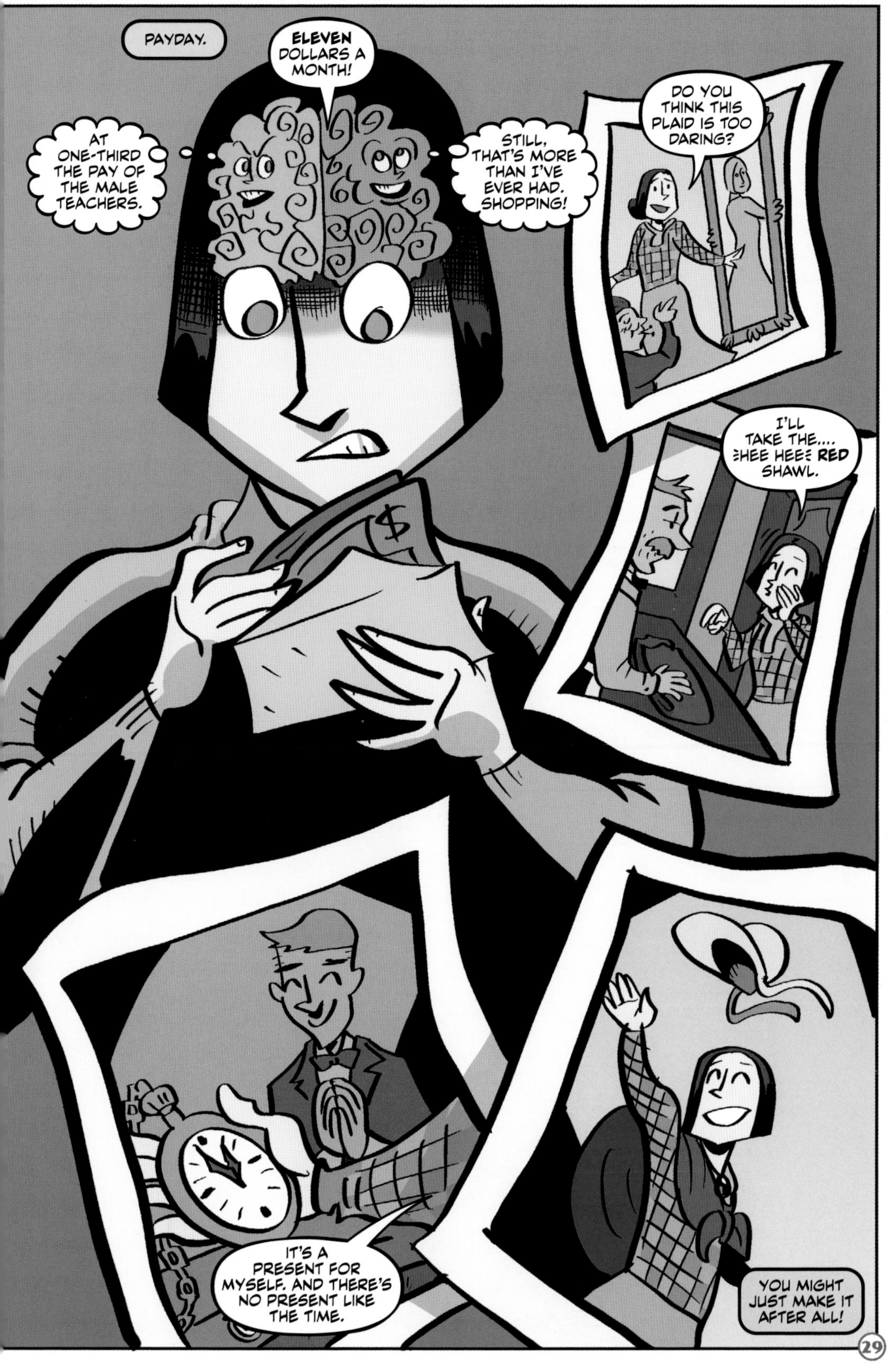
PAYDAY.
ELEVEN DOLLARS A MONTH!
AT ONE-THIRD THE PAY OF THE MALE TEACHERS.
STILL, THAT'S MORE THAN I'VE EVER HAD. SHOPPING!
DO YOU THINK THIS PLAID IS TOO DARING?
I'LL TAKE THE.... ≷HEE HEE≷ RED SHAWL.
IT'S A PRESENT FOR MYSELF. AND THERE'S NO PRESENT LIKE THE TIME.
YOU MIGHT JUST MAKE IT AFTER ALL!

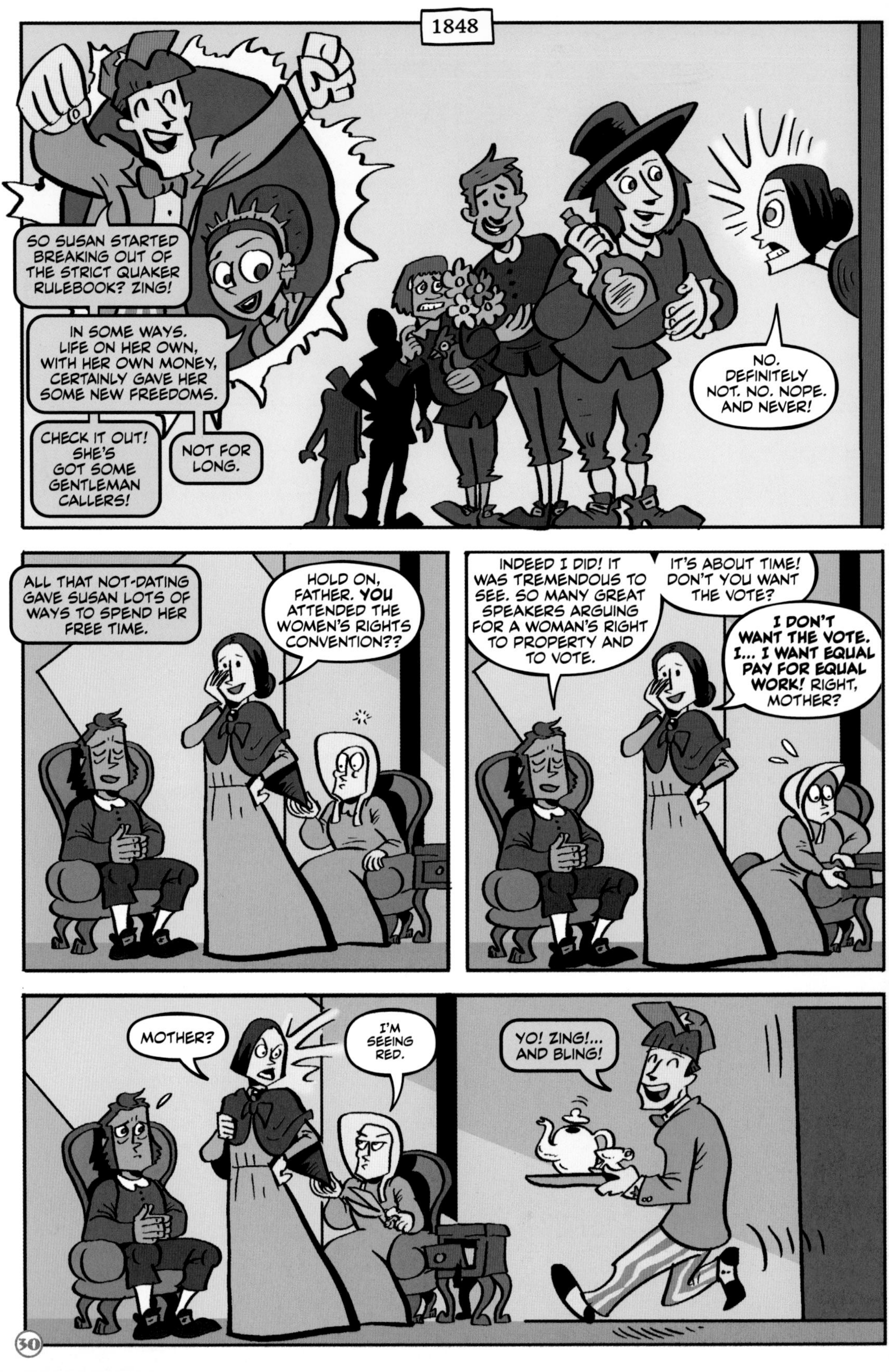
1848
SO SUSAN STARTED BREAKING OUT OF THE STRICT QUAKER RULEBOOK? ZING!
IN SOME WAYS. LIFE ON HER OWN, WITH HER OWN MONEY, CERTAINLY GAVE HER SOME NEW FREEDOMS.
CHECK IT OUT! SHE'S GOT SOME GENTLEMAN CALLERS!
NOT FOR LONG.
NO. DEFINITELY NOT. NO. NOPE. AND NEVER!
ALL THAT NOT-DATING GAVE SUSAN LOTS OF WAYS TO SPEND HER FREE TIME.
HOLD ON, FATHER. YOU ATTENDED THE WOMEN'S RIGHTS CONVENTION??
INDEED I DID! IT WAS TREMENDOUS TO SEE. SO MANY GREAT SPEAKERS ARGUING FOR A WOMAN'S RIGHT TO PROPERTY AND TO VOTE.
IT'S ABOUT TIME! DON'T YOU WANT THE VOTE?
I DON'T WANT THE VOTE. I... I WANT EQUAL PAY FOR EQUAL WORK! RIGHT, MOTHER?
MOTHER?
I'M SEEING RED.
YO! ZING!... AND BLING!

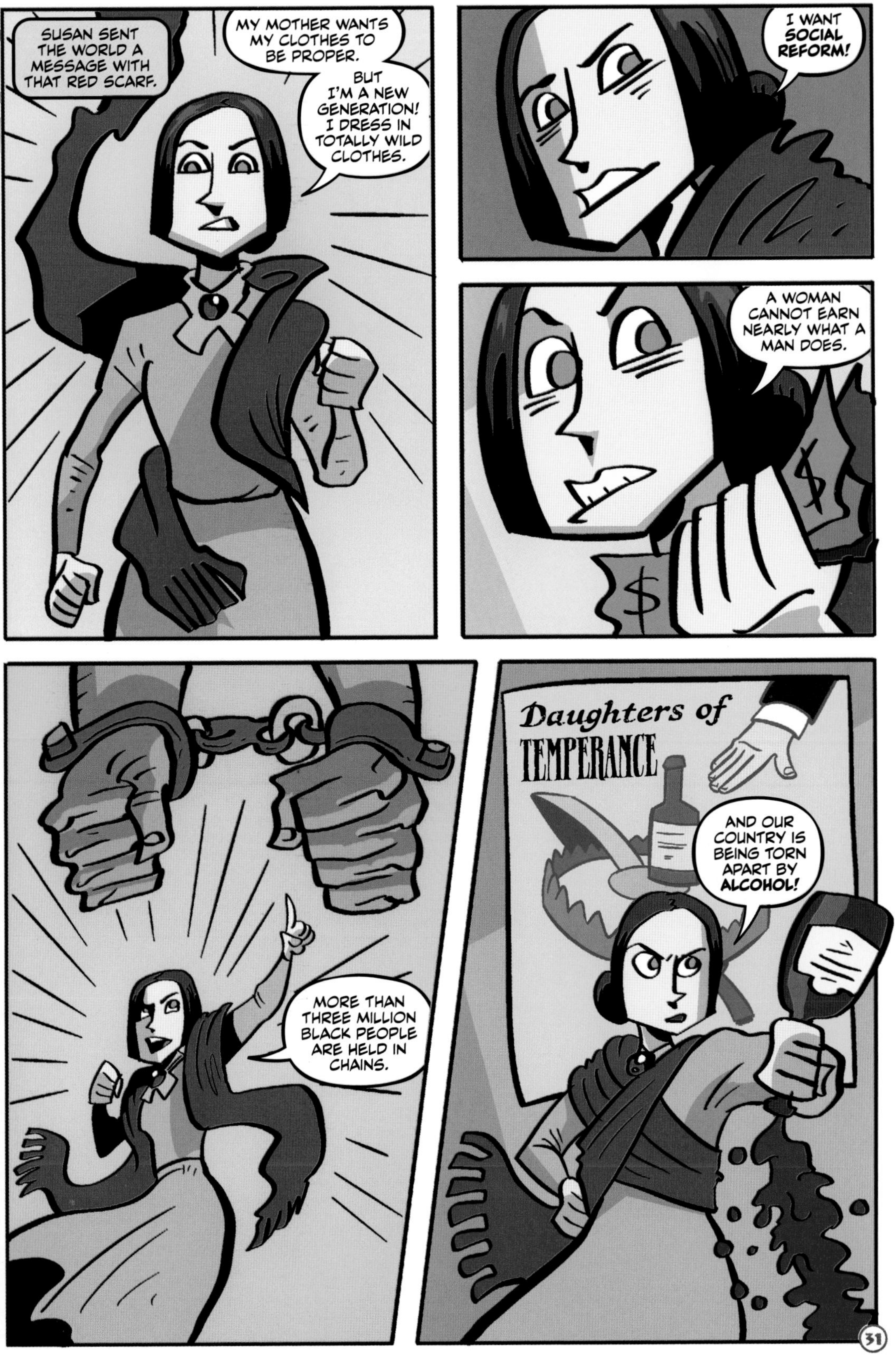
SUSAN SENT THE WORLD A MESSAGE WITH THAT RED SCARF.
MY MOTHER WANTS MY CLOTHES TO BE PROPER.
BUT I'M A NEW GENERATION! I DRESS IN TOTALLY WILD CLOTHES.
I WANT SOCIAL REFORM!
A WOMAN CANNOT EARN NEARLY WHAT A MAN DOES.
MORE THAN THREE MILLION BLACK PEOPLE ARE HELD IN CHAINS.
Daughters of TEMPERANCE
AND OUR COUNTRY IS BEING TORN APART BY ALCOHOL!

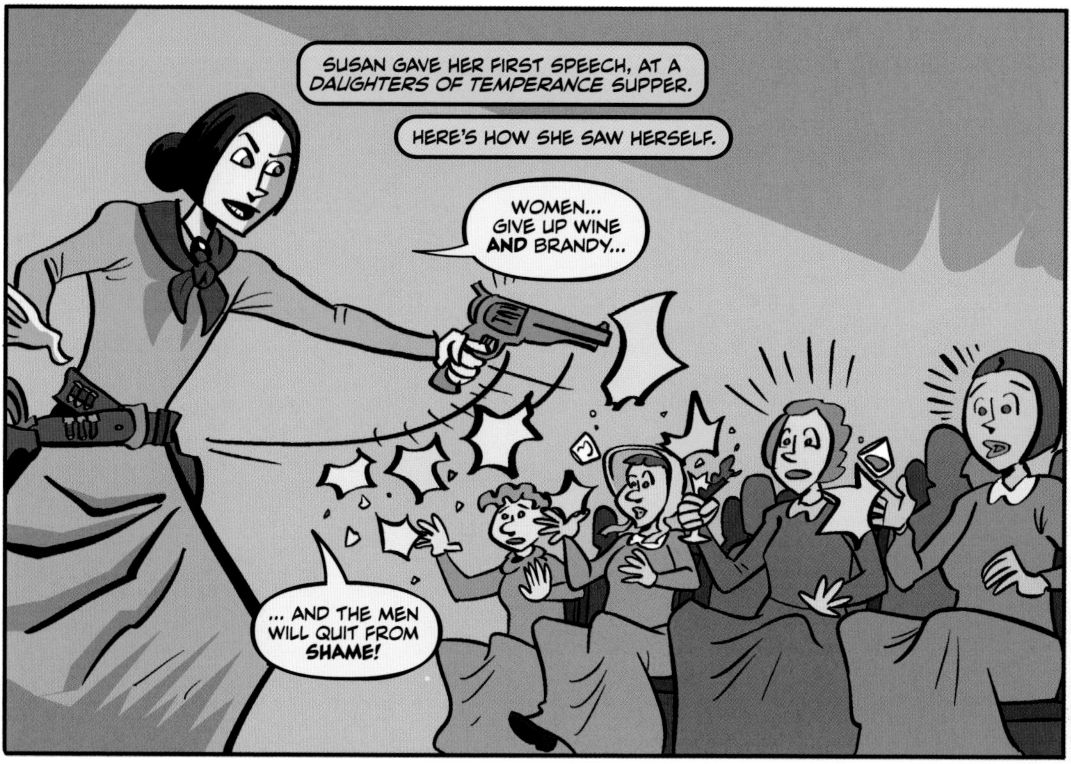
SUSAN GAVE HER FIRST SPEECH, AT A *DAUGHTERS OF TEMPERANCE* SUPPER.
HERE'S HOW SHE SAW HERSELF.
WOMEN... GIVE UP WINE **AND** BRANDY...
... AND THE MEN WILL QUIT FROM **SHAME!**

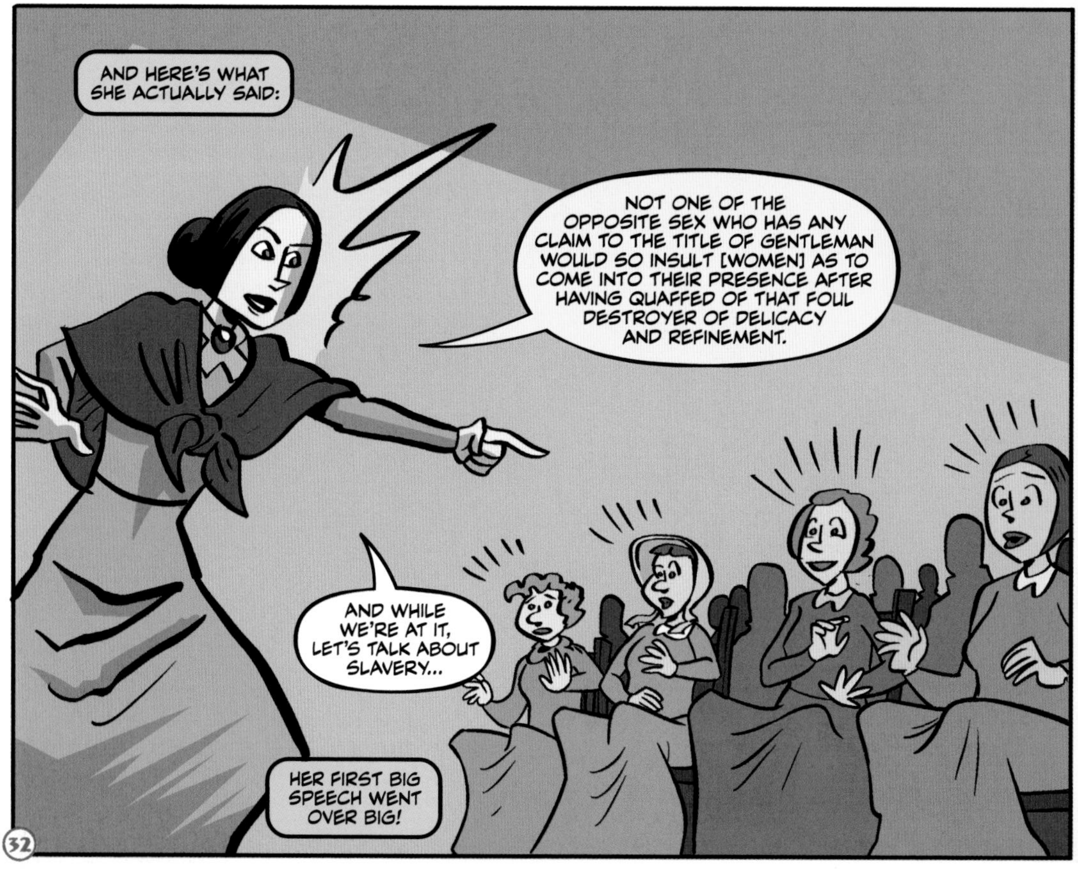
AND HERE'S WHAT SHE ACTUALLY SAID:
NOT ONE OF THE OPPOSITE SEX WHO HAS ANY CLAIM TO THE TITLE OF GENTLEMAN WOULD SO INSULT [WOMEN] AS TO COME INTO THEIR PRESENCE AFTER HAVING QUAFFED OF THAT FOUL DESTROYER OF DELICACY AND REFINEMENT.
AND WHILE WE'RE AT IT, LET'S TALK ABOUT SLAVERY...
HER FIRST BIG SPEECH WENT OVER BIG!

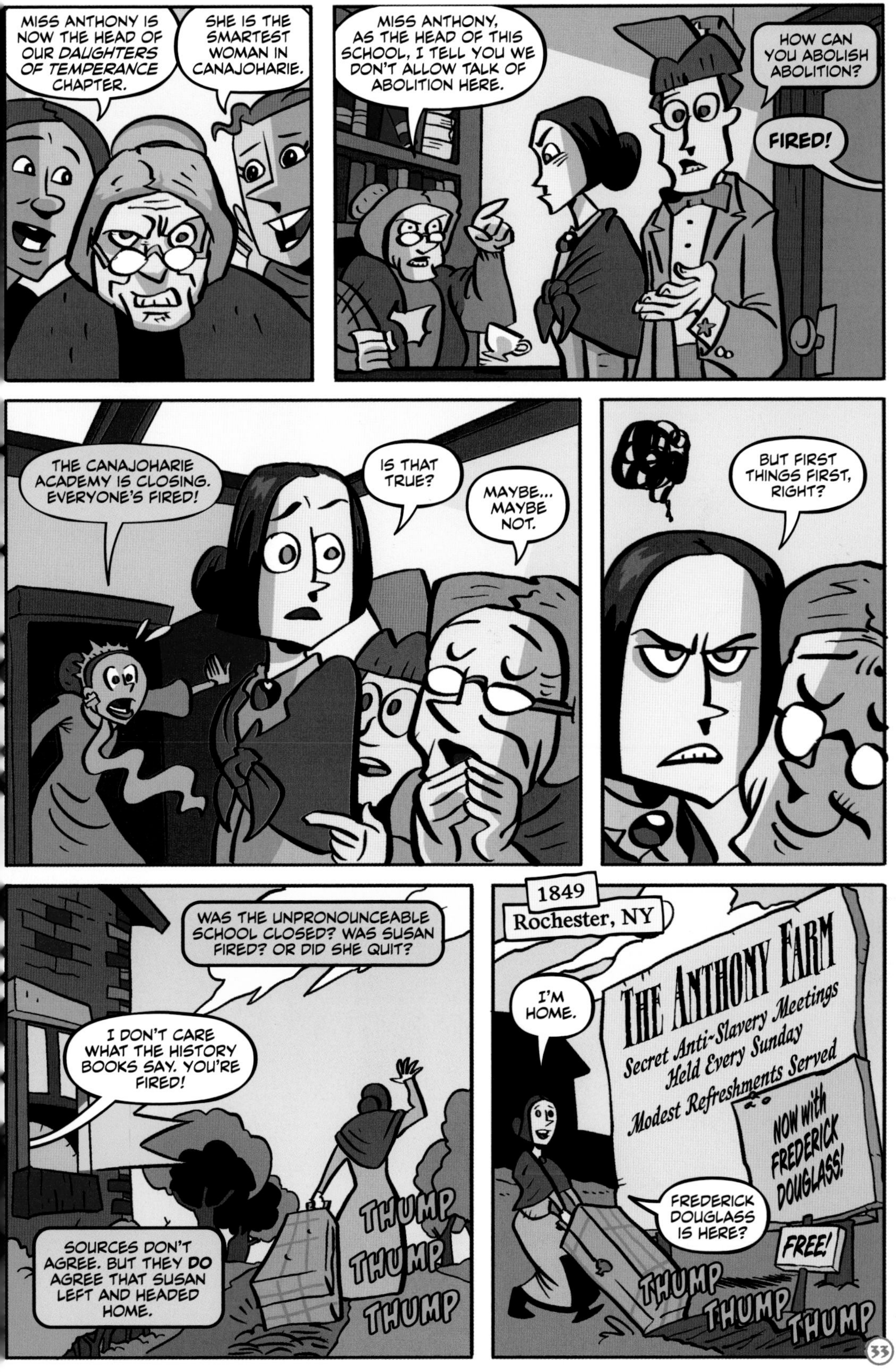
MISS ANTHONY IS NOW THE HEAD OF OUR DAUGHTERS OF TEMPERANCE CHAPTER.
SHE IS THE SMARTEST WOMAN IN CANAJOHARIE.
MISS ANTHONY, AS THE HEAD OF THIS SCHOOL, I TELL YOU WE DON'T ALLOW TALK OF ABOLITION HERE.
HOW CAN YOU ABOLISH ABOLITION?
FIRED!
THE CANAJOHARIE ACADEMY IS CLOSING. EVERYONE'S FIRED!
IS THAT TRUE?
MAYBE... MAYBE NOT.
BUT FIRST THINGS FIRST, RIGHT?
WAS THE UNPRONOUNCEABLE SCHOOL CLOSED? WAS SUSAN FIRED? OR DID SHE QUIT?
I DON'T CARE WHAT THE HISTORY BOOKS SAY. YOU'RE FIRED!
SOURCES DON'T AGREE. BUT THEY DO AGREE THAT SUSAN LEFT AND HEADED HOME.
THUMP
THUMP
THUMP
1849
Rochester, NY
THE ANTHONY FARM
Secret Anti-Slavery Meetings
Held Every Sunday
Modest Refreshments Served
NOW WITH FREDERICK DOUGLASS!
FREE!
I'M HOME.
FREDERICK DOUGLASS IS HERE?
THUMP
THUMP
THUMP

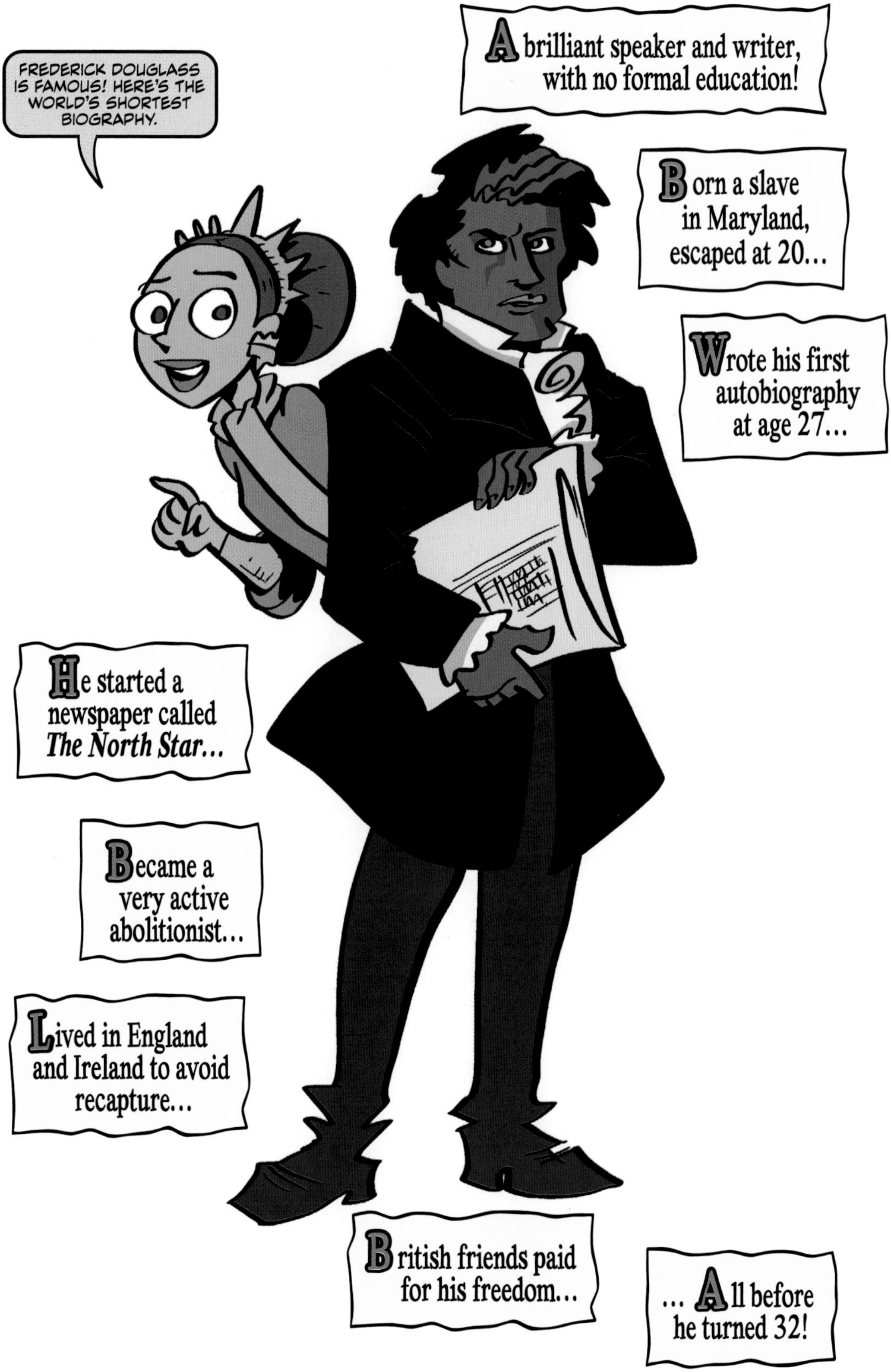
FREDERICK DOUGLASS IS FAMOUS! HERE'S THE WORLD'S SHORTEST BIOGRAPHY.
A brilliant speaker and writer, with no formal education!
Born a slave in Maryland, escaped at 20...
Wrote his first autobiography at age 27...
He started a newspaper called *The North Star*...
Became a very active abolitionist...
Lived in England and Ireland to avoid recapture...
British friends paid for his freedom...
... All before he turned 32!

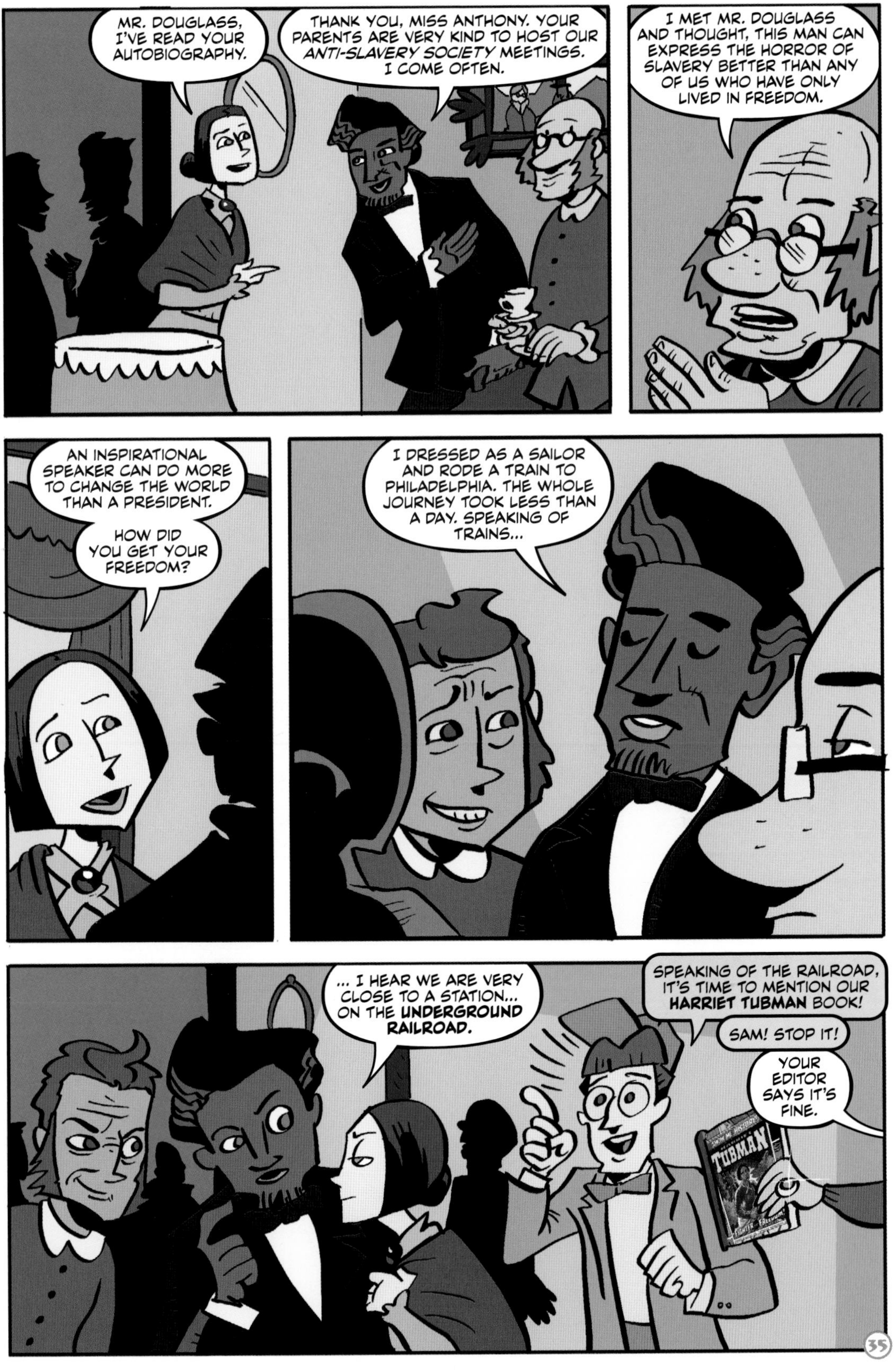
MR. DOUGLASS, I'VE READ YOUR AUTOBIOGRAPHY.
THANK YOU, MISS ANTHONY. YOUR PARENTS ARE VERY KIND TO HOST OUR *ANTI-SLAVERY SOCIETY* MEETINGS. I COME OFTEN.
I MET MR. DOUGLASS AND THOUGHT, THIS MAN CAN EXPRESS THE HORROR OF SLAVERY BETTER THAN ANY OF US WHO HAVE ONLY LIVED IN FREEDOM.
AN INSPIRATIONAL SPEAKER CAN DO MORE TO CHANGE THE WORLD THAN A PRESIDENT.
HOW DID YOU GET YOUR FREEDOM?
I DRESSED AS A SAILOR AND RODE A TRAIN TO PHILADELPHIA. THE WHOLE JOURNEY TOOK LESS THAN A DAY. SPEAKING OF TRAINS...
... I HEAR WE ARE VERY CLOSE TO A STATION... ON THE **UNDERGROUND RAILROAD.**
SPEAKING OF THE RAILROAD, IT'S TIME TO MENTION OUR **HARRIET TUBMAN** BOOK!
SAM! STOP IT!
YOUR EDITOR SAYS IT'S FINE.
TUBMAN

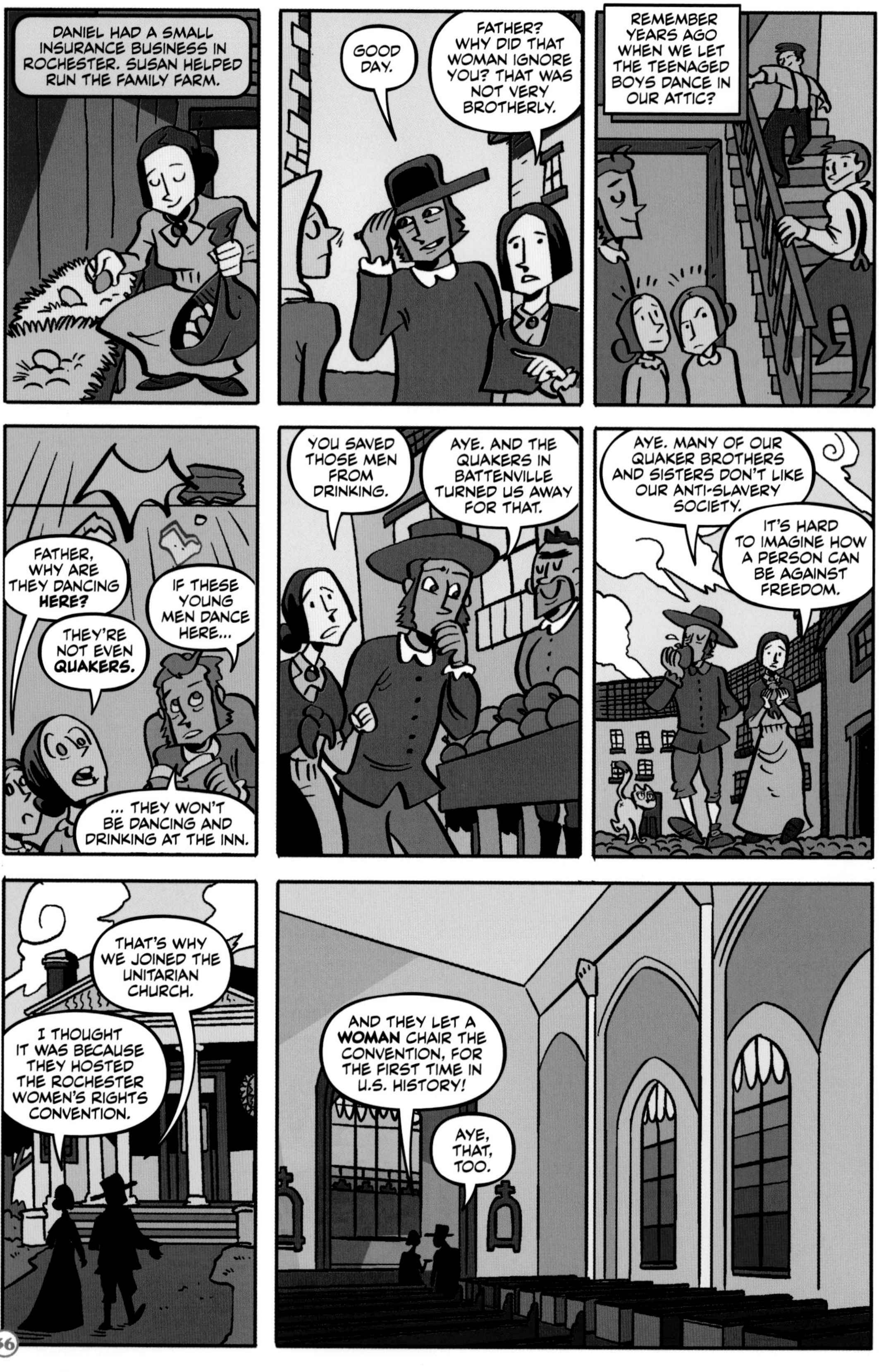
DANIEL HAD A SMALL INSURANCE BUSINESS IN ROCHESTER. SUSAN HELPED RUN THE FAMILY FARM.
GOOD DAY.
FATHER? WHY DID THAT WOMAN IGNORE YOU? THAT WAS NOT VERY BROTHERLY.
REMEMBER YEARS AGO WHEN WE LET THE TEENAGED BOYS DANCE IN OUR ATTIC?
FATHER, WHY ARE THEY DANCING HERE?
THEY'RE NOT EVEN QUAKERS.
IF THESE YOUNG MEN DANCE HERE...
... THEY WON'T BE DANCING AND DRINKING AT THE INN.
YOU SAVED THOSE MEN FROM DRINKING.
AYE. AND THE QUAKERS IN BATTENVILLE TURNED US AWAY FOR THAT.
AYE. MANY OF OUR QUAKER BROTHERS AND SISTERS DON'T LIKE OUR ANTI-SLAVERY SOCIETY.
IT'S HARD TO IMAGINE HOW A PERSON CAN BE AGAINST FREEDOM.
THAT'S WHY WE JOINED THE UNITARIAN CHURCH.
I THOUGHT IT WAS BECAUSE THEY HOSTED THE ROCHESTER WOMEN'S RIGHTS CONVENTION.
AND THEY LET A WOMAN CHAIR THE CONVENTION, FOR THE FIRST TIME IN U.S. HISTORY!
AYE, THAT, TOO.

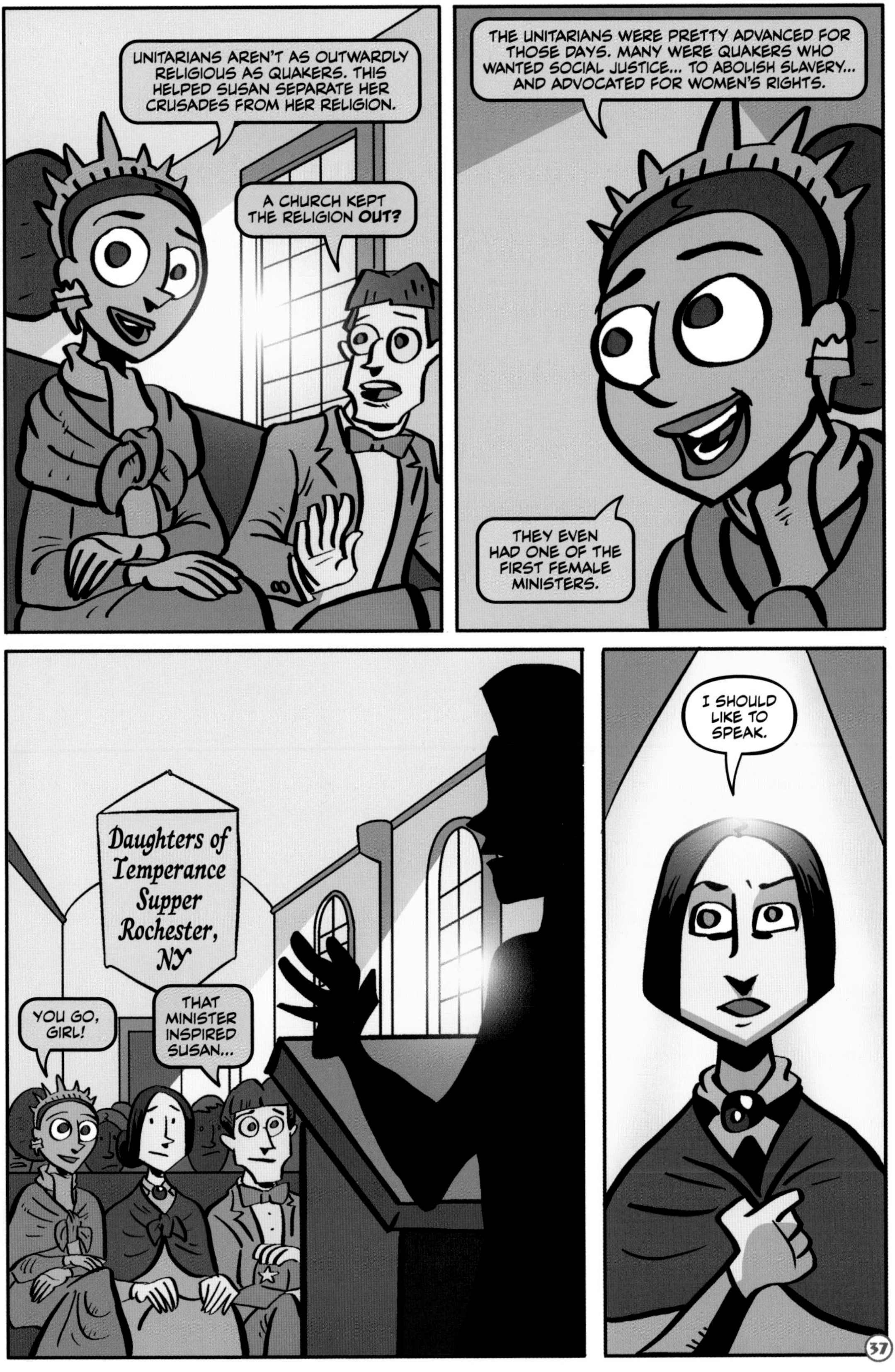
UNITARIANS AREN'T AS OUTWARDLY RELIGIOUS AS QUAKERS. THIS HELPED SUSAN SEPARATE HER CRUSADES FROM HER RELIGION.
A CHURCH KEPT THE RELIGION **OUT?**
THE UNITARIANS WERE PRETTY ADVANCED FOR THOSE DAYS. MANY WERE QUAKERS WHO WANTED SOCIAL JUSTICE... TO ABOLISH SLAVERY... AND ADVOCATED FOR WOMEN'S RIGHTS.
THEY EVEN HAD ONE OF THE FIRST FEMALE MINISTERS.
Daughters of Temperance Supper Rochester, NY
YOU GO, GIRL!
THAT MINISTER INSPIRED SUSAN...
I SHOULD LIKE TO SPEAK.

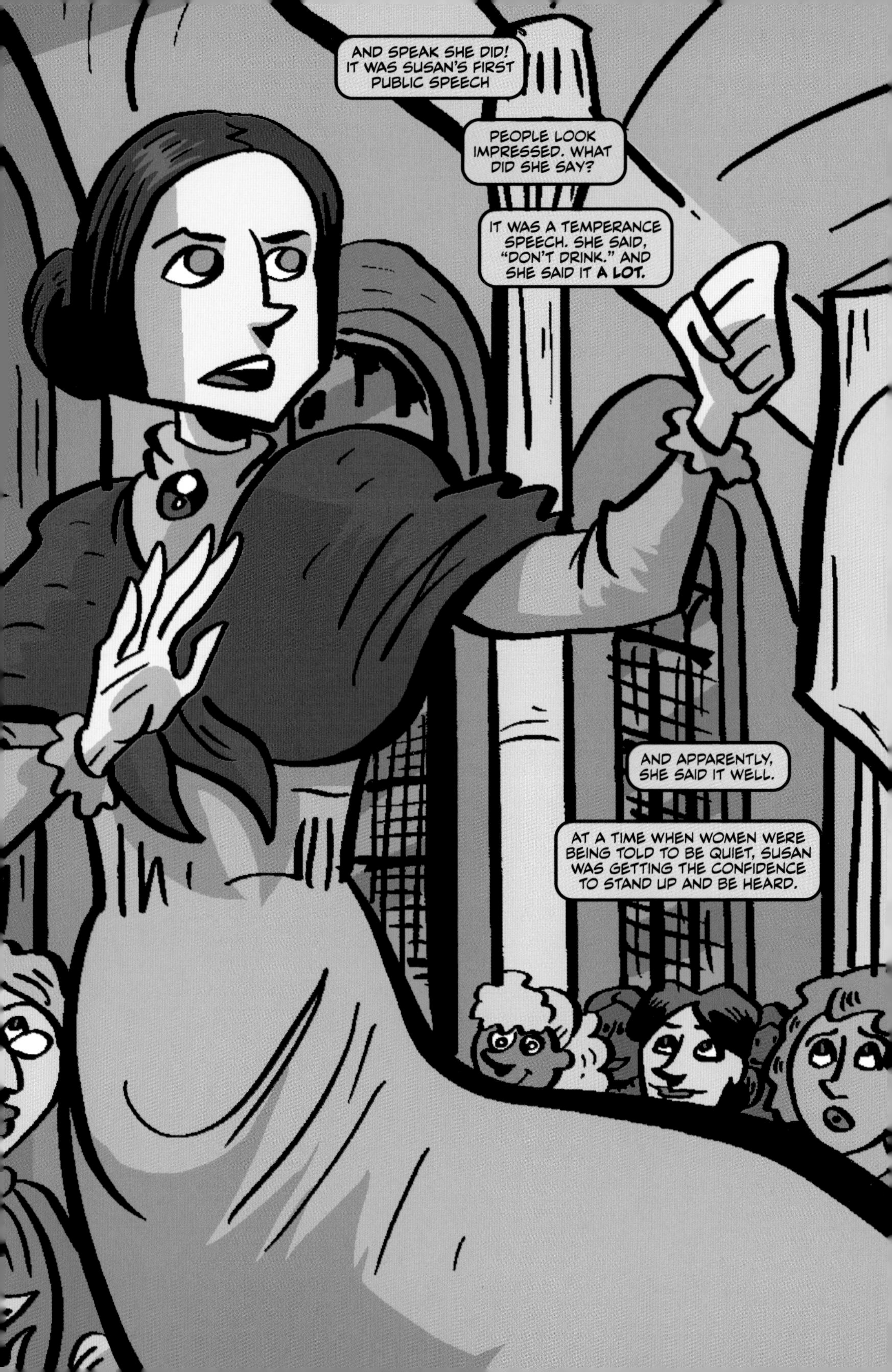
AND SPEAK SHE DID! IT WAS SUSAN'S FIRST PUBLIC SPEECH
PEOPLE LOOK IMPRESSED. WHAT DID SHE SAY?
IT WAS A TEMPERANCE SPEECH. SHE SAID, "DON'T DRINK." AND SHE SAID IT **A LOT.**
AND APPARENTLY, SHE SAID IT WELL.
AT A TIME WHEN WOMEN WERE BEING TOLD TO BE QUIET, SUSAN WAS GETTING THE CONFIDENCE TO STAND UP AND BE HEARD.

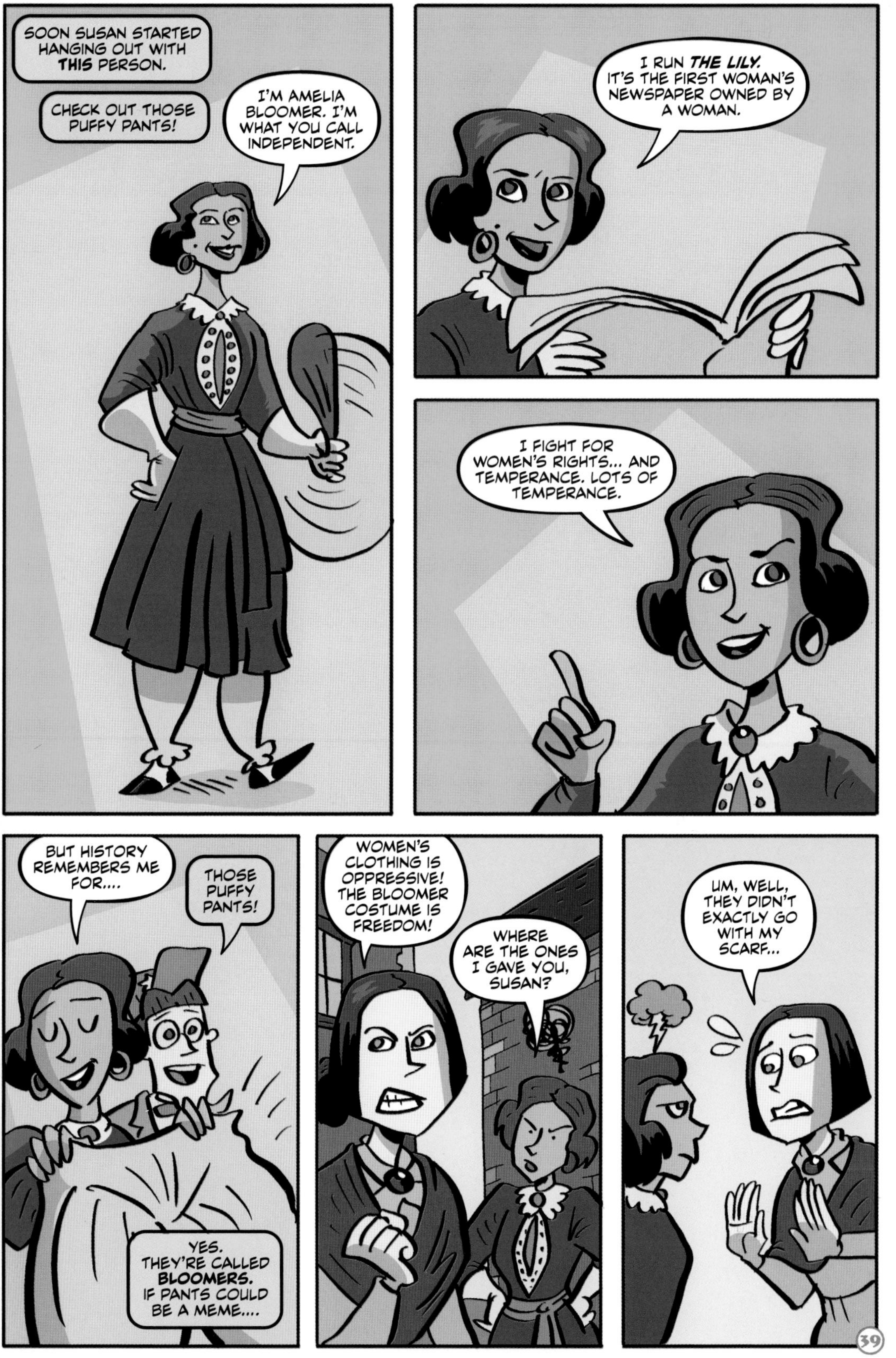

SOON SUSAN STARTED HANGING OUT WITH **THIS** PERSON.
CHECK OUT THOSE PUFFY PANTS!
I'M AMELIA BLOOMER. I'M WHAT YOU CALL INDEPENDENT.
I RUN ***THE LILY.*** IT'S THE FIRST WOMAN'S NEWSPAPER OWNED BY A WOMAN.
I FIGHT FOR WOMEN'S RIGHTS... AND TEMPERANCE. LOTS OF TEMPERANCE.
BUT HISTORY REMEMBERS ME FOR....
THOSE PUFFY PANTS!
YES. THEY'RE CALLED **BLOOMERS.** IF PANTS COULD BE A MEME....
WOMEN'S CLOTHING IS OPPRESSIVE! THE BLOOMER COSTUME IS FREEDOM!
WHERE ARE THE ONES I GAVE YOU, SUSAN?
UM, WELL, THEY DIDN'T EXACTLY GO WITH MY SCARF...

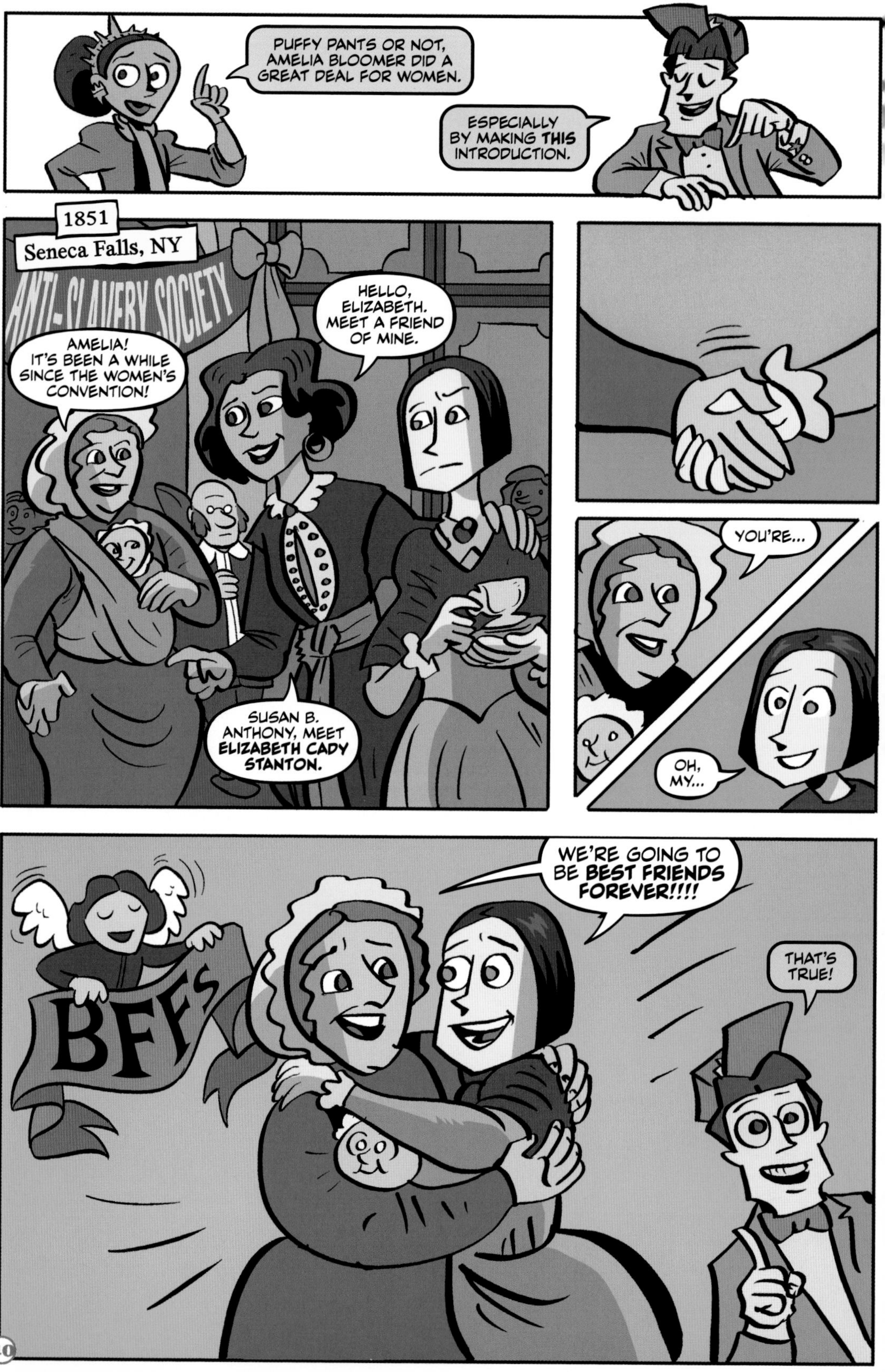
PUFFY PANTS OR NOT, AMELIA BLOOMER DID A GREAT DEAL FOR WOMEN.
ESPECIALLY BY MAKING **THIS** INTRODUCTION.
1851
Seneca Falls, NY
ANTI-SLAVERY SOCIETY
AMELIA! IT'S BEEN A WHILE SINCE THE WOMEN'S CONVENTION!
HELLO, ELIZABETH. MEET A FRIEND OF MINE.
SUSAN B. ANTHONY, MEET **ELIZABETH CADY STANTON.**
YOU'RE...
OH, MY...
WE'RE GOING TO BE **BEST FRIENDS FOREVER!!!!**
BFFs
THAT'S TRUE!

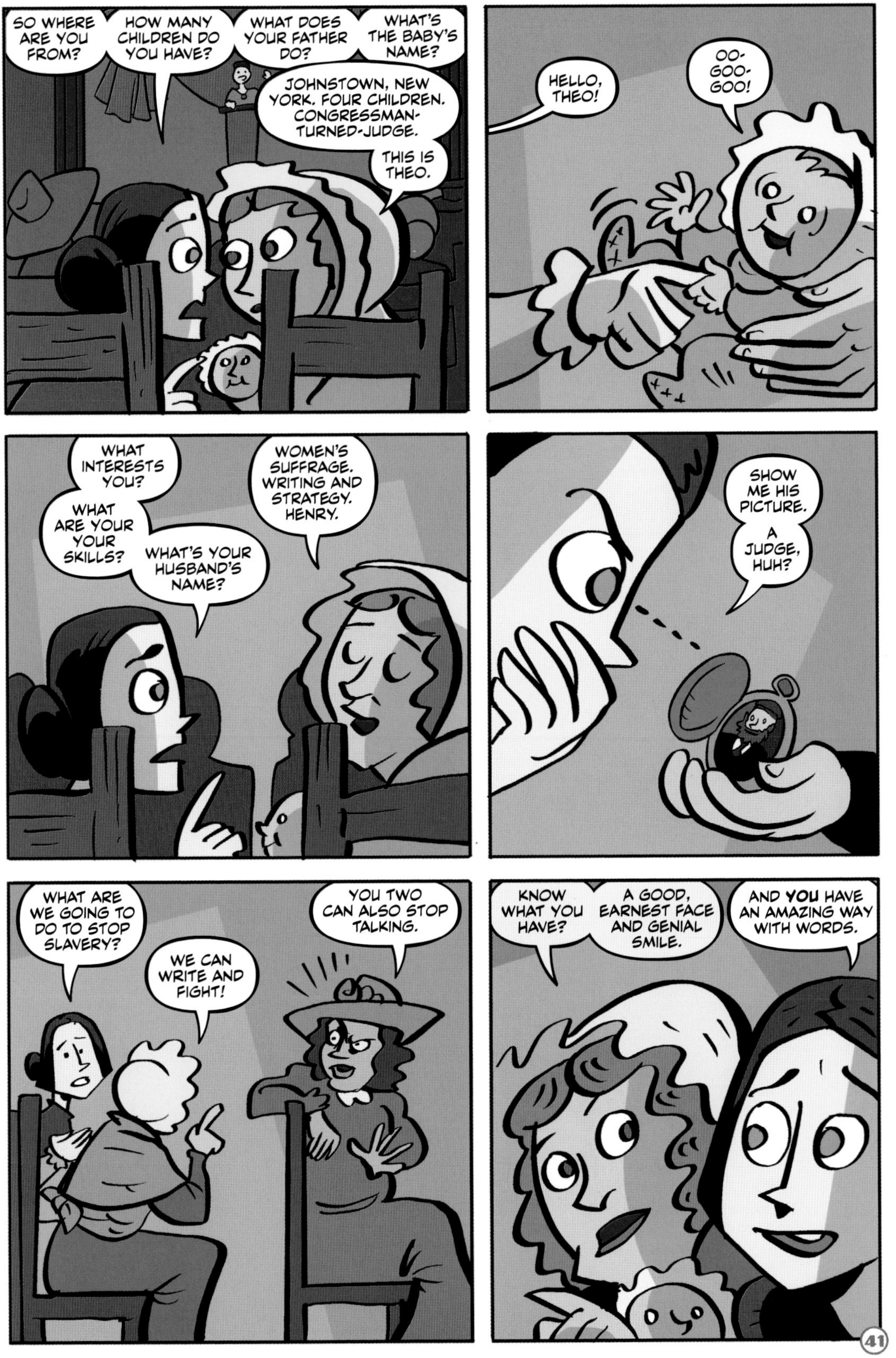
SO WHERE ARE YOU FROM?
HOW MANY CHILDREN DO YOU HAVE?
WHAT DOES YOUR FATHER DO?
WHAT'S THE BABY'S NAME?
JOHNSTOWN, NEW YORK. FOUR CHILDREN. CONGRESSMAN-TURNED-JUDGE.
THIS IS THEO.
HELLO, THEO!
OO-GOO-GOO!
WHAT INTERESTS YOU?
WHAT ARE YOUR YOUR SKILLS?
WHAT'S YOUR HUSBAND'S NAME?
WOMEN'S SUFFRAGE. WRITING AND STRATEGY. HENRY.
SHOW ME HIS PICTURE.
A JUDGE, HUH?
WHAT ARE WE GOING TO DO TO STOP SLAVERY?
WE CAN WRITE AND FIGHT!
YOU TWO CAN ALSO STOP TALKING.
KNOW WHAT YOU HAVE?
A GOOD, EARNEST FACE AND GENIAL SMILE.
AND **YOU** HAVE AN AMAZING WAY WITH WORDS.

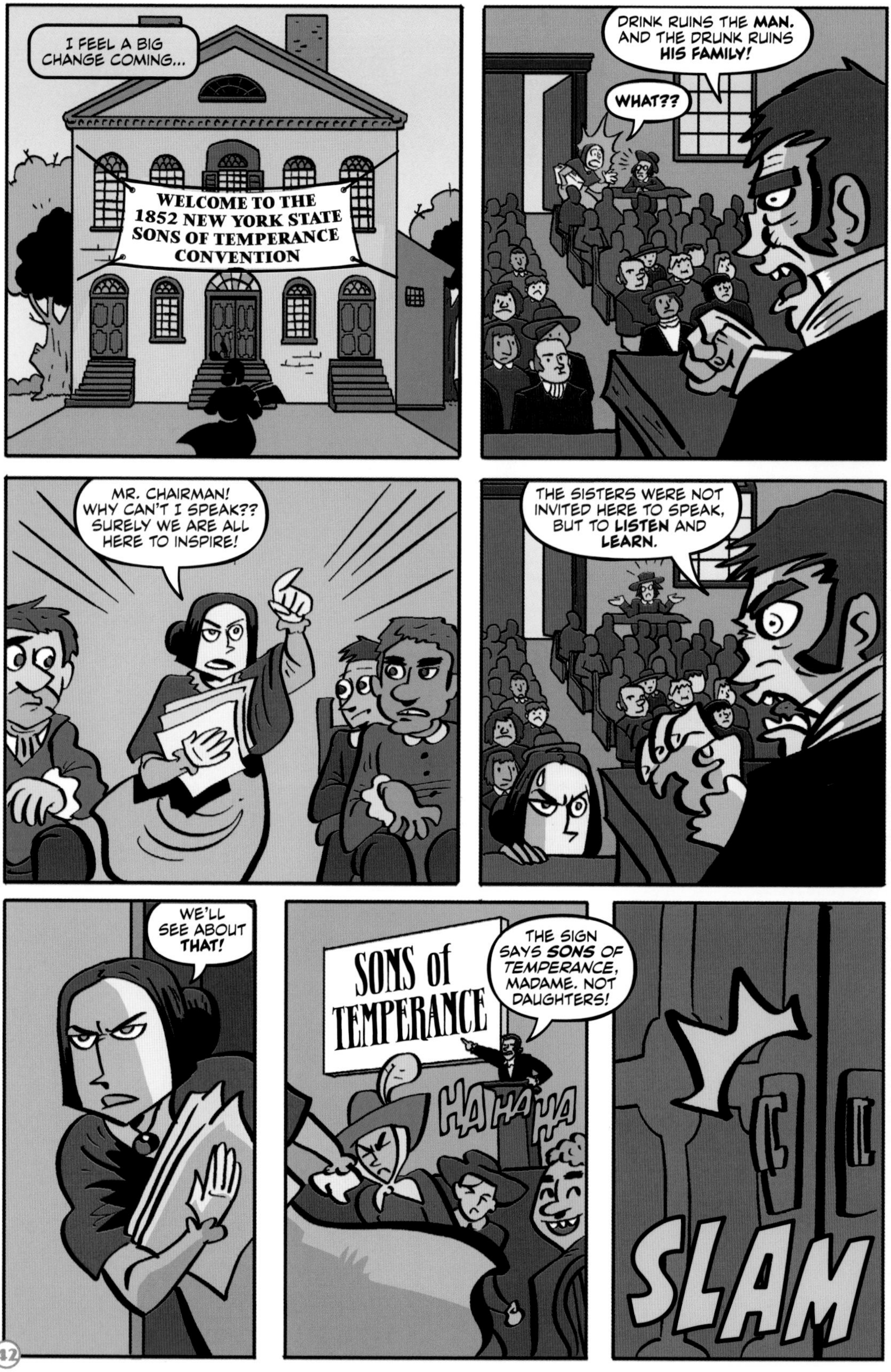
I FEEL A BIG CHANGE COMING...
WELCOME TO THE 1852 NEW YORK STATE SONS OF TEMPERANCE CONVENTION
DRINK RUINS THE MAN. AND THE DRUNK RUINS HIS FAMILY!
WHAT??
MR. CHAIRMAN! WHY CAN'T I SPEAK?? SURELY WE ARE ALL HERE TO INSPIRE!
THE SISTERS WERE NOT INVITED HERE TO SPEAK, BUT TO LISTEN AND LEARN.
WE'LL SEE ABOUT THAT!
SONS of TEMPERANCE
THE SIGN SAYS SONS OF TEMPERANCE, MADAME. NOT DAUGHTERS!
HA HA HA
SLAM

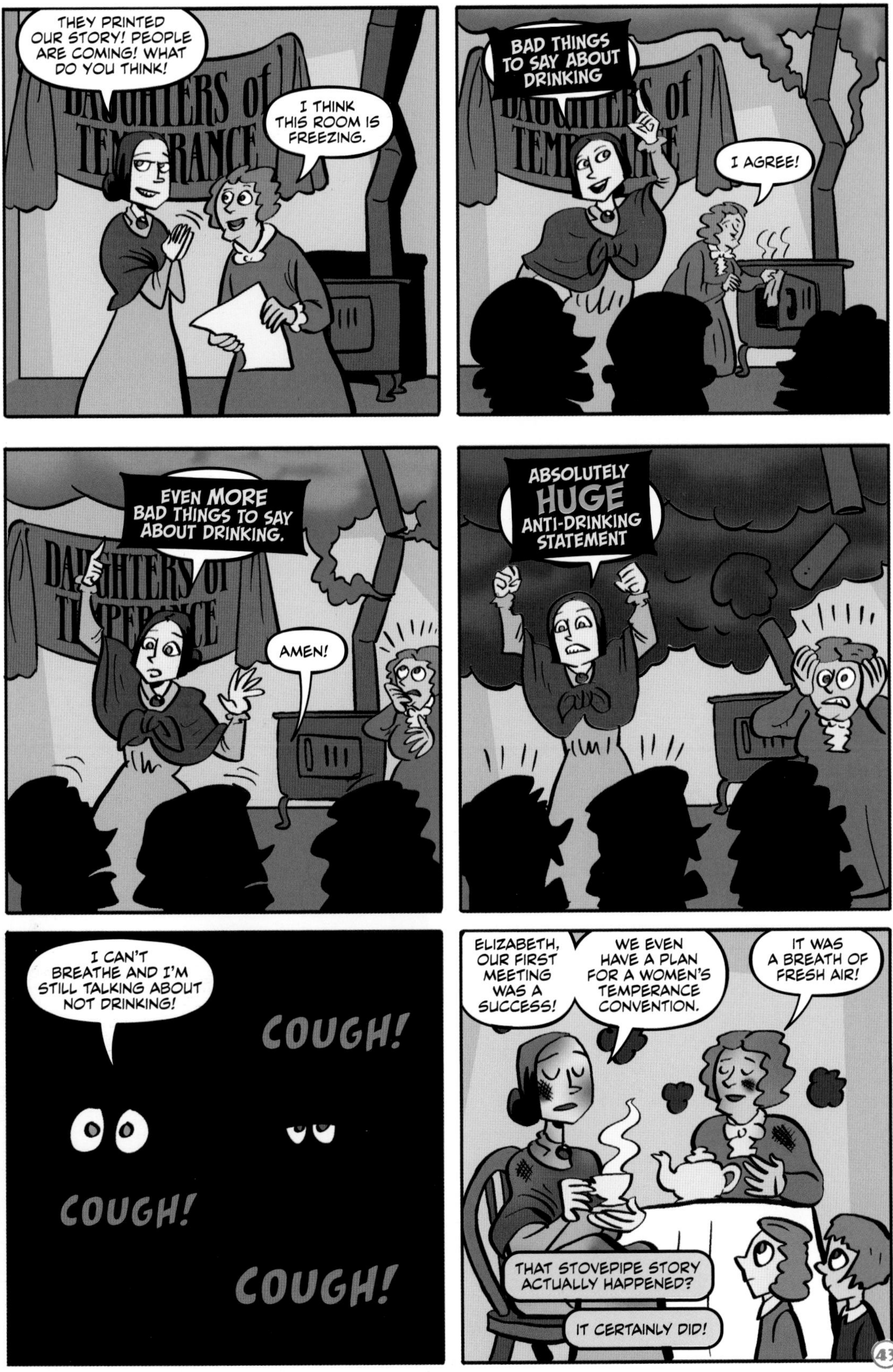
THEY PRINTED OUR STORY! PEOPLE ARE COMING! WHAT DO YOU THINK!
DAUGHTERS of TEMPERANCE
I THINK THIS ROOM IS FREEZING.
BAD THINGS TO SAY ABOUT DRINKING
I AGREE!
EVEN MORE BAD THINGS TO SAY ABOUT DRINKING.
AMEN!
ABSOLUTELY HUGE ANTI-DRINKING STATEMENT
I CAN'T BREATHE AND I'M STILL TALKING ABOUT NOT DRINKING!
COUGH!
COUGH!
COUGH!
ELIZABETH, OUR FIRST MEETING WAS A SUCCESS!
WE EVEN HAVE A PLAN FOR A WOMEN'S TEMPERANCE CONVENTION.
IT WAS A BREATH OF FRESH AIR!
THAT STOVEPIPE STORY ACTUALLY HAPPENED?
IT CERTAINLY DID!

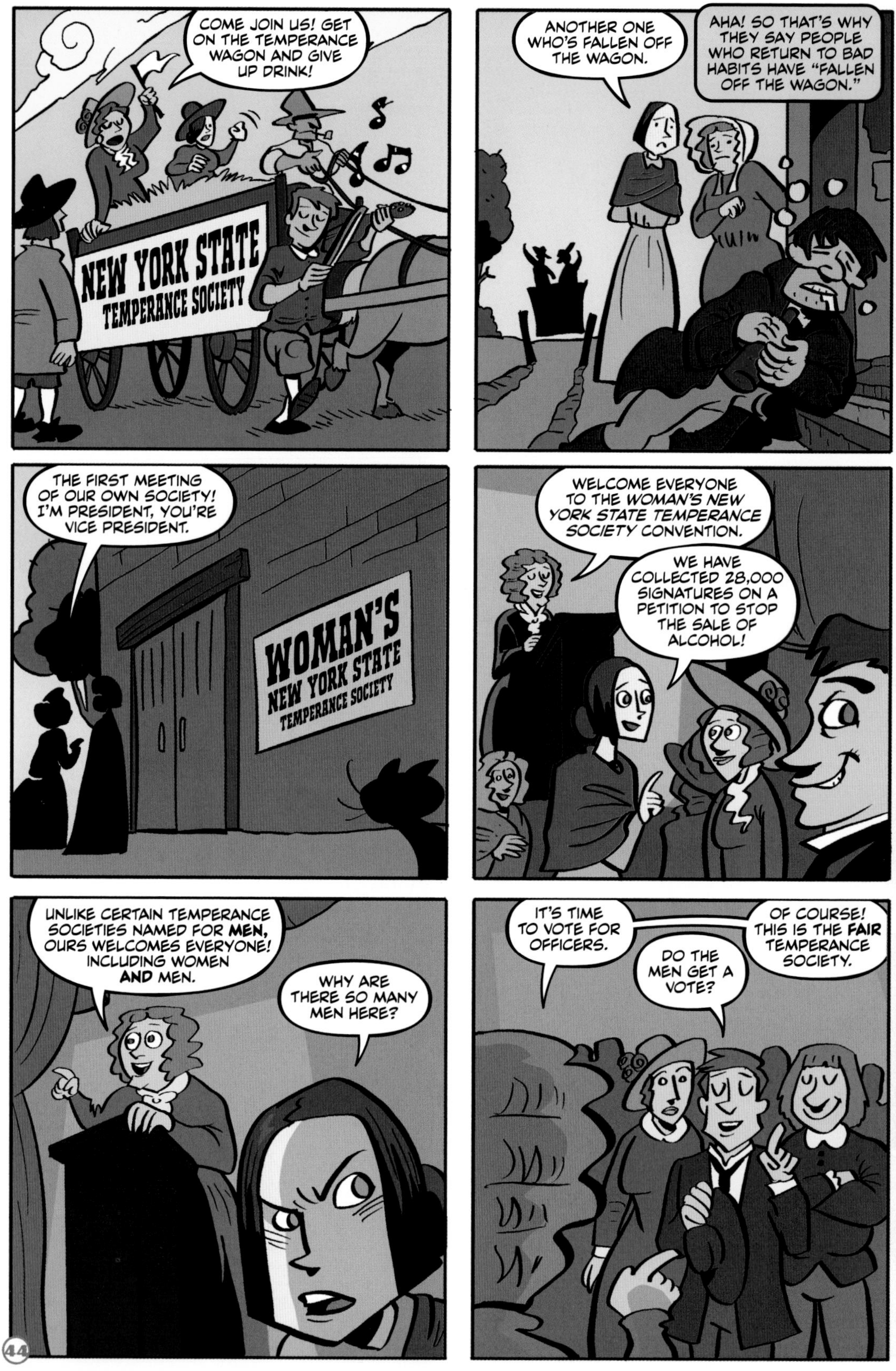
COME JOIN US! GET ON THE TEMPERANCE WAGON AND GIVE UP DRINK!
NEW YORK STATE TEMPERANCE SOCIETY
ANOTHER ONE WHO'S FALLEN OFF THE WAGON.
AHA! SO THAT'S WHY THEY SAY PEOPLE WHO RETURN TO BAD HABITS HAVE "FALLEN OFF THE WAGON."
THE FIRST MEETING OF OUR OWN SOCIETY! I'M PRESIDENT, YOU'RE VICE PRESIDENT.
WOMAN'S NEW YORK STATE TEMPERANCE SOCIETY
WELCOME EVERYONE TO THE *WOMAN'S NEW YORK STATE TEMPERANCE SOCIETY* CONVENTION.
WE HAVE COLLECTED 28,000 SIGNATURES ON A PETITION TO STOP THE SALE OF ALCOHOL!
UNLIKE CERTAIN TEMPERANCE SOCIETIES NAMED FOR **MEN**, OURS WELCOMES EVERYONE! INCLUDING WOMEN **AND** MEN.
WHY ARE THERE SO MANY MEN HERE?
IT'S TIME TO VOTE FOR OFFICERS.
DO THE MEN GET A VOTE?
OF COURSE! THIS IS THE **FAIR** TEMPERANCE SOCIETY.

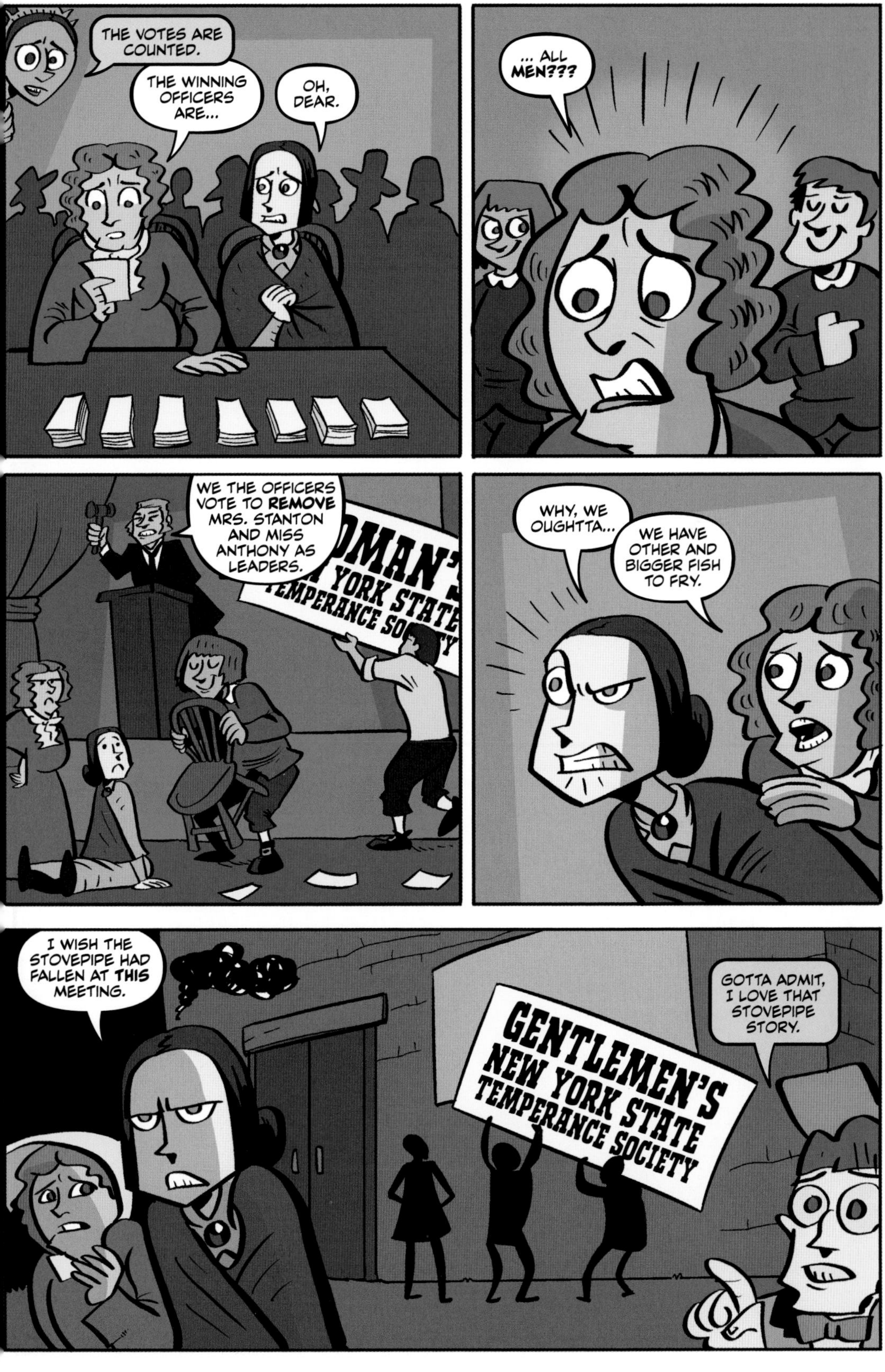
THE VOTES ARE COUNTED.
THE WINNING OFFICERS ARE...
OH, DEAR.
... ALL MEN???
WE THE OFFICERS VOTE TO REMOVE MRS. STANTON AND MISS ANTHONY AS LEADERS.
WHY, WE OUGHTTA...
WE HAVE OTHER AND BIGGER FISH TO FRY.
I WISH THE STOVEPIPE HAD FALLEN AT THIS MEETING.
GENTLEMEN'S NEW YORK STATE TEMPERANCE SOCIETY
GOTTA ADMIT, I LOVE THAT STOVEPIPE STORY.

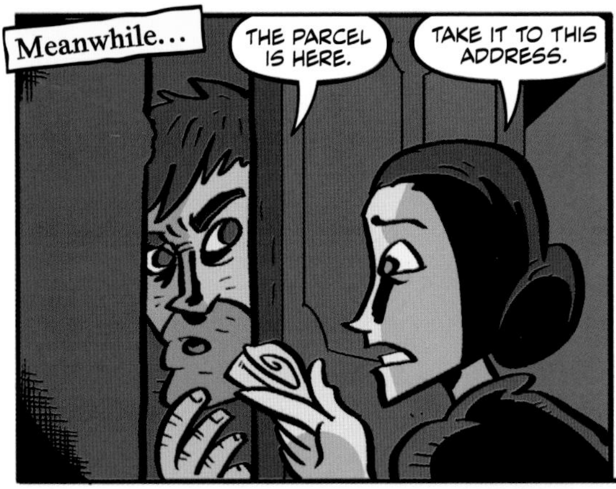
Meanwhile…
THE PARCEL IS HERE.
TAKE IT TO THIS ADDRESS.

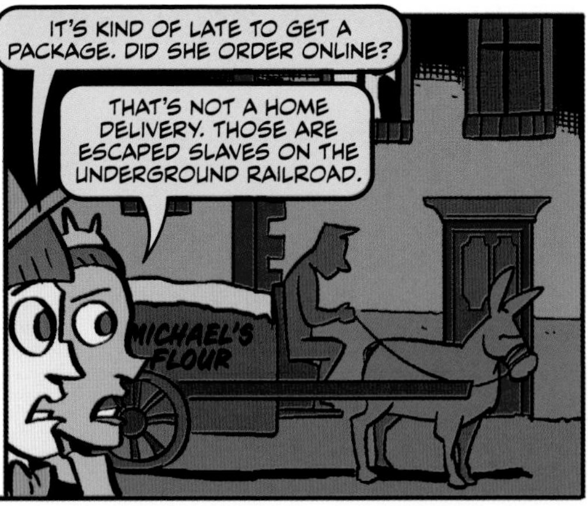
IT'S KIND OF LATE TO GET A PACKAGE. DID SHE ORDER ONLINE?
THAT'S NOT A HOME DELIVERY. THOSE ARE ESCAPED SLAVES ON THE UNDERGROUND RAILROAD.
MICHAEL'S FLOUR

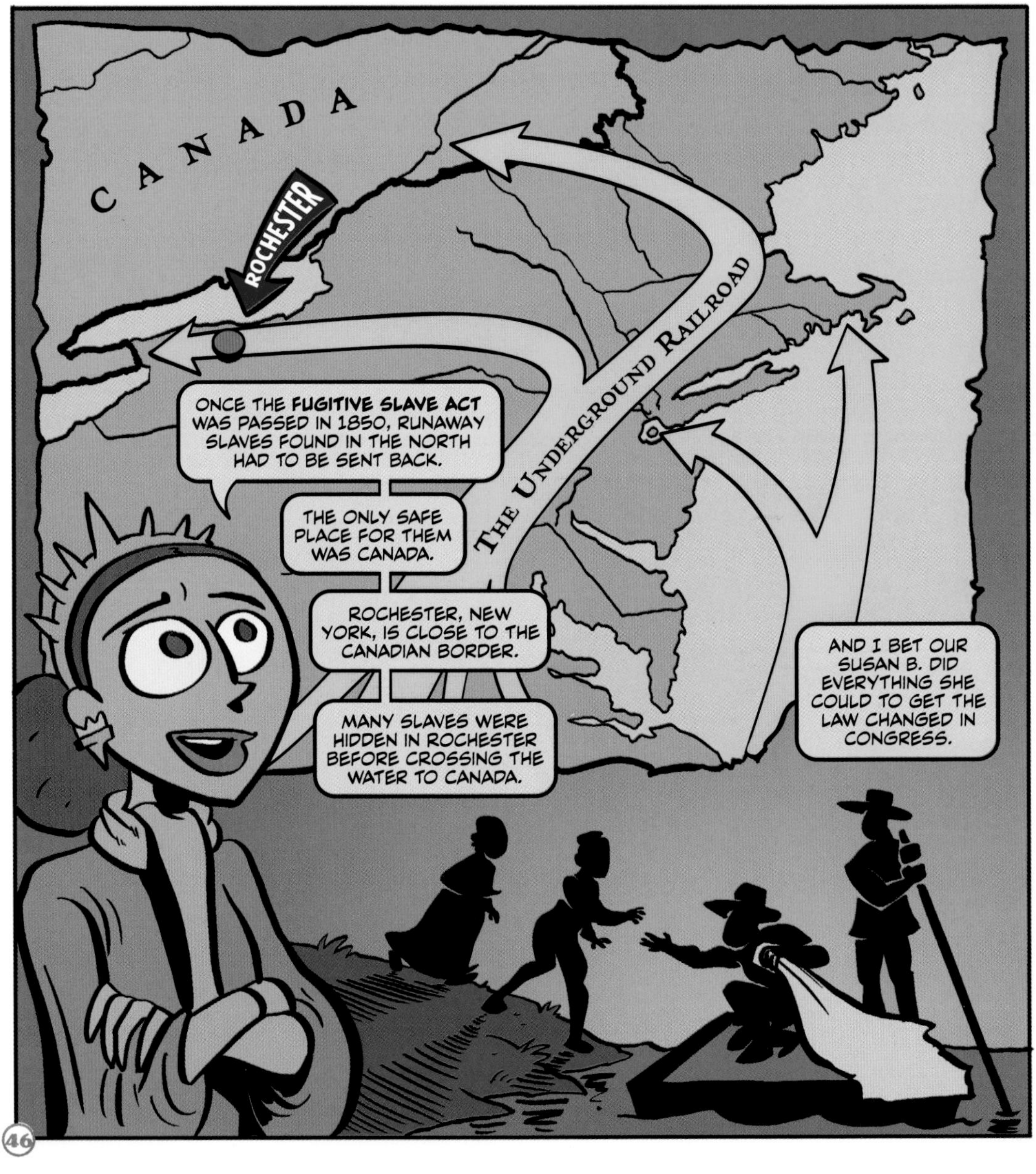
CANADA
ROCHESTER
THE UNDERGROUND RAILROAD
ONCE THE FUGITIVE SLAVE ACT WAS PASSED IN 1850, RUNAWAY SLAVES FOUND IN THE NORTH HAD TO BE SENT BACK.
THE ONLY SAFE PLACE FOR THEM WAS CANADA.
ROCHESTER, NEW YORK, IS CLOSE TO THE CANADIAN BORDER.
MANY SLAVES WERE HIDDEN IN ROCHESTER BEFORE CROSSING THE WATER TO CANADA.
AND I BET OUR SUSAN B. DID EVERYTHING SHE COULD TO GET THE LAW CHANGED IN CONGRESS.

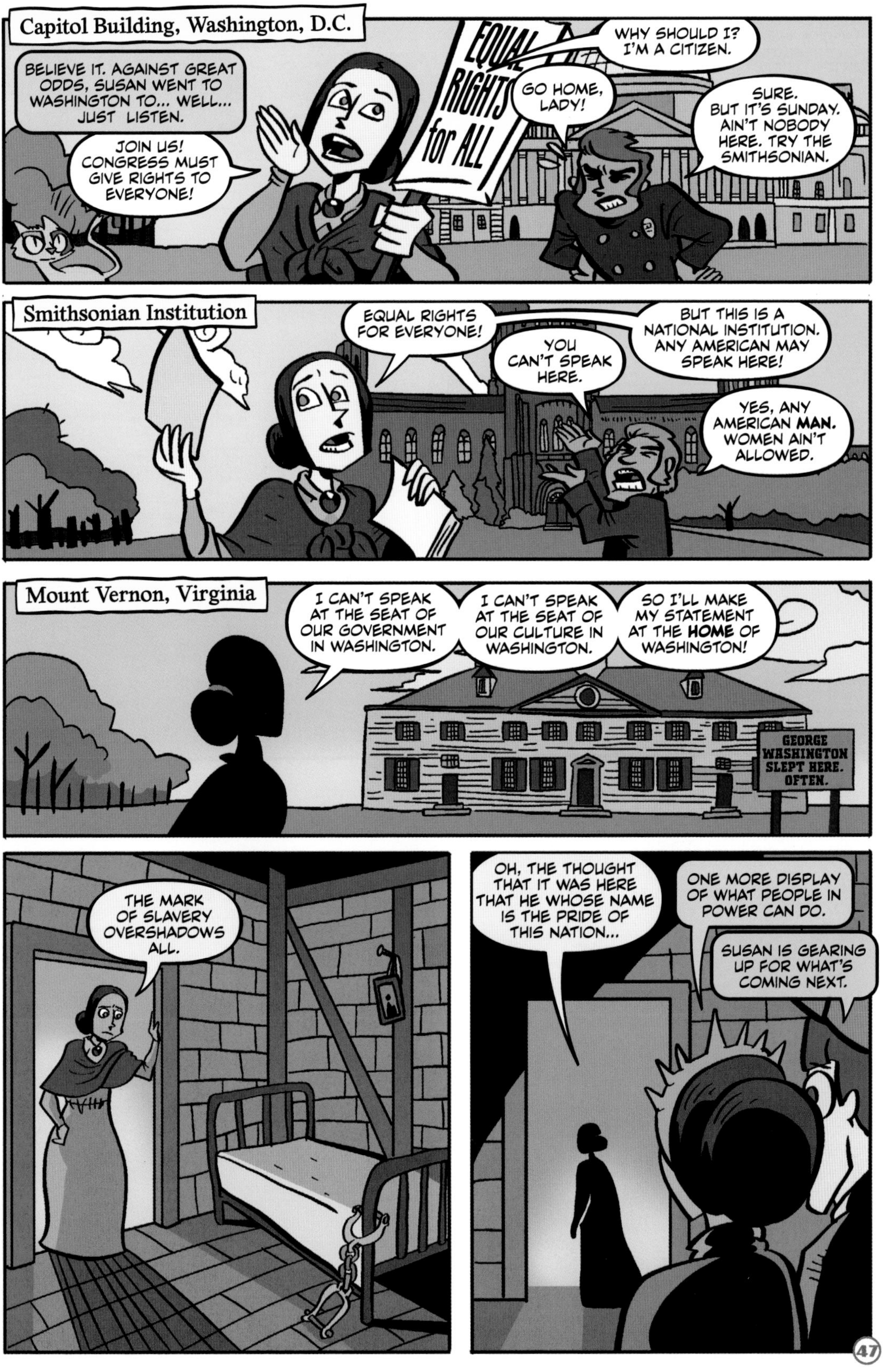

Capitol Building, Washington, D.C.
BELIEVE IT. AGAINST GREAT ODDS, SUSAN WENT TO WASHINGTON TO... WELL... JUST LISTEN.
JOIN US! CONGRESS MUST GIVE RIGHTS TO EVERYONE!
EQUAL RIGHTS for ALL
GO HOME, LADY!
WHY SHOULD I? I'M A CITIZEN.
SURE. BUT IT'S SUNDAY. AIN'T NOBODY HERE. TRY THE SMITHSONIAN.
Smithsonian Institution
EQUAL RIGHTS FOR EVERYONE!
YOU CAN'T SPEAK HERE.
BUT THIS IS A NATIONAL INSTITUTION. ANY AMERICAN MAY SPEAK HERE!
YES, ANY AMERICAN **MAN.** WOMEN AIN'T ALLOWED.
Mount Vernon, Virginia
I CAN'T SPEAK AT THE SEAT OF OUR GOVERNMENT IN WASHINGTON.
I CAN'T SPEAK AT THE SEAT OF OUR CULTURE IN WASHINGTON.
SO I'LL MAKE MY STATEMENT AT THE **HOME** OF WASHINGTON!
GEORGE WASHINGTON SLEPT HERE. OFTEN.
THE MARK OF SLAVERY OVERSHADOWS ALL.
OH, THE THOUGHT THAT IT WAS HERE THAT HE WHOSE NAME IS THE PRIDE OF THIS NATION...
ONE MORE DISPLAY OF WHAT PEOPLE IN POWER CAN DO.
SUSAN IS GEARING UP FOR WHAT'S COMING NEXT.

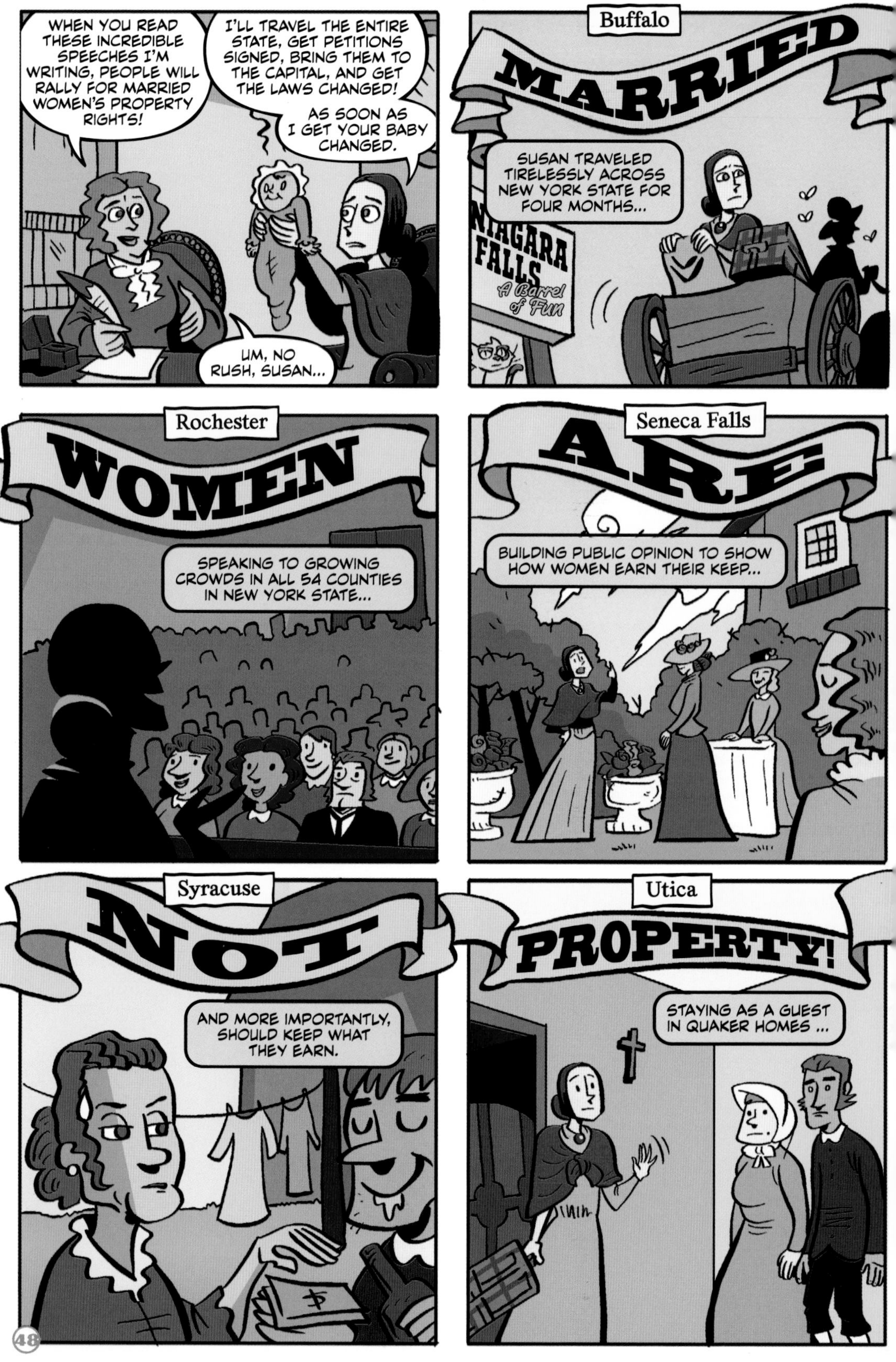
WHEN YOU READ THESE INCREDIBLE SPEECHES I'M WRITING, PEOPLE WILL RALLY FOR MARRIED WOMEN'S PROPERTY RIGHTS!
I'LL TRAVEL THE ENTIRE STATE, GET PETITIONS SIGNED, BRING THEM TO THE CAPITAL, AND GET THE LAWS CHANGED!
AS SOON AS I GET YOUR BABY CHANGED.
UM, NO RUSH, SUSAN...
Buffalo
MARRIED
SUSAN TRAVELED TIRELESSLY ACROSS NEW YORK STATE FOR FOUR MONTHS...
NIAGARA FALLS
A Barrel of Fun
Rochester
WOMEN
SPEAKING TO GROWING CROWDS IN ALL 54 COUNTIES IN NEW YORK STATE...
Seneca Falls
ARE
BUILDING PUBLIC OPINION TO SHOW HOW WOMEN EARN THEIR KEEP...
Syracuse
NOT
AND MORE IMPORTANTLY, SHOULD KEEP WHAT THEY EARN.
Utica
PROPERTY!
STAYING AS A GUEST IN QUAKER HOMES ...

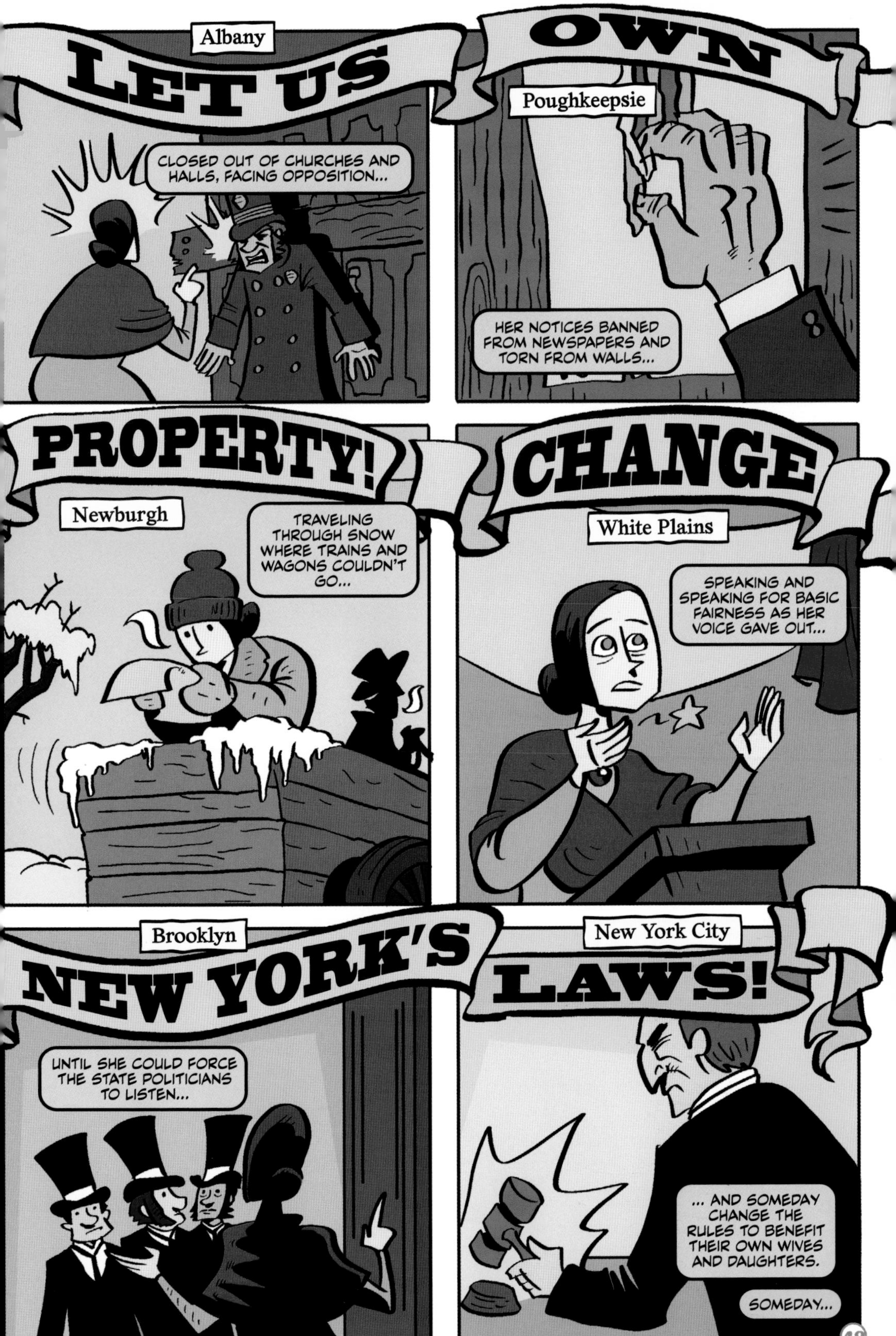
Albany
LET US
CLOSED OUT OF CHURCHES AND HALLS, FACING OPPOSITION...
OWN
Poughkeepsie
HER NOTICES BANNED FROM NEWSPAPERS AND TORN FROM WALLS...
PROPERTY!
Newburgh
TRAVELING THROUGH SNOW WHERE TRAINS AND WAGONS COULDN'T GO...
CHANGE
White Plains
SPEAKING AND SPEAKING FOR BASIC FAIRNESS AS HER VOICE GAVE OUT...
Brooklyn
NEW YORK'S
UNTIL SHE COULD FORCE THE STATE POLITICIANS TO LISTEN...
New York City
LAWS!
... AND SOMEDAY CHANGE THE RULES TO BENEFIT THEIR OWN WIVES AND DAUGHTERS.
SOMEDAY...

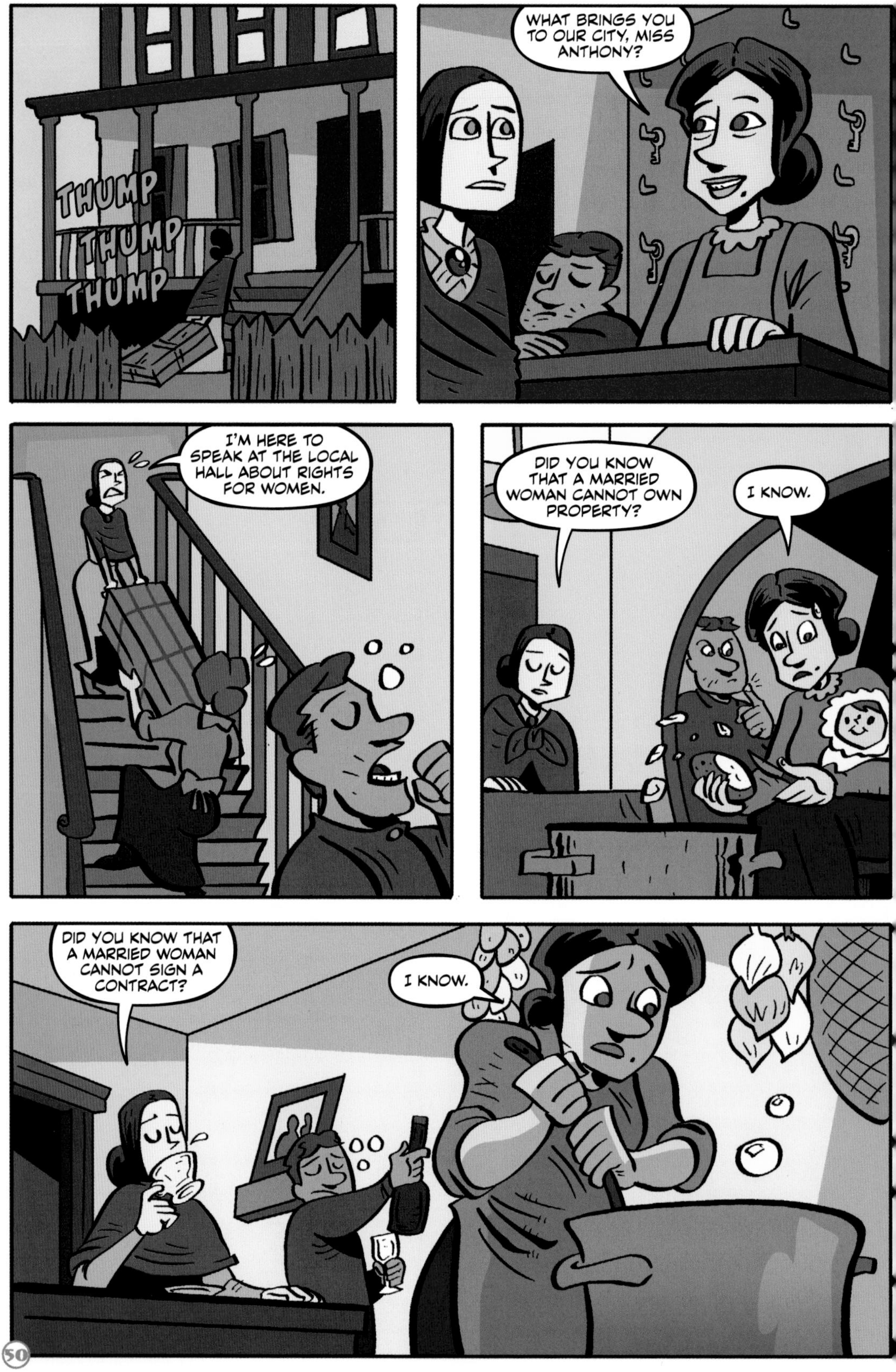
THUMP
THUMP
THUMP
WHAT BRINGS YOU TO OUR CITY, MISS ANTHONY?
I'M HERE TO SPEAK AT THE LOCAL HALL ABOUT RIGHTS FOR WOMEN.
DID YOU KNOW THAT A MARRIED WOMAN CANNOT OWN PROPERTY?
I KNOW.
DID YOU KNOW THAT A MARRIED WOMAN CANNOT SIGN A CONTRACT?
I KNOW.

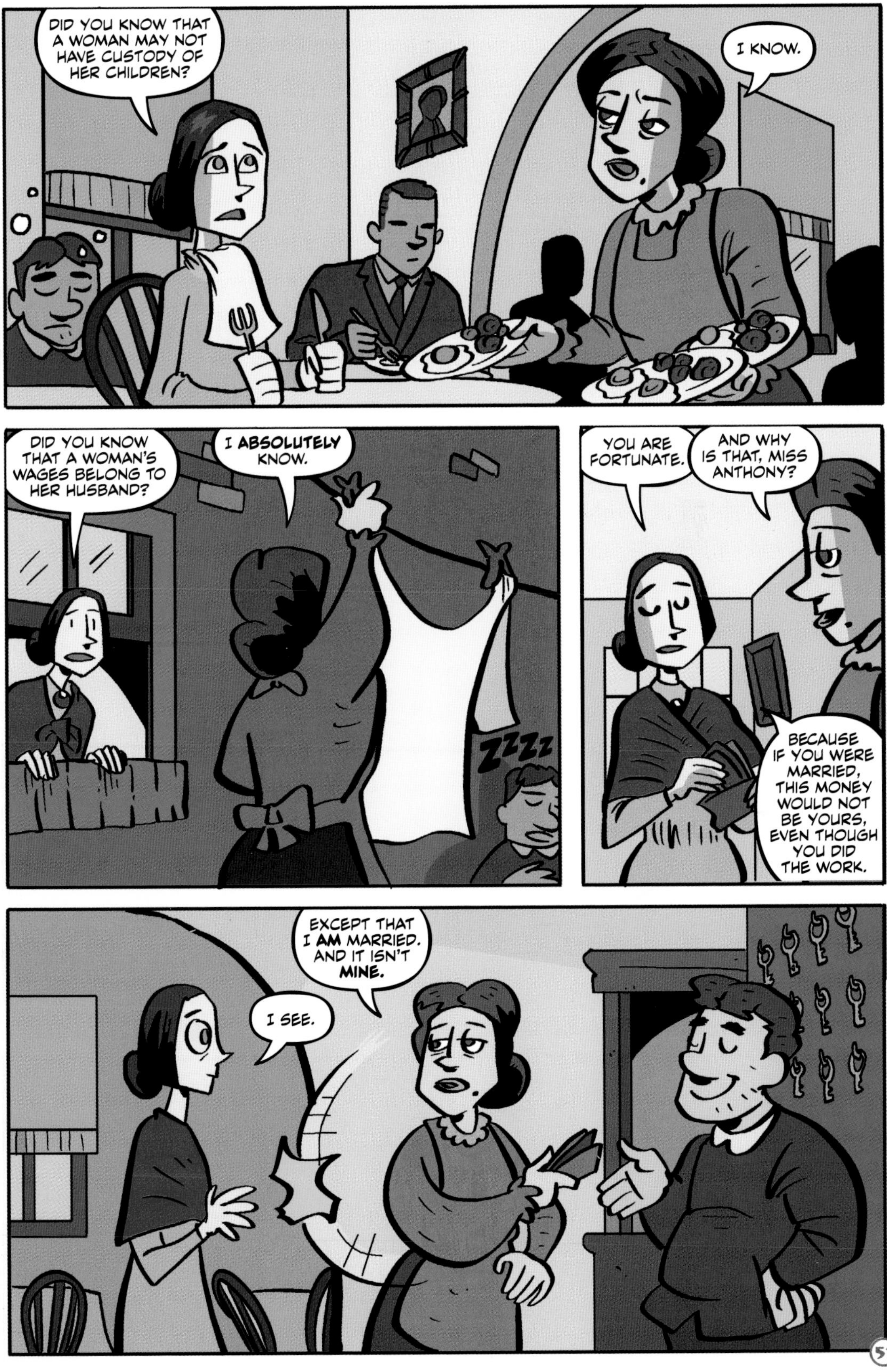

DID YOU KNOW THAT A WOMAN MAY NOT HAVE CUSTODY OF HER CHILDREN?
I KNOW.
DID YOU KNOW THAT A WOMAN'S WAGES BELONG TO HER HUSBAND?
I **ABSOLUTELY** KNOW.
ZZZZ
YOU ARE FORTUNATE.
AND WHY IS THAT, MISS ANTHONY?
BECAUSE IF YOU WERE MARRIED, THIS MONEY WOULD NOT BE YOURS, EVEN THOUGH YOU DID THE WORK.
EXCEPT THAT I **AM** MARRIED. AND IT ISN'T **MINE.**
I SEE.

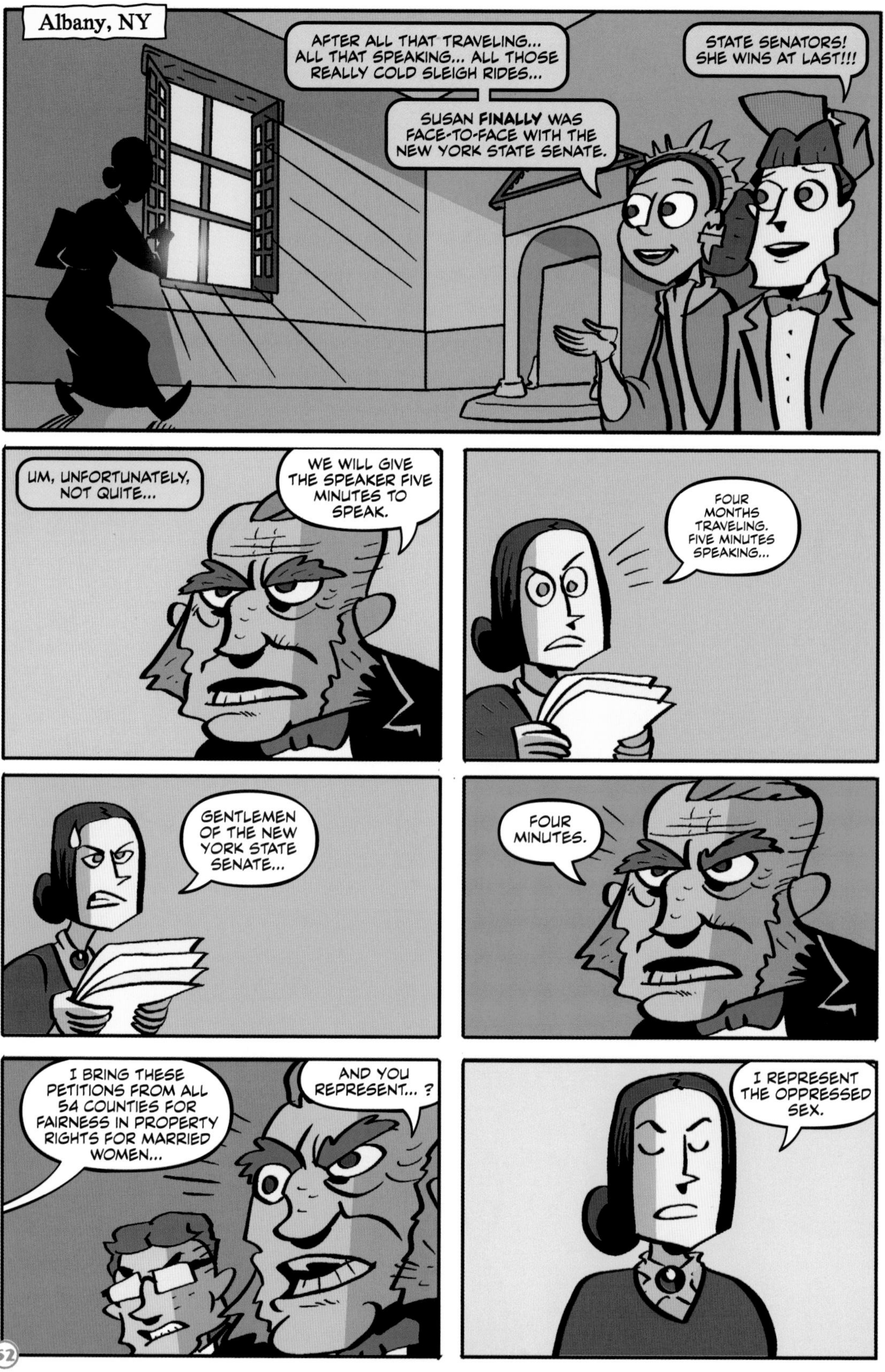
Albany, NY
AFTER ALL THAT TRAVELING... ALL THAT SPEAKING... ALL THOSE REALLY COLD SLEIGH RIDES...
SUSAN FINALLY WAS FACE-TO-FACE WITH THE NEW YORK STATE SENATE.
STATE SENATORS! SHE WINS AT LAST!!!
UM, UNFORTUNATELY, NOT QUITE...
WE WILL GIVE THE SPEAKER FIVE MINUTES TO SPEAK.
FOUR MONTHS TRAVELING. FIVE MINUTES SPEAKING...
GENTLEMEN OF THE NEW YORK STATE SENATE...
FOUR MINUTES.
I BRING THESE PETITIONS FROM ALL 54 COUNTIES FOR FAIRNESS IN PROPERTY RIGHTS FOR MARRIED WOMEN...
AND YOU REPRESENT... ?
I REPRESENT THE OPPRESSED SEX.

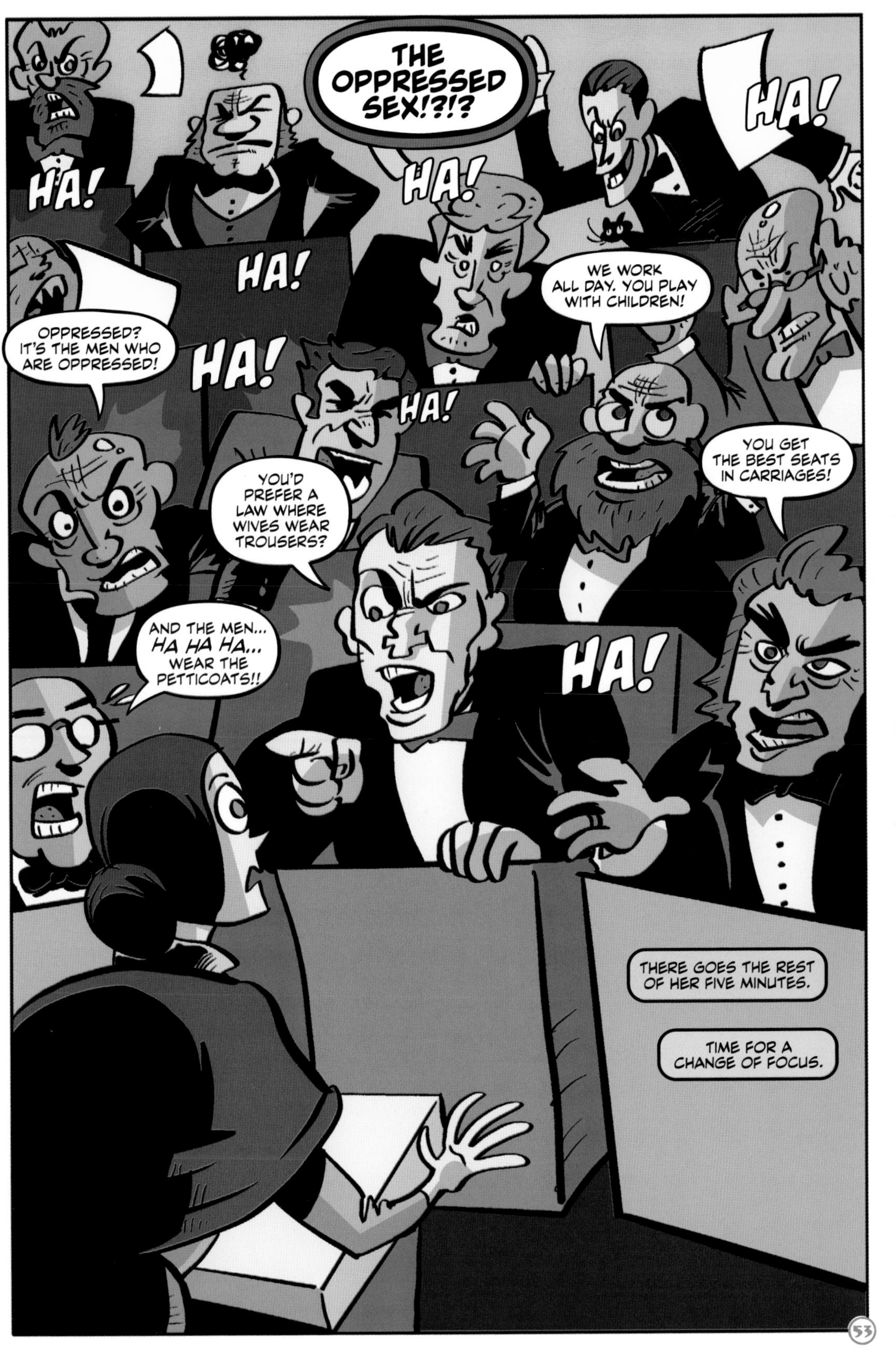
THE OPPRESSED SEX!?!?
HA!
HA!
HA!
HA!
WE WORK ALL DAY. YOU PLAY WITH CHILDREN!
OPPRESSED? IT'S THE MEN WHO ARE OPPRESSED!
HA!
HA!
YOU GET THE BEST SEATS IN CARRIAGES!
YOU'D PREFER A LAW WHERE WIVES WEAR TROUSERS?
AND THE MEN... HA HA HA... WEAR THE PETTICOATS!!
HA!
THERE GOES THE REST OF HER FIVE MINUTES.
TIME FOR A CHANGE OF FOCUS.

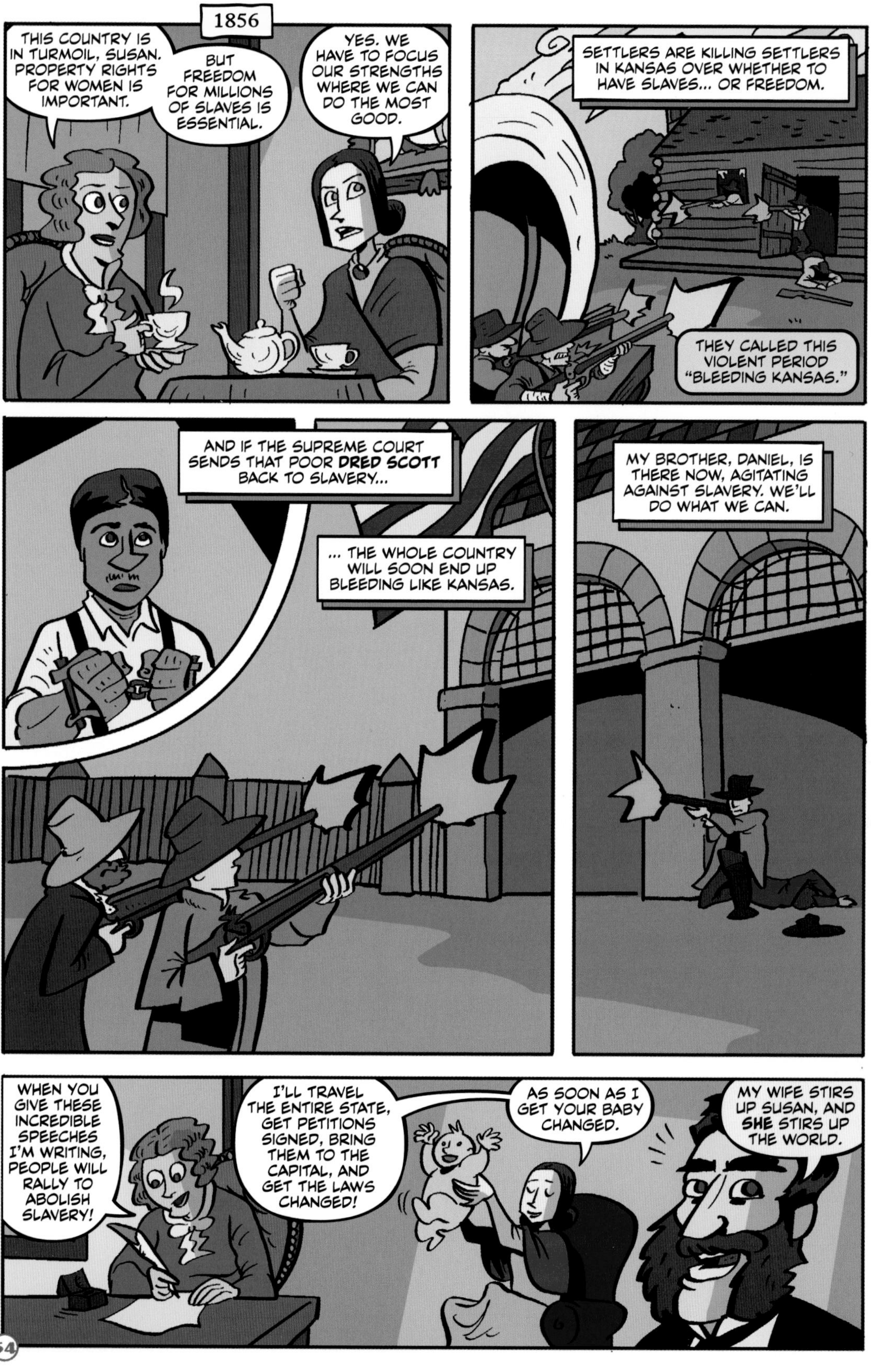
1856
THIS COUNTRY IS IN TURMOIL, SUSAN. PROPERTY RIGHTS FOR WOMEN IS IMPORTANT.
BUT FREEDOM FOR MILLIONS OF SLAVES IS ESSENTIAL.
YES. WE HAVE TO FOCUS OUR STRENGTHS WHERE WE CAN DO THE MOST GOOD.
SETTLERS ARE KILLING SETTLERS IN KANSAS OVER WHETHER TO HAVE SLAVES... OR FREEDOM.
THEY CALLED THIS VIOLENT PERIOD "BLEEDING KANSAS."
AND IF THE SUPREME COURT SENDS THAT POOR **DRED SCOTT** BACK TO SLAVERY...
... THE WHOLE COUNTRY WILL SOON END UP BLEEDING LIKE KANSAS.
MY BROTHER, DANIEL, IS THERE NOW, AGITATING AGAINST SLAVERY. WE'LL DO WHAT WE CAN.
WHEN YOU GIVE THESE INCREDIBLE SPEECHES I'M WRITING, PEOPLE WILL RALLY TO ABOLISH SLAVERY!
I'LL TRAVEL THE ENTIRE STATE, GET PETITIONS SIGNED, BRING THEM TO THE CAPITAL, AND GET THE LAWS CHANGED!
AS SOON AS I GET YOUR BABY CHANGED.
MY WIFE STIRS UP SUSAN, AND **SHE** STIRS UP THE WORLD.

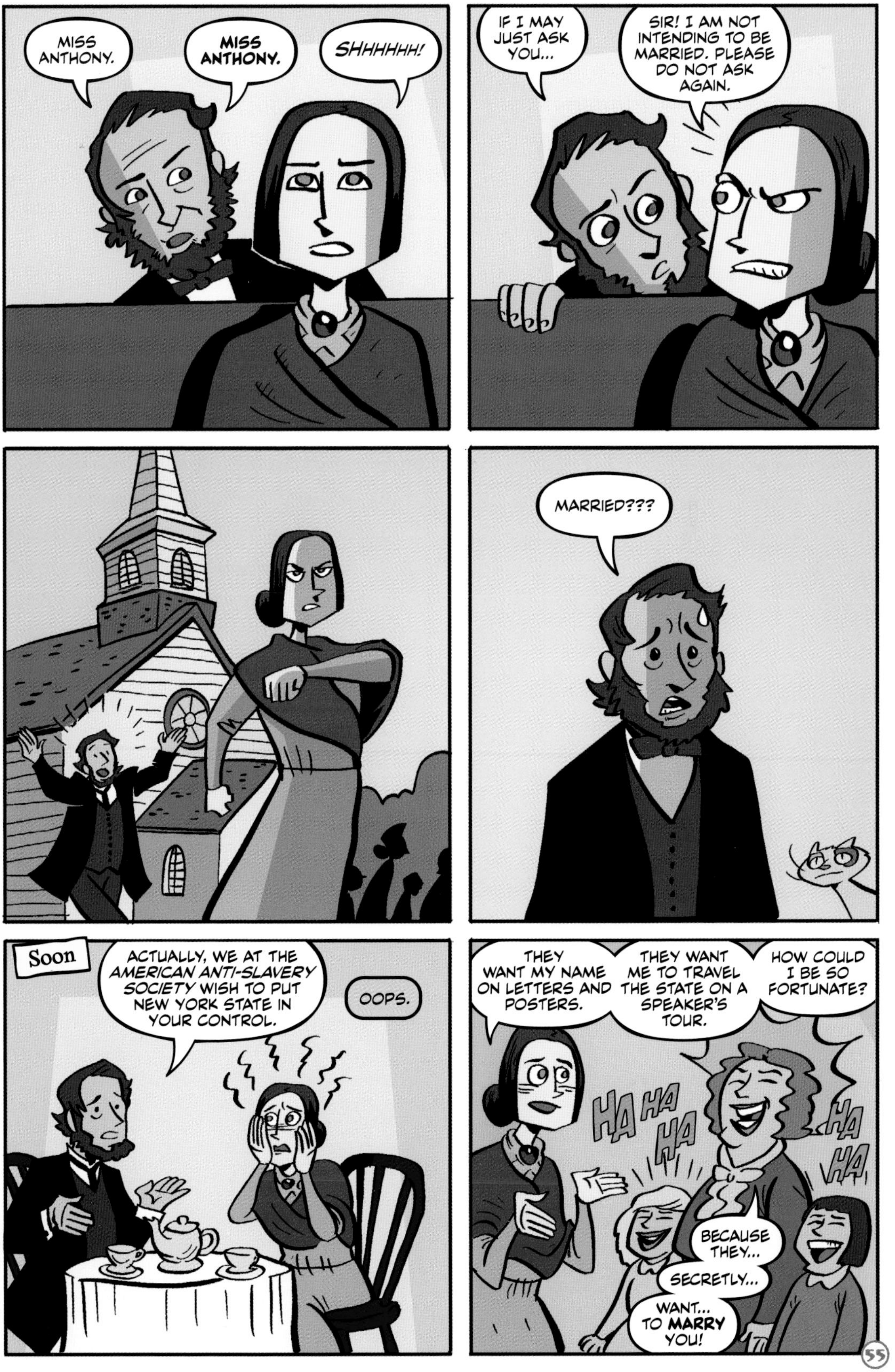
MISS ANTHONY.
**MISS ANTHONY.**
*SHHHHHH!*
IF I MAY JUST ASK YOU...
SIR! I AM NOT INTENDING TO BE MARRIED. PLEASE DO NOT ASK AGAIN.
MARRIED???
Soon
ACTUALLY, WE AT THE *AMERICAN ANTI-SLAVERY SOCIETY* WISH TO PUT NEW YORK STATE IN YOUR CONTROL.
OOPS.
THEY WANT MY NAME ON LETTERS AND POSTERS.
THEY WANT ME TO TRAVEL THE STATE ON A SPEAKER'S TOUR.
HOW COULD I BE SO FORTUNATE?
HA HA HA
HA HA
BECAUSE THEY...
SECRETLY...
WANT... TO **MARRY** YOU!

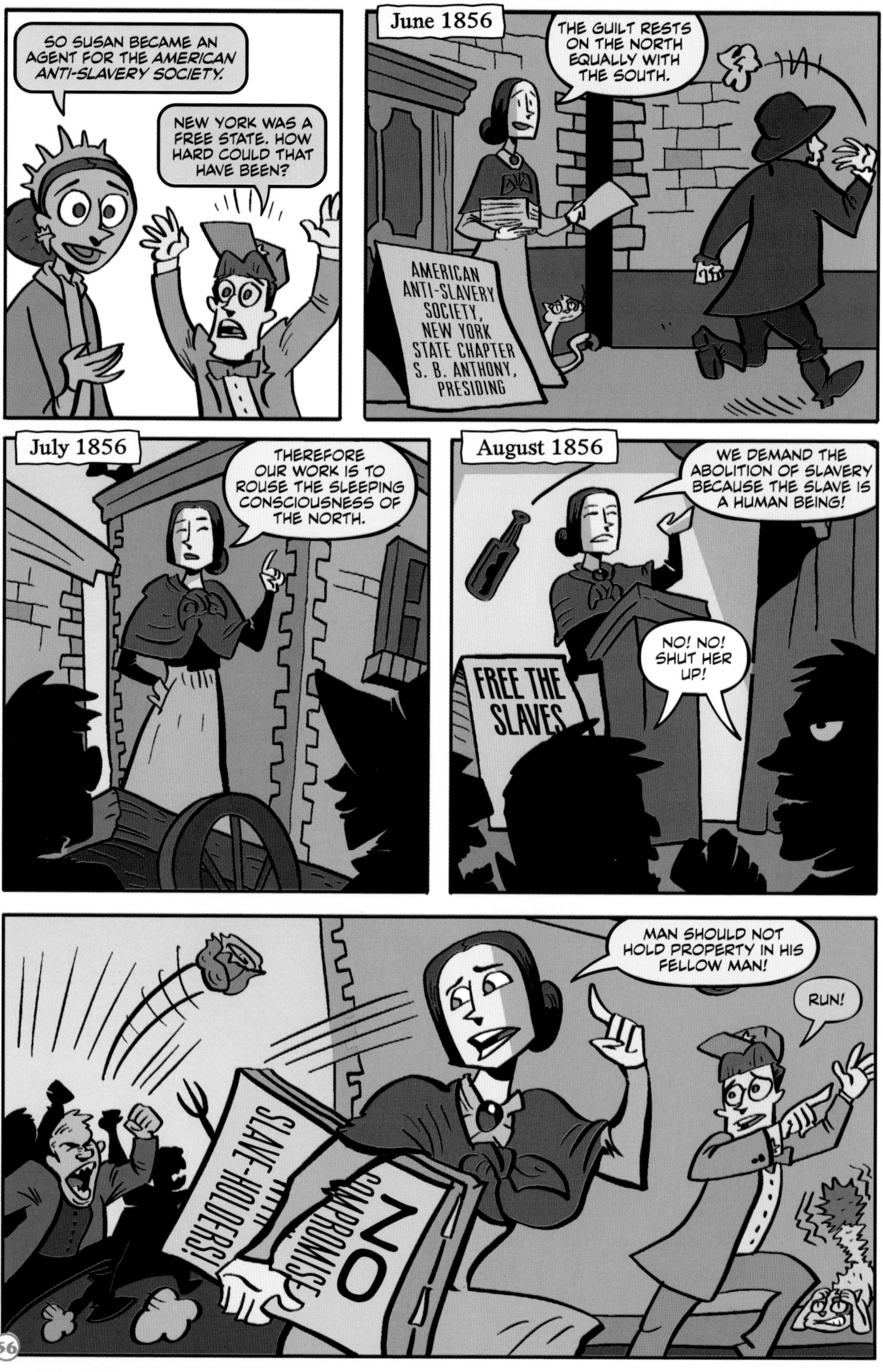
SO SUSAN BECAME AN AGENT FOR THE AMERICAN ANTI-SLAVERY SOCIETY.
NEW YORK WAS A FREE STATE. HOW HARD COULD THAT HAVE BEEN?
June 1856
THE GUILT RESTS ON THE NORTH EQUALLY WITH THE SOUTH.
AMERICAN ANTI-SLAVERY SOCIETY, NEW YORK STATE CHAPTER S. B. ANTHONY, PRESIDING
July 1856
THEREFORE OUR WORK IS TO ROUSE THE SLEEPING CONSCIOUSNESS OF THE NORTH.
August 1856
WE DEMAND THE ABOLITION OF SLAVERY BECAUSE THE SLAVE IS A HUMAN BEING!
FREE THE SLAVES
NO! NO! SHUT HER UP!
MAN SHOULD NOT HOLD PROPERTY IN HIS FELLOW MAN!
RUN!
SLAVE-HOLDERS!
NO COMPROMISE

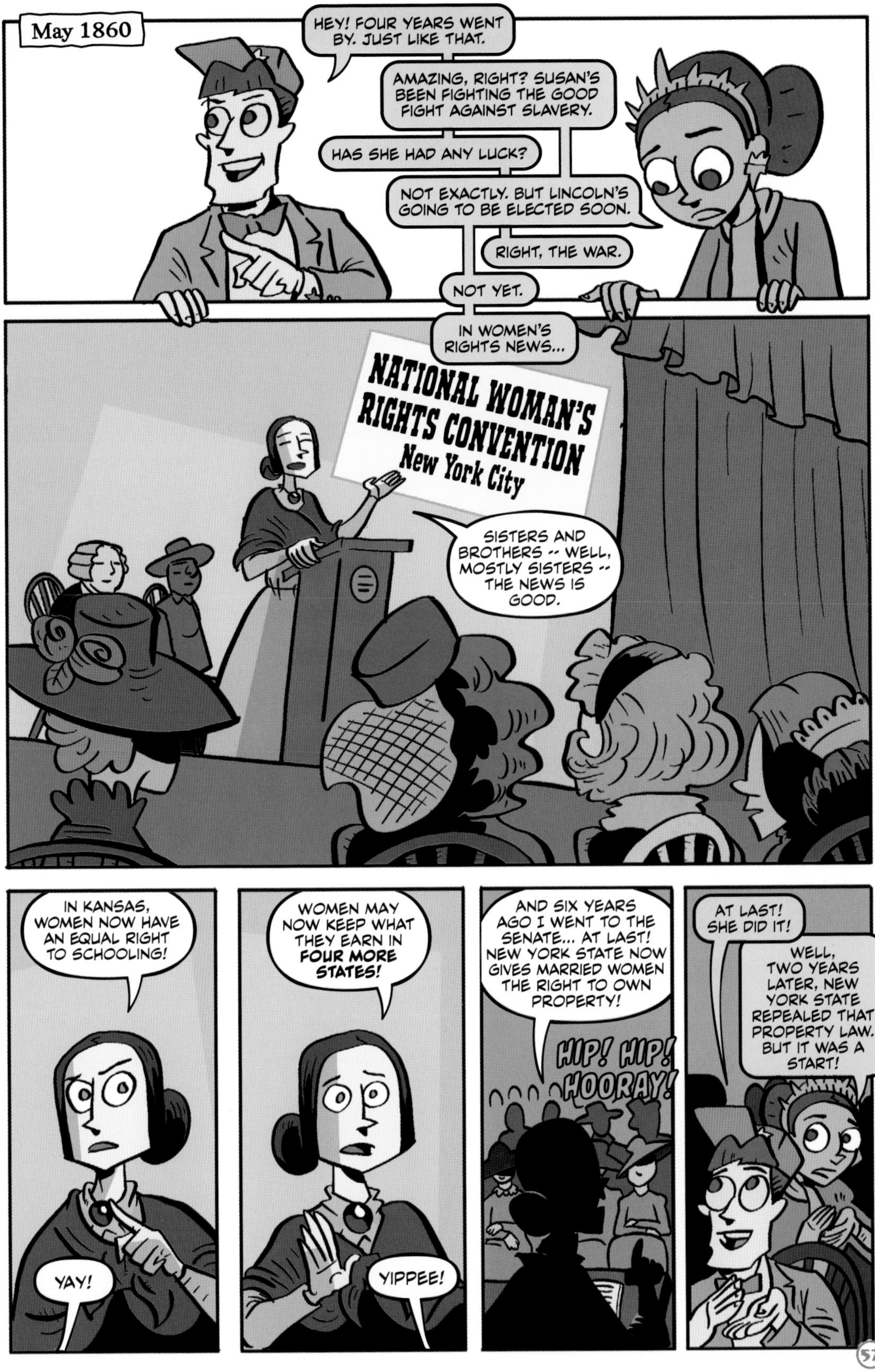

May 1860
HEY! FOUR YEARS WENT BY. JUST LIKE THAT.
AMAZING, RIGHT? SUSAN'S BEEN FIGHTING THE GOOD FIGHT AGAINST SLAVERY.
HAS SHE HAD ANY LUCK?
NOT EXACTLY. BUT LINCOLN'S GOING TO BE ELECTED SOON.
RIGHT, THE WAR.
NOT YET.
IN WOMEN'S RIGHTS NEWS...
NATIONAL WOMAN'S RIGHTS CONVENTION New York City
SISTERS AND BROTHERS -- WELL, MOSTLY SISTERS -- THE NEWS IS GOOD.
IN KANSAS, WOMEN NOW HAVE AN EQUAL RIGHT TO SCHOOLING!
YAY!
WOMEN MAY NOW KEEP WHAT THEY EARN IN FOUR MORE STATES!
YIPPEE!
AND SIX YEARS AGO I WENT TO THE SENATE... AT LAST! NEW YORK STATE NOW GIVES MARRIED WOMEN THE RIGHT TO OWN PROPERTY!
HIP! HIP! HOORAY!
AT LAST! SHE DID IT!
WELL, TWO YEARS LATER, NEW YORK STATE REPEALED THAT PROPERTY LAW. BUT IT WAS A START!

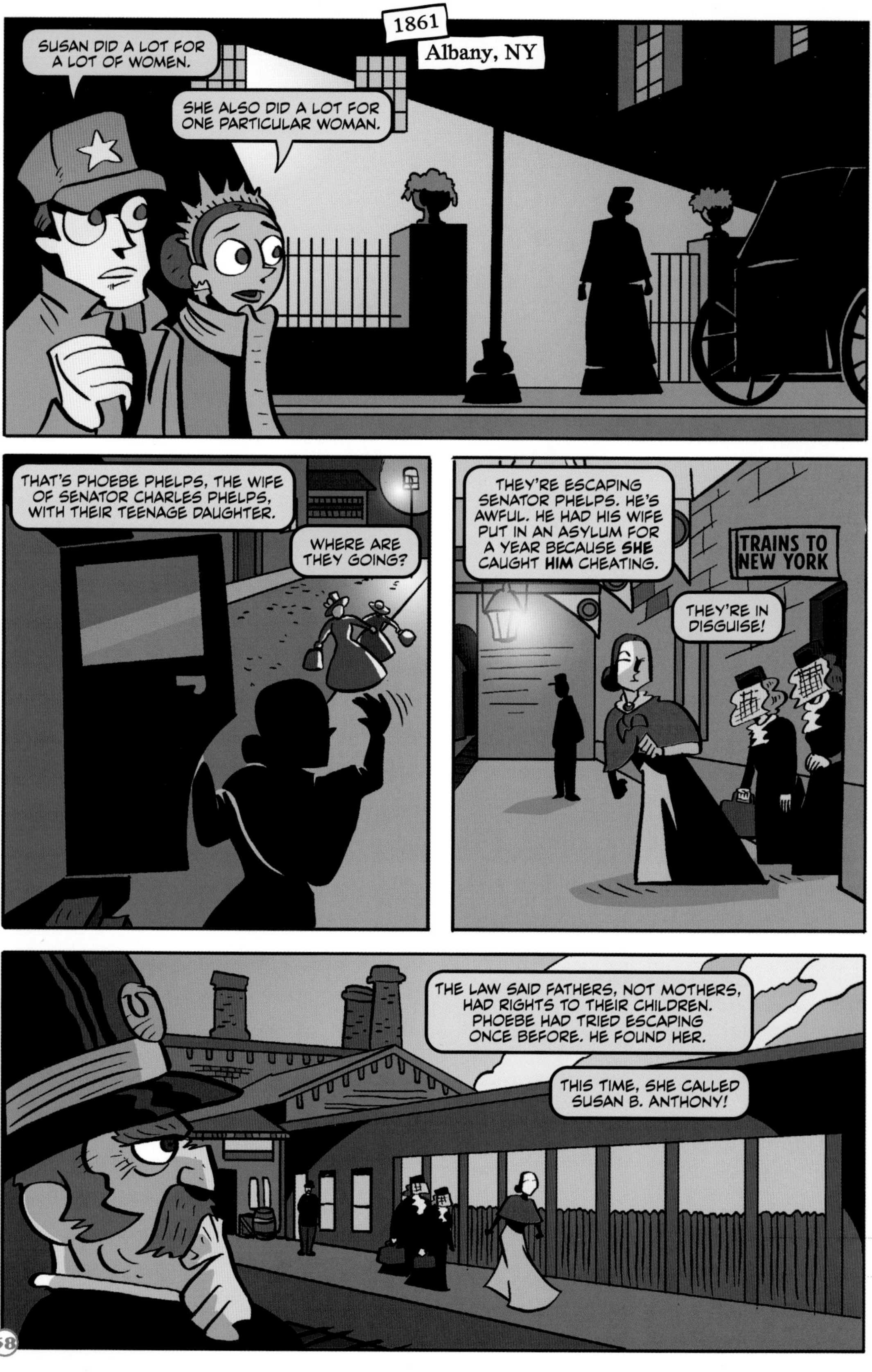
1861
Albany, NY
SUSAN DID A LOT FOR A LOT OF WOMEN.
SHE ALSO DID A LOT FOR ONE PARTICULAR WOMAN.
THAT'S PHOEBE PHELPS, THE WIFE OF SENATOR CHARLES PHELPS, WITH THEIR TEENAGE DAUGHTER.
WHERE ARE THEY GOING?
THEY'RE ESCAPING SENATOR PHELPS. HE'S AWFUL. HE HAD HIS WIFE PUT IN AN ASYLUM FOR A YEAR BECAUSE SHE CAUGHT HIM CHEATING.
TRAINS TO NEW YORK
THEY'RE IN DISGUISE!
THE LAW SAID FATHERS, NOT MOTHERS, HAD RIGHTS TO THEIR CHILDREN. PHOEBE HAD TRIED ESCAPING ONCE BEFORE. HE FOUND HER.
THIS TIME, SHE CALLED SUSAN B. ANTHONY!

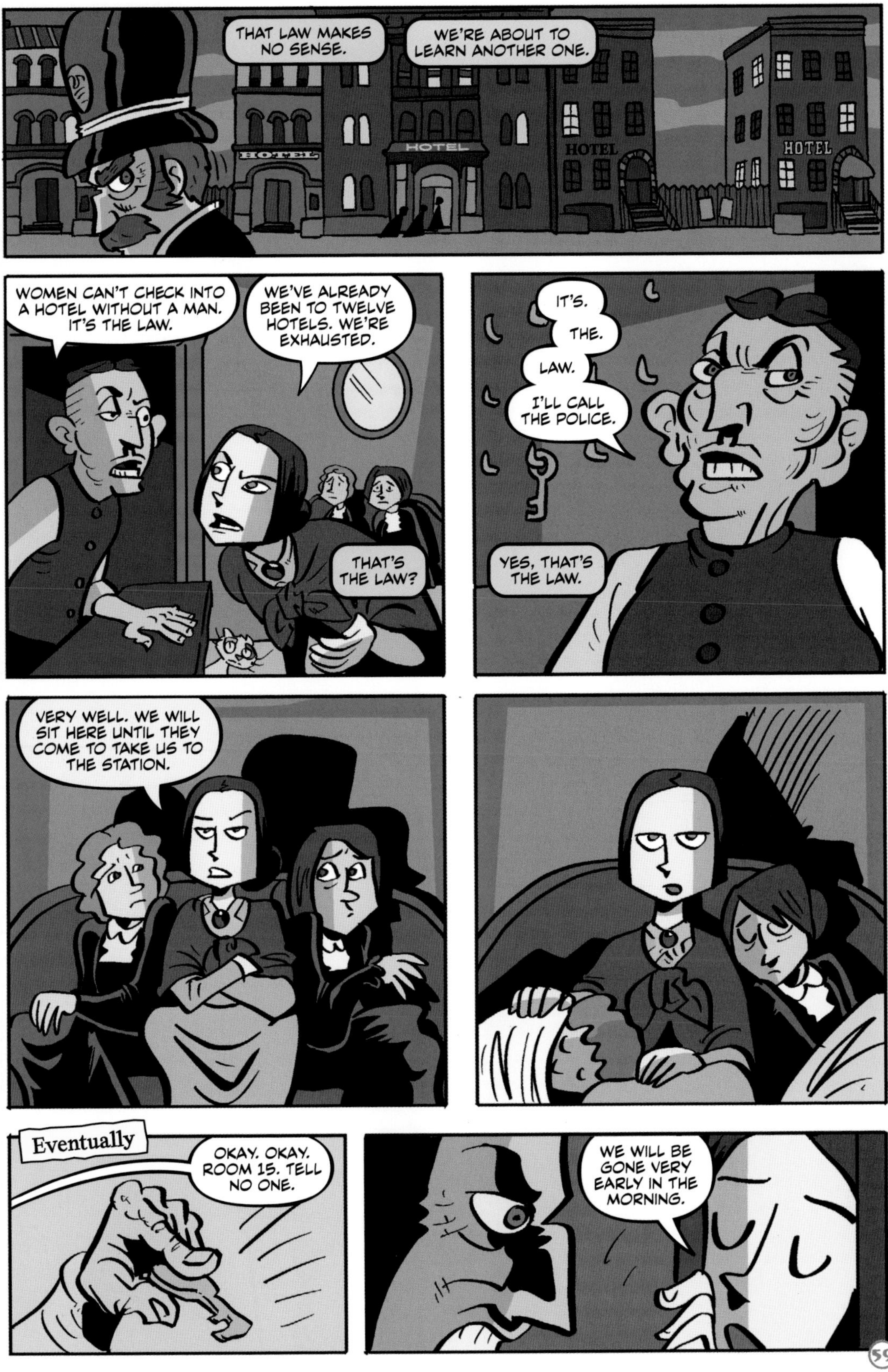
THAT LAW MAKES NO SENSE.
WE'RE ABOUT TO LEARN ANOTHER ONE.
HOTEL
HOTEL
HOTEL
HOTEL
WOMEN CAN'T CHECK INTO A HOTEL WITHOUT A MAN. IT'S THE LAW.
WE'VE ALREADY BEEN TO TWELVE HOTELS. WE'RE EXHAUSTED.
THAT'S THE LAW?
IT'S.
THE.
LAW.
I'LL CALL THE POLICE.
YES, THAT'S THE LAW.
VERY WELL. WE WILL SIT HERE UNTIL THEY COME TO TAKE US TO THE STATION.
Eventually
OKAY. OKAY. ROOM 15. TELL NO ONE.
WE WILL BE GONE VERY EARLY IN THE MORNING.

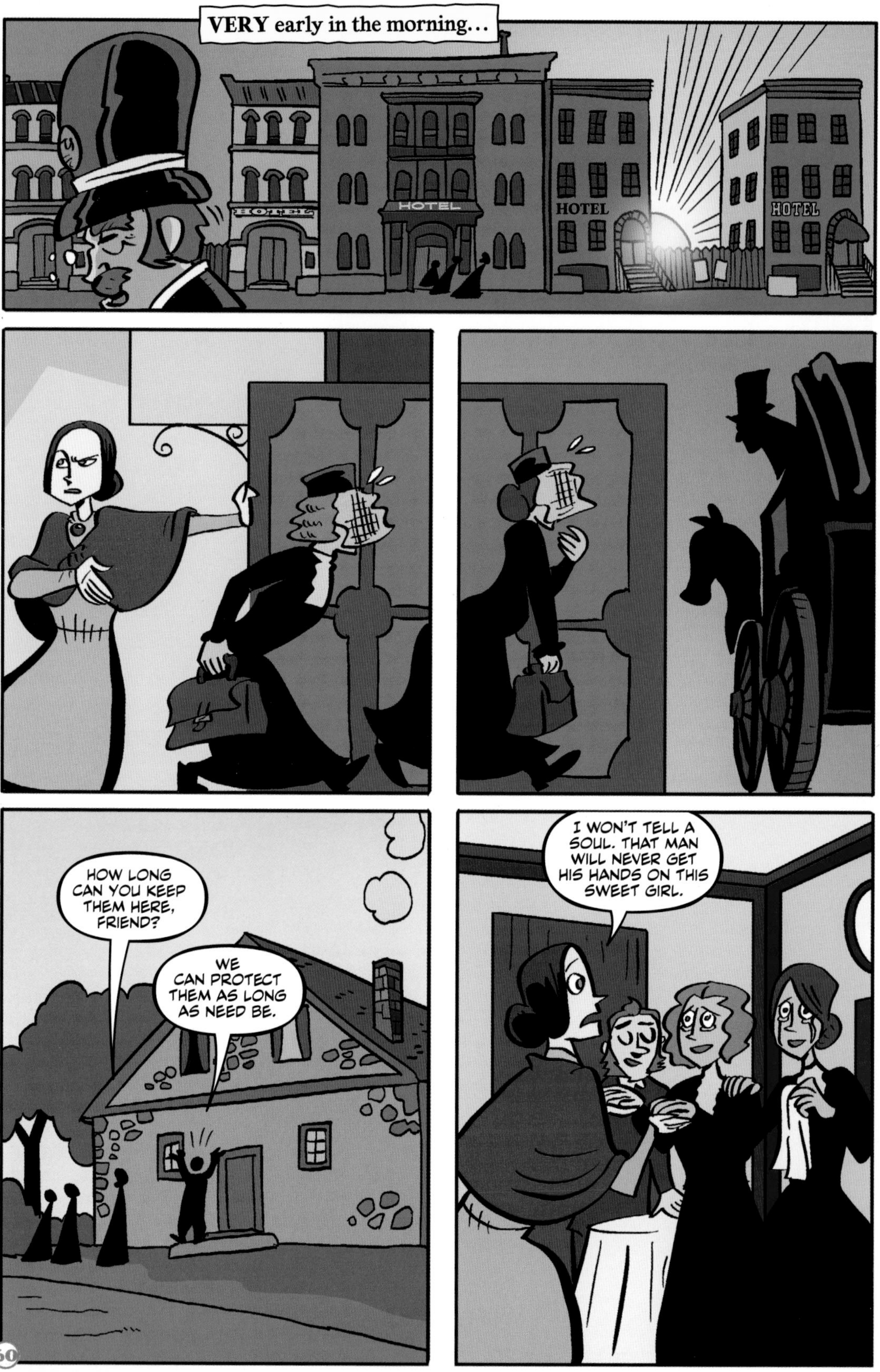
VERY early in the morning...
HOTEL
HOTEL
HOTEL
HOTEL
HOW LONG CAN YOU KEEP THEM HERE, FRIEND?
WE CAN PROTECT THEM AS LONG AS NEED BE.
I WON'T TELL A SOUL. THAT MAN WILL NEVER GET HIS HANDS ON THIS SWEET GIRL.

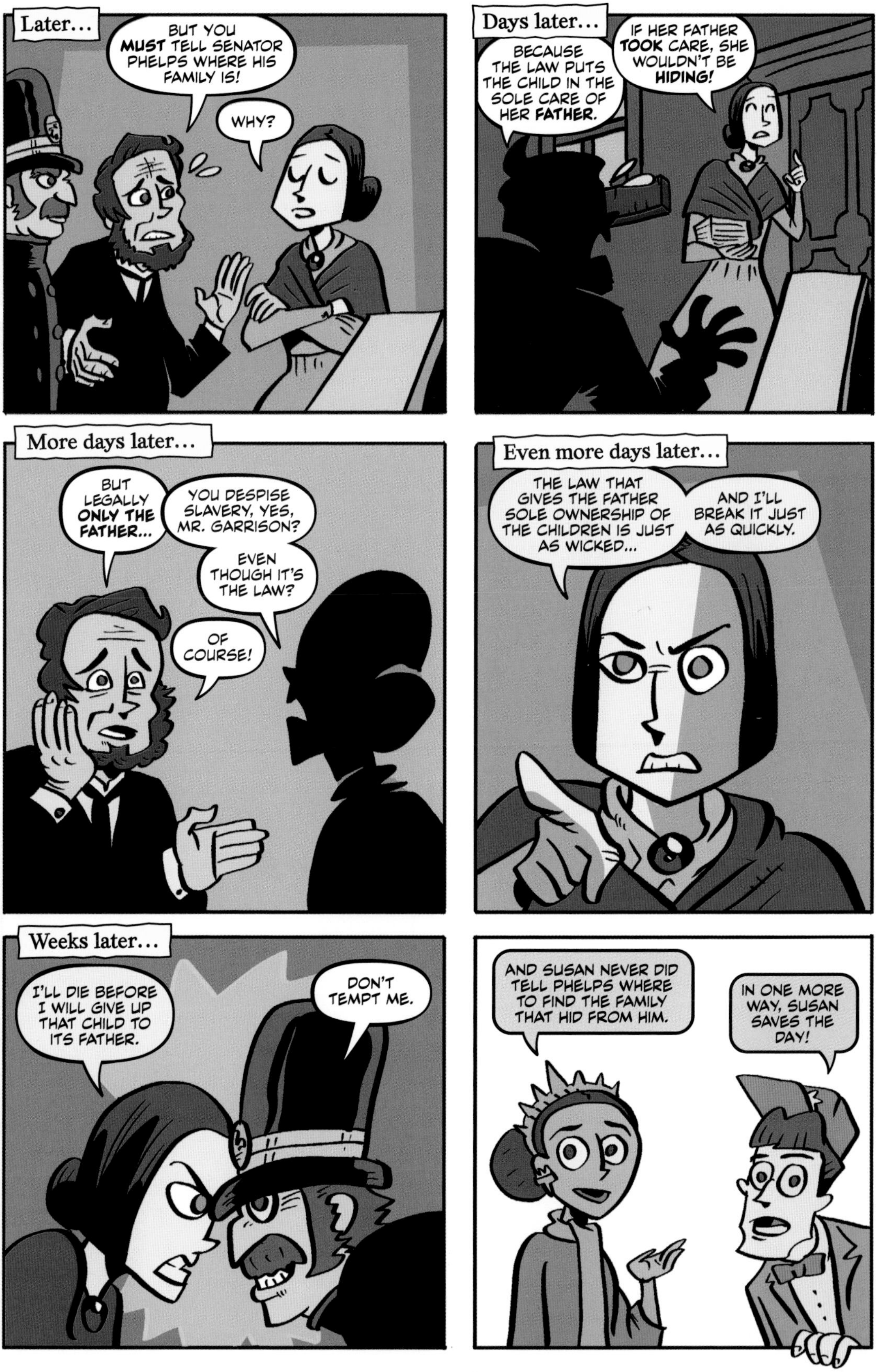
Later…
BUT YOU MUST TELL SENATOR PHELPS WHERE HIS FAMILY IS!
WHY?
Days later…
BECAUSE THE LAW PUTS THE CHILD IN THE SOLE CARE OF HER FATHER.
IF HER FATHER TOOK CARE, SHE WOULDN'T BE HIDING!
More days later…
BUT LEGALLY ONLY THE FATHER…
YOU DESPISE SLAVERY, YES, MR. GARRISON?
EVEN THOUGH IT'S THE LAW?
OF COURSE!
Even more days later…
THE LAW THAT GIVES THE FATHER SOLE OWNERSHIP OF THE CHILDREN IS JUST AS WICKED…
AND I'LL BREAK IT JUST AS QUICKLY.
Weeks later…
I'LL DIE BEFORE I WILL GIVE UP THAT CHILD TO ITS FATHER.
DON'T TEMPT ME.
AND SUSAN NEVER DID TELL PHELPS WHERE TO FIND THE FAMILY THAT HID FROM HIM.
IN ONE MORE WAY, SUSAN SAVES THE DAY!

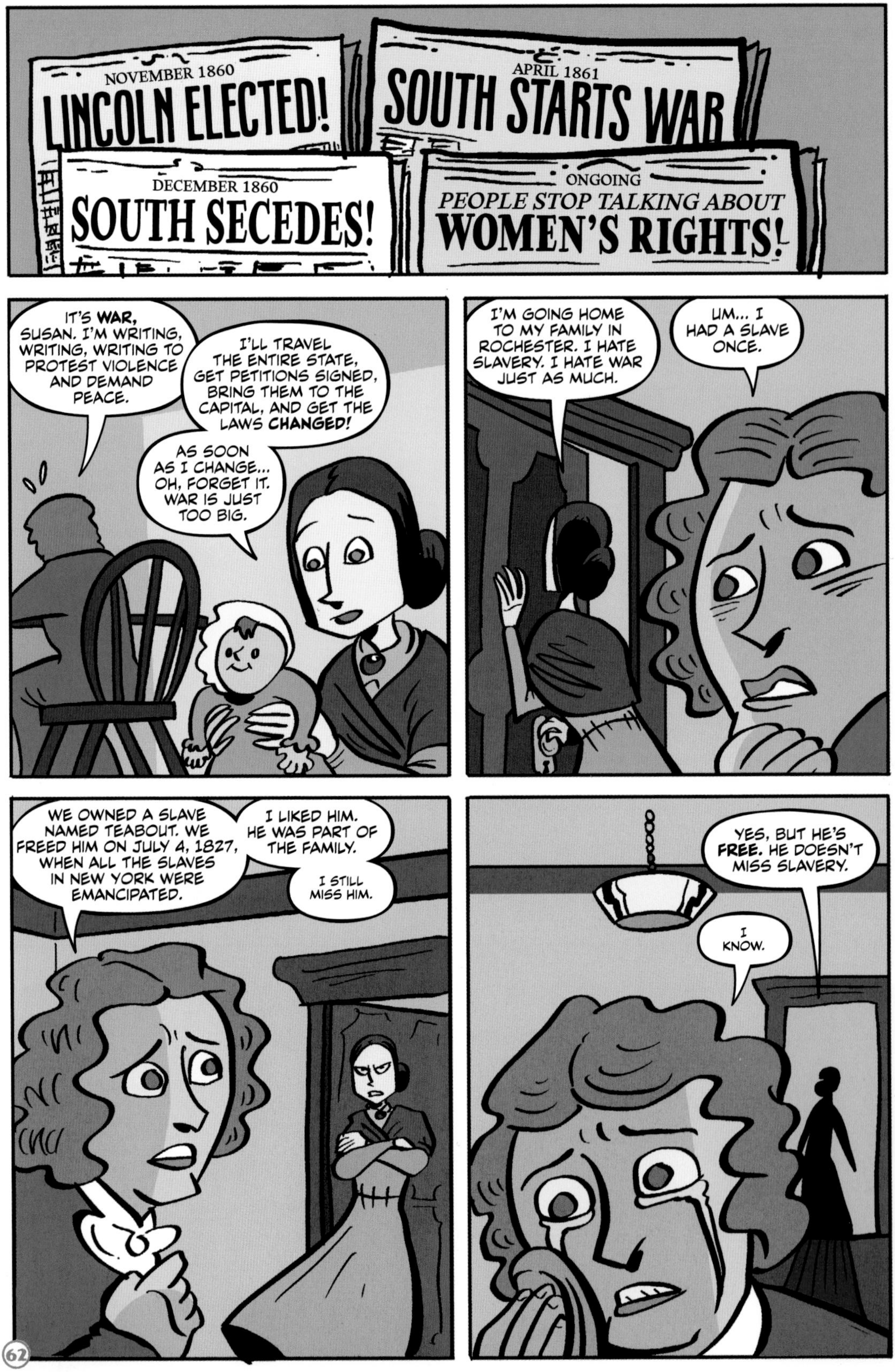
NOVEMBER 1860
LINCOLN ELECTED!
APRIL 1861
SOUTH STARTS WAR
DECEMBER 1860
SOUTH SECEDES!
ONGOING
PEOPLE STOP TALKING ABOUT WOMEN'S RIGHTS!
IT'S WAR, SUSAN. I'M WRITING, WRITING, WRITING TO PROTEST VIOLENCE AND DEMAND PEACE.
I'LL TRAVEL THE ENTIRE STATE, GET PETITIONS SIGNED, BRING THEM TO THE CAPITAL, AND GET THE LAWS CHANGED!
AS SOON AS I CHANGE... OH, FORGET IT. WAR IS JUST TOO BIG.
I'M GOING HOME TO MY FAMILY IN ROCHESTER. I HATE SLAVERY. I HATE WAR JUST AS MUCH.
UM... I HAD A SLAVE ONCE.
WE OWNED A SLAVE NAMED TEABOUT. WE FREED HIM ON JULY 4, 1827, WHEN ALL THE SLAVES IN NEW YORK WERE EMANCIPATED.
I LIKED HIM. HE WAS PART OF THE FAMILY.
I STILL MISS HIM.
YES, BUT HE'S FREE. HE DOESN'T MISS SLAVERY.
I KNOW.

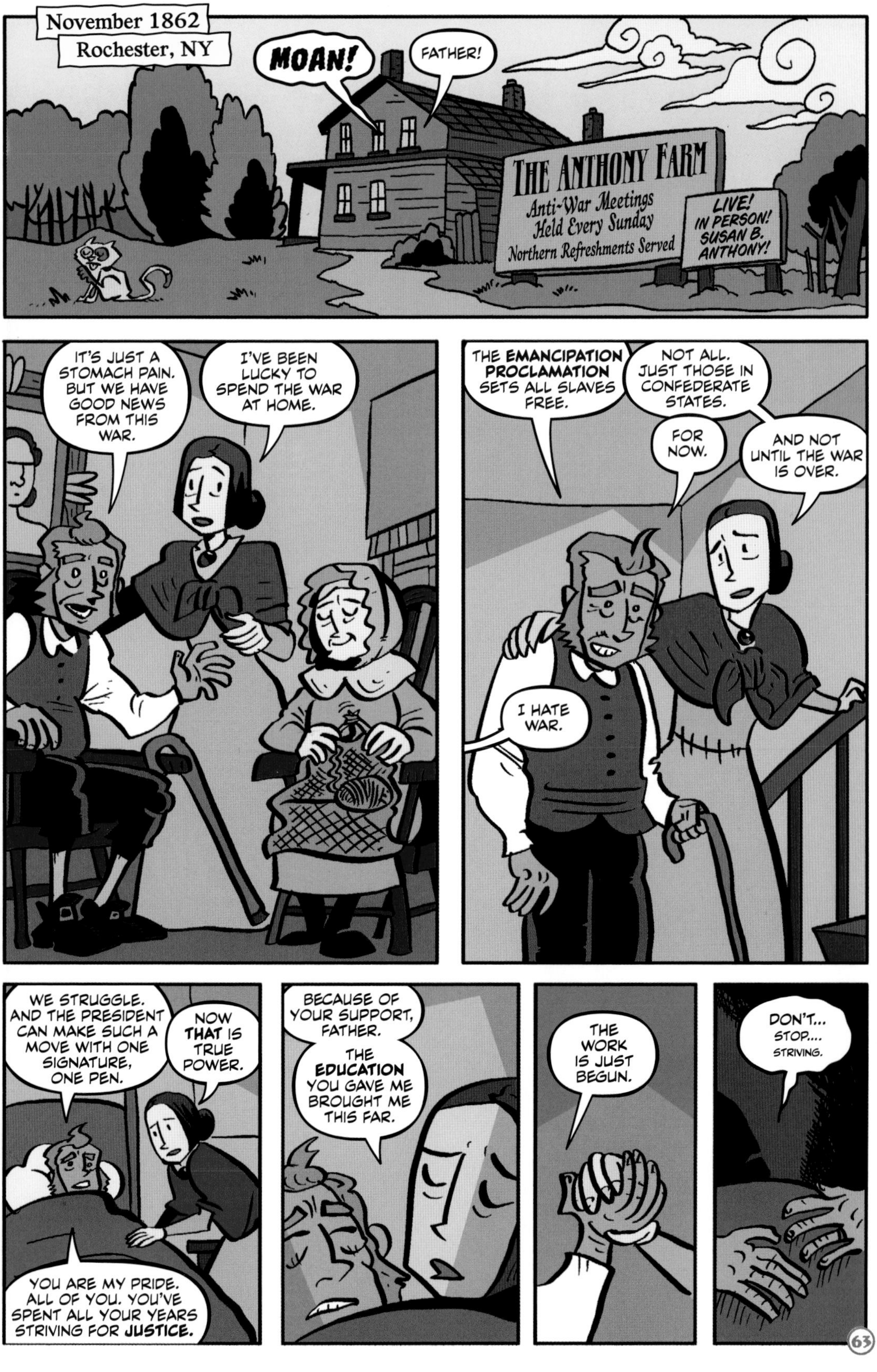
November 1862
Rochester, NY
MOAN!
FATHER!
THE ANTHONY FARM
Anti-War Meetings
Held Every Sunday
Northern Refreshments Served
LIVE! IN PERSON! SUSAN B. ANTHONY!
IT'S JUST A STOMACH PAIN. BUT WE HAVE GOOD NEWS FROM THIS WAR.
I'VE BEEN LUCKY TO SPEND THE WAR AT HOME.
THE **EMANCIPATION PROCLAMATION** SETS ALL SLAVES FREE.
NOT ALL. JUST THOSE IN CONFEDERATE STATES.
FOR NOW.
AND NOT UNTIL THE WAR IS OVER.
I HATE WAR.
WE STRUGGLE. AND THE PRESIDENT CAN MAKE SUCH A MOVE WITH ONE SIGNATURE, ONE PEN.
NOW **THAT** IS TRUE POWER.
YOU ARE MY PRIDE. ALL OF YOU. YOU'VE SPENT ALL YOUR YEARS STRIVING FOR **JUSTICE.**
BECAUSE OF YOUR SUPPORT, FATHER.
THE **EDUCATION** YOU GAVE ME BROUGHT ME THIS FAR.
THE WORK IS JUST BEGUN.
DON'T... STOP.... STRIVING.

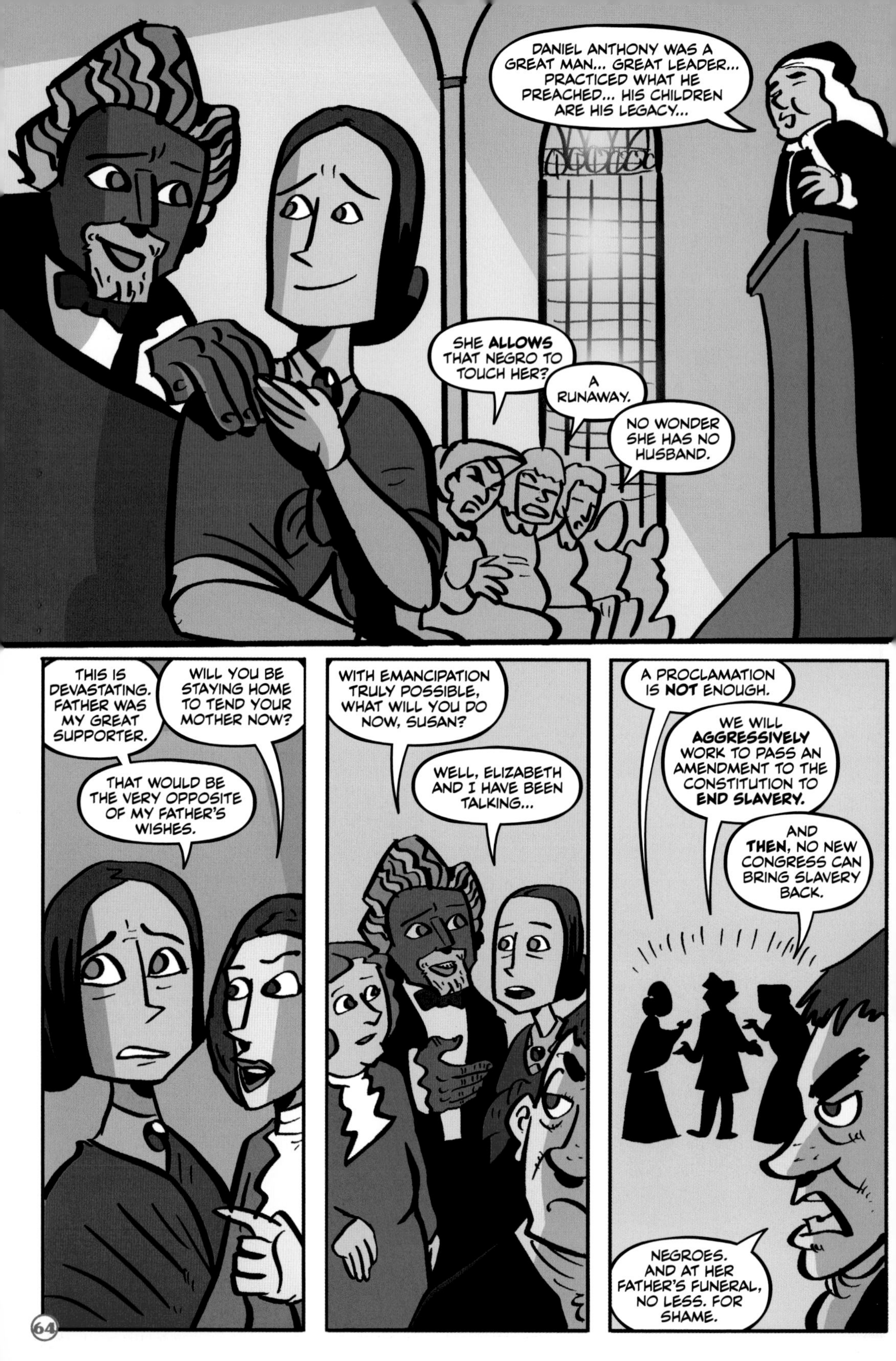

DANIEL ANTHONY WAS A GREAT MAN... GREAT LEADER... PRACTICED WHAT HE PREACHED... HIS CHILDREN ARE HIS LEGACY...
SHE **ALLOWS** THAT NEGRO TO TOUCH HER?
A RUNAWAY.
NO WONDER SHE HAS NO HUSBAND.
THIS IS DEVASTATING. FATHER WAS MY GREAT SUPPORTER.
WILL YOU BE STAYING HOME TO TEND YOUR MOTHER NOW?
THAT WOULD BE THE VERY OPPOSITE OF MY FATHER'S WISHES.
WITH EMANCIPATION TRULY POSSIBLE, WHAT WILL YOU DO NOW, SUSAN?
WELL, ELIZABETH AND I HAVE BEEN TALKING...
A PROCLAMATION IS **NOT** ENOUGH.
WE WILL **AGGRESSIVELY** WORK TO PASS AN AMENDMENT TO THE CONSTITUTION TO **END SLAVERY.**
AND **THEN**, NO NEW CONGRESS CAN BRING SLAVERY BACK.
NEGROES. AND AT HER FATHER'S FUNERAL, NO LESS. FOR SHAME.

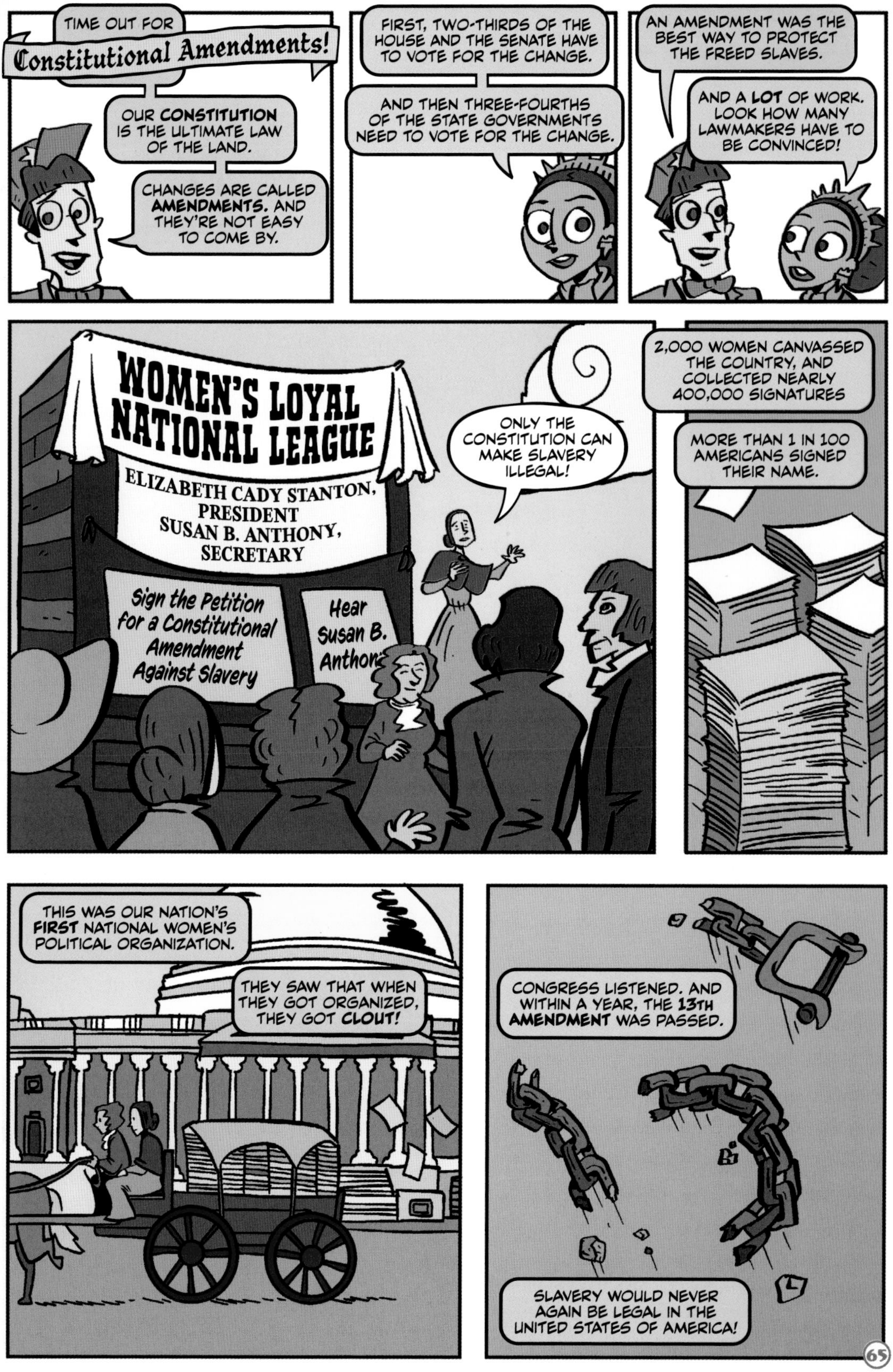
TIME OUT FOR
Constitutional Amendments!
OUR CONSTITUTION IS THE ULTIMATE LAW OF THE LAND.
CHANGES ARE CALLED AMENDMENTS. AND THEY'RE NOT EASY TO COME BY.
FIRST, TWO-THIRDS OF THE HOUSE AND THE SENATE HAVE TO VOTE FOR THE CHANGE.
AND THEN THREE-FOURTHS OF THE STATE GOVERNMENTS NEED TO VOTE FOR THE CHANGE.
AN AMENDMENT WAS THE BEST WAY TO PROTECT THE FREED SLAVES.
AND A LOT OF WORK. LOOK HOW MANY LAWMAKERS HAVE TO BE CONVINCED!
WOMEN'S LOYAL NATIONAL LEAGUE
ELIZABETH CADY STANTON, PRESIDENT
SUSAN B. ANTHONY, SECRETARY
Sign the Petition for a Constitutional Amendment Against Slavery
Hear Susan B. Anthon
ONLY THE CONSTITUTION CAN MAKE SLAVERY ILLEGAL!
2,000 WOMEN CANVASSED THE COUNTRY, AND COLLECTED NEARLY 400,000 SIGNATURES
MORE THAN 1 IN 100 AMERICANS SIGNED THEIR NAME.
THIS WAS OUR NATION'S FIRST NATIONAL WOMEN'S POLITICAL ORGANIZATION.
THEY SAW THAT WHEN THEY GOT ORGANIZED, THEY GOT CLOUT!
CONGRESS LISTENED. AND WITHIN A YEAR, THE 13TH AMENDMENT WAS PASSED.
SLAVERY WOULD NEVER AGAIN BE LEGAL IN THE UNITED STATES OF AMERICA!

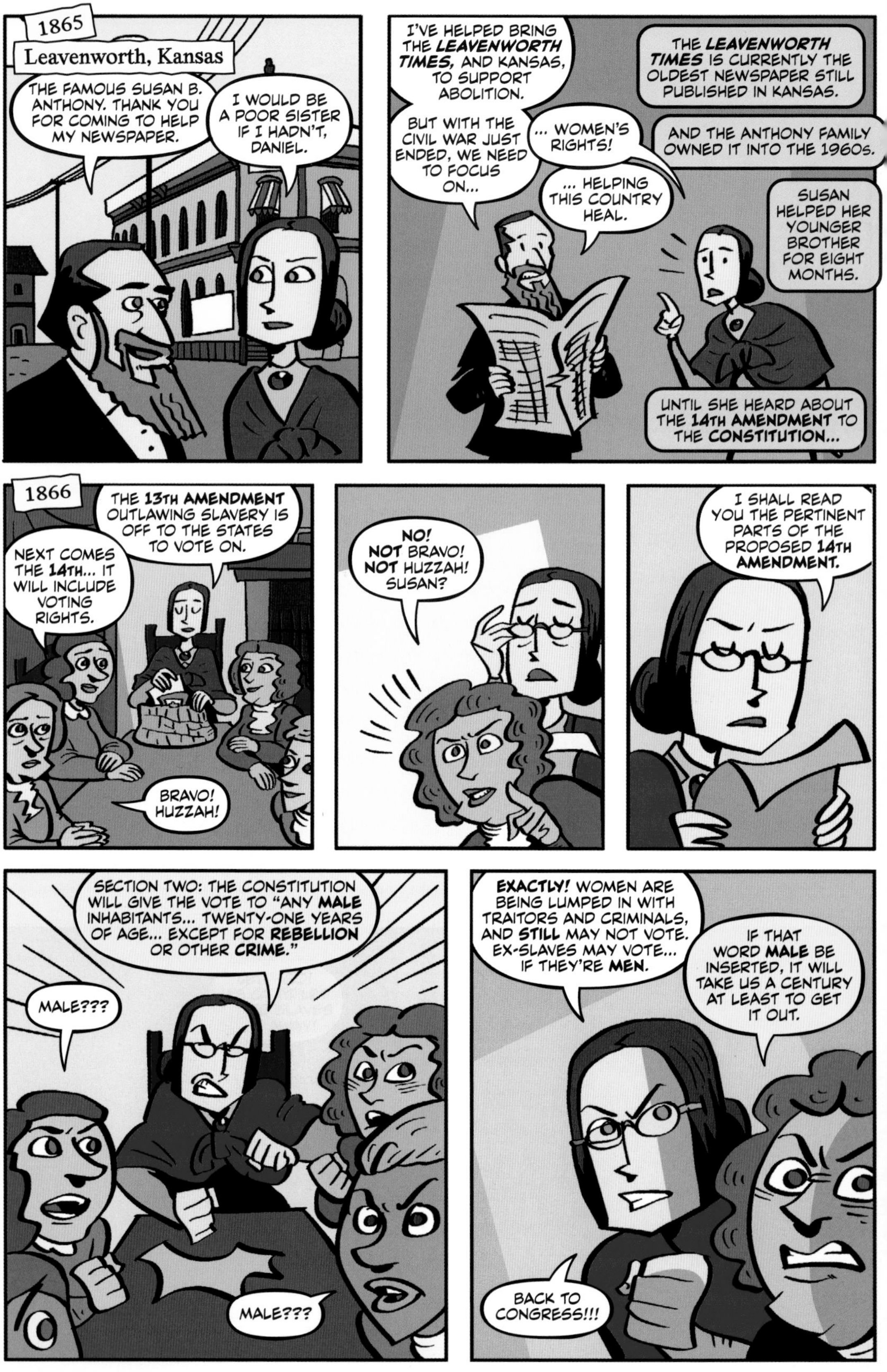
1865
Leavenworth, Kansas
THE FAMOUS SUSAN B. ANTHONY. THANK YOU FOR COMING TO HELP MY NEWSPAPER.
I WOULD BE A POOR SISTER IF I HADN'T, DANIEL.
I'VE HELPED BRING THE LEAVENWORTH TIMES, AND KANSAS, TO SUPPORT ABOLITION.
BUT WITH THE CIVIL WAR JUST ENDED, WE NEED TO FOCUS ON...
... WOMEN'S RIGHTS!
... HELPING THIS COUNTRY HEAL.
THE LEAVENWORTH TIMES IS CURRENTLY THE OLDEST NEWSPAPER STILL PUBLISHED IN KANSAS.
AND THE ANTHONY FAMILY OWNED IT INTO THE 1960s.
SUSAN HELPED HER YOUNGER BROTHER FOR EIGHT MONTHS.
UNTIL SHE HEARD ABOUT THE 14TH AMENDMENT TO THE CONSTITUTION...
1866
THE 13TH AMENDMENT OUTLAWING SLAVERY IS OFF TO THE STATES TO VOTE ON.
NEXT COMES THE 14TH... IT WILL INCLUDE VOTING RIGHTS.
BRAVO! HUZZAH!
NO! NOT BRAVO! NOT HUZZAH! SUSAN?
I SHALL READ YOU THE PERTINENT PARTS OF THE PROPOSED 14TH AMENDMENT.
SECTION TWO: THE CONSTITUTION WILL GIVE THE VOTE TO "ANY MALE INHABITANTS... TWENTY-ONE YEARS OF AGE... EXCEPT FOR REBELLION OR OTHER CRIME."
MALE???
MALE???
EXACTLY! WOMEN ARE BEING LUMPED IN WITH TRAITORS AND CRIMINALS, AND STILL MAY NOT VOTE. EX-SLAVES MAY VOTE... IF THEY'RE MEN.
IF THAT WORD MALE BE INSERTED, IT WILL TAKE US A CENTURY AT LEAST TO GET IT OUT.
BACK TO CONGRESS!!!

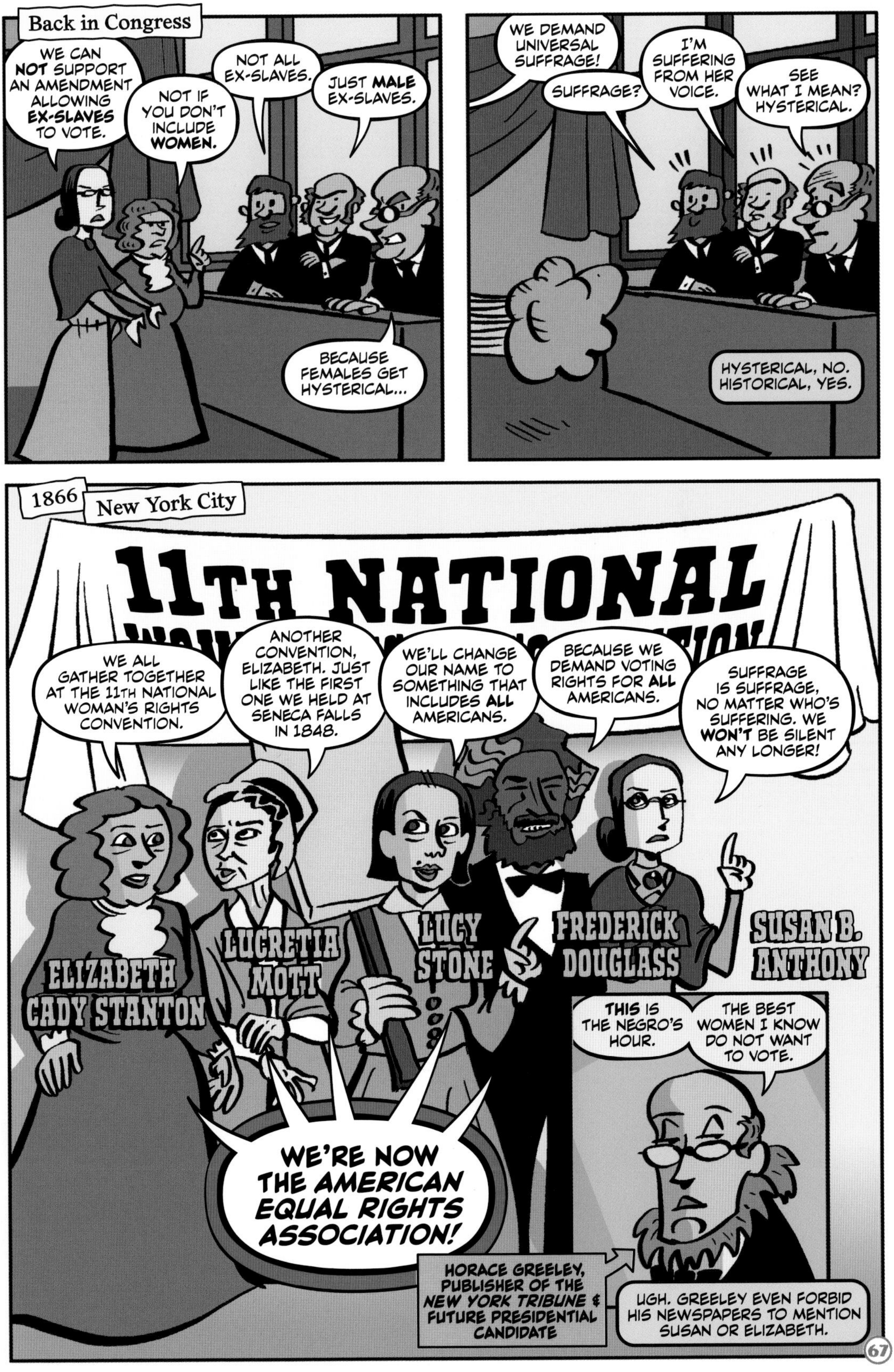
Back in Congress
WE CAN NOT SUPPORT AN AMENDMENT ALLOWING EX-SLAVES TO VOTE.
NOT IF YOU DON'T INCLUDE WOMEN.
NOT ALL EX-SLAVES.
JUST MALE EX-SLAVES.
BECAUSE FEMALES GET HYSTERICAL...
WE DEMAND UNIVERSAL SUFFRAGE!
SUFFRAGE?
I'M SUFFERING FROM HER VOICE.
SEE WHAT I MEAN? HYSTERICAL.
HYSTERICAL, NO. HISTORICAL, YES.
1866
New York City
11TH NATIONAL
WE ALL GATHER TOGETHER AT THE 11TH NATIONAL WOMAN'S RIGHTS CONVENTION.
ANOTHER CONVENTION, ELIZABETH. JUST LIKE THE FIRST ONE WE HELD AT SENECA FALLS IN 1848.
WE'LL CHANGE OUR NAME TO SOMETHING THAT INCLUDES ALL AMERICANS.
BECAUSE WE DEMAND VOTING RIGHTS FOR ALL AMERICANS.
SUFFRAGE IS SUFFRAGE, NO MATTER WHO'S SUFFERING. WE WON'T BE SILENT ANY LONGER!
ELIZABETH CADY STANTON
LUCRETIA MOTT
LUCY STONE
FREDERICK DOUGLASS
SUSAN B. ANTHONY
THIS IS THE NEGRO'S HOUR.
THE BEST WOMEN I KNOW DO NOT WANT TO VOTE.
WE'RE NOW THE AMERICAN EQUAL RIGHTS ASSOCIATION!
HORACE GREELEY, PUBLISHER OF THE NEW YORK TRIBUNE & FUTURE PRESIDENTIAL CANDIDATE
UGH. GREELEY EVEN FORBID HIS NEWSPAPERS TO MENTION SUSAN OR ELIZABETH.

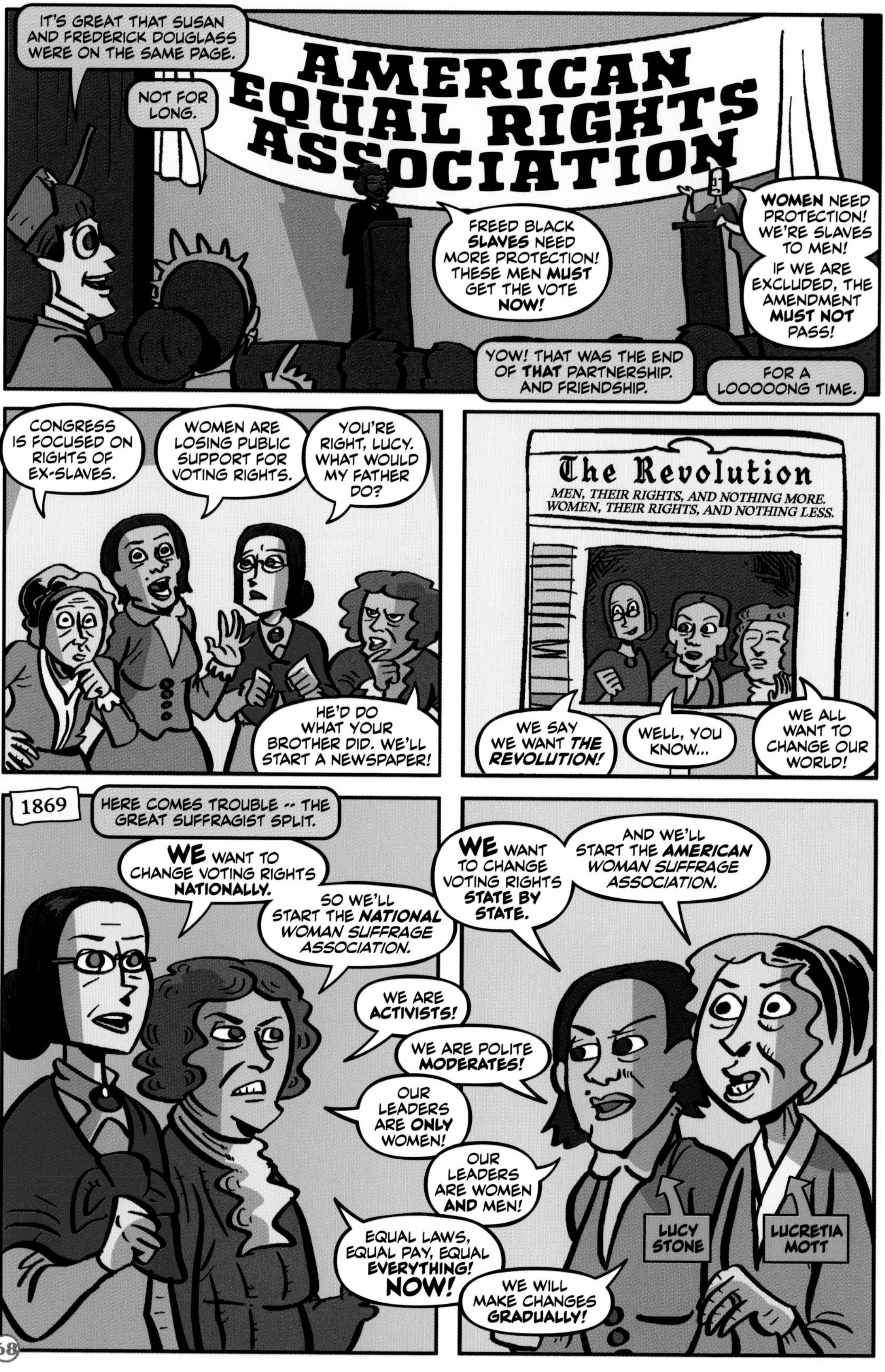
IT'S GREAT THAT SUSAN AND FREDERICK DOUGLASS WERE ON THE SAME PAGE.
NOT FOR LONG.
AMERICAN EQUAL RIGHTS ASSOCIATION
FREED BLACK SLAVES NEED MORE PROTECTION! THESE MEN MUST GET THE VOTE NOW!
WOMEN NEED PROTECTION! WE'RE SLAVES TO MEN!
IF WE ARE EXCLUDED, THE AMENDMENT MUST NOT PASS!
YOW! THAT WAS THE END OF THAT PARTNERSHIP. AND FRIENDSHIP.
FOR A LOOOOONG TIME.
CONGRESS IS FOCUSED ON RIGHTS OF EX-SLAVES.
WOMEN ARE LOSING PUBLIC SUPPORT FOR VOTING RIGHTS.
YOU'RE RIGHT, LUCY. WHAT WOULD MY FATHER DO?
HE'D DO WHAT YOUR BROTHER DID. WE'LL START A NEWSPAPER!
The Revolution
MEN, THEIR RIGHTS, AND NOTHING MORE. WOMEN, THEIR RIGHTS, AND NOTHING LESS.
WE SAY WE WANT THE REVOLUTION!
WELL, YOU KNOW...
WE ALL WANT TO CHANGE OUR WORLD!
1869
HERE COMES TROUBLE -- THE GREAT SUFFRAGIST SPLIT.
WE WANT TO CHANGE VOTING RIGHTS NATIONALLY.
SO WE'LL START THE NATIONAL WOMAN SUFFRAGE ASSOCIATION.
WE WANT TO CHANGE VOTING RIGHTS STATE BY STATE.
AND WE'LL START THE AMERICAN WOMAN SUFFRAGE ASSOCIATION.
WE ARE ACTIVISTS!
WE ARE POLITE MODERATES!
OUR LEADERS ARE ONLY WOMEN!
OUR LEADERS ARE WOMEN AND MEN!
EQUAL LAWS, EQUAL PAY, EQUAL EVERYTHING! NOW!
WE WILL MAKE CHANGES GRADUALLY!
LUCY STONE
LUCRETIA MOTT

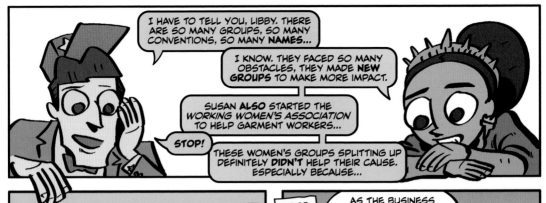

I HAVE TO TELL YOU, LIBBY. THERE ARE SO MANY GROUPS, SO MANY CONVENTIONS, SO MANY **NAMES**...

I KNOW. THEY FACED SO MANY OBSTACLES, THEY MADE **NEW GROUPS** TO MAKE MORE IMPACT.

SUSAN **ALSO** STARTED THE *WORKING WOMEN'S ASSOCIATION* TO HELP GARMENT WORKERS...

STOP!

THESE WOMEN'S GROUPS SPLITTING UP DEFINITELY **DIDN'T** HELP THEIR CAUSE. ESPECIALLY BECAUSE...

## The Revolution

I'M STARTING MY OWN NEWSPAPER, THE **WOMAN'S JOURNAL**.

WE'LL COMPETE WITH SUSAN'S *THE REVOLUTION.*

LUCY AND LUCRETIA. AGAIN!

1869

AS THE BUSINESS MANAGER, I HAVE TO SAY, WE'RE BROKE. WE NEED A WEALTHY PATRON, ELIZABETH.

GEORGE TRAIN IS OUR GUY. HE'S HELPED US BEFORE.

NO! HE'S **PRO-SLAVERY!** HE FIGHTS THE NEGRO VOTE.

WE CAN TAME HIS AWFUL INSTINCTS.

WE CAN??

WOMAN FIRST AND NEGRO **LAST!**

HE'S THE MOST WONDERFUL MAN OF THE CENTURY.

WILL DENYING BLACKS THE VOTE INCREASE CHANCES FOR WOMEN?

HOW'D THIS HAPPEN? WHO IS THIS GUY?

A RACIST. AND A FEMINIST. AND A RICH ONE. TRAIN MADE BIG MONEY BUILDING THE TRANS-CONTINENTAL RAILROAD.

AND HIS NAME IS TRAIN? SERIOUSLY?

1870

WE'RE SCARING THE ADVERTISERS. FAMOUS PEOPLE WON'T CONTRIBUTE TO A PAPER CALLED *THE REVOLUTION.*

EVEN WORSE, TRAIN ISN'T FUNDING US ANYMORE. WE'RE THROUGH. AND $10,000 IN DEBT.

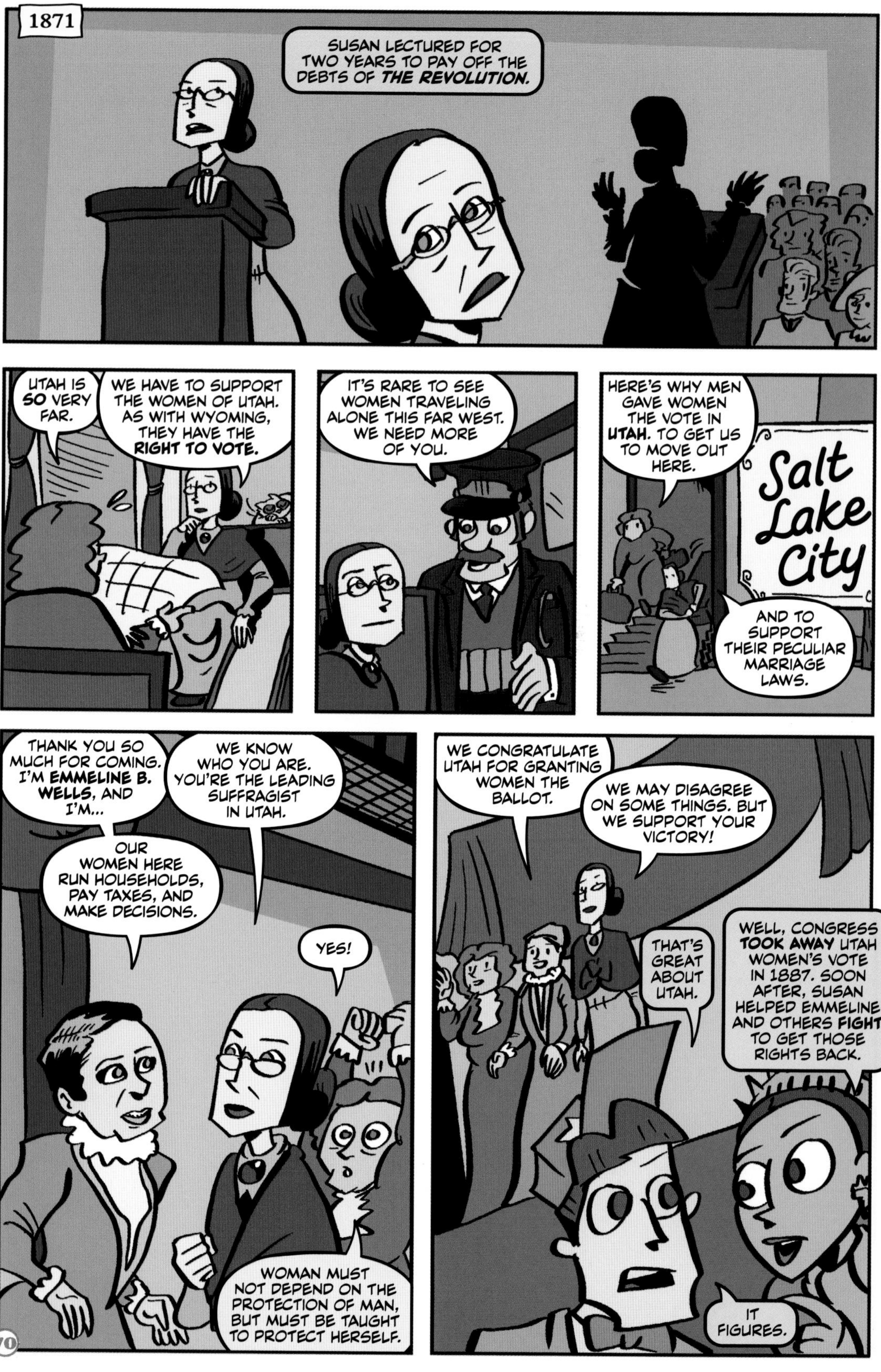
1871
SUSAN LECTURED FOR TWO YEARS TO PAY OFF THE DEBTS OF ***THE REVOLUTION.***
UTAH IS **SO** VERY FAR.
WE HAVE TO SUPPORT THE WOMEN OF UTAH. AS WITH WYOMING, THEY HAVE THE **RIGHT TO VOTE.**
IT'S RARE TO SEE WOMEN TRAVELING ALONE THIS FAR WEST. WE NEED MORE OF YOU.
HERE'S WHY MEN GAVE WOMEN THE VOTE IN **UTAH**. TO GET US TO MOVE OUT HERE.
Salt Lake City
AND TO SUPPORT THEIR PECULIAR MARRIAGE LAWS.
THANK YOU SO MUCH FOR COMING. I'M **EMMELINE B. WELLS**, AND I'M...
WE KNOW WHO YOU ARE. YOU'RE THE LEADING SUFFRAGIST IN UTAH.
OUR WOMEN HERE RUN HOUSEHOLDS, PAY TAXES, AND MAKE DECISIONS.
YES!
WOMAN MUST NOT DEPEND ON THE PROTECTION OF MAN, BUT MUST BE TAUGHT TO PROTECT HERSELF.
WE CONGRATULATE UTAH FOR GRANTING WOMEN THE BALLOT.
WE MAY DISAGREE ON SOME THINGS. BUT WE SUPPORT YOUR VICTORY!
THAT'S GREAT ABOUT UTAH.
WELL, CONGRESS **TOOK AWAY** UTAH WOMEN'S VOTE IN 1887. SOON AFTER, SUSAN HELPED EMMELINE AND OTHERS **FIGHT** TO GET THOSE RIGHTS BACK.
IT FIGURES.

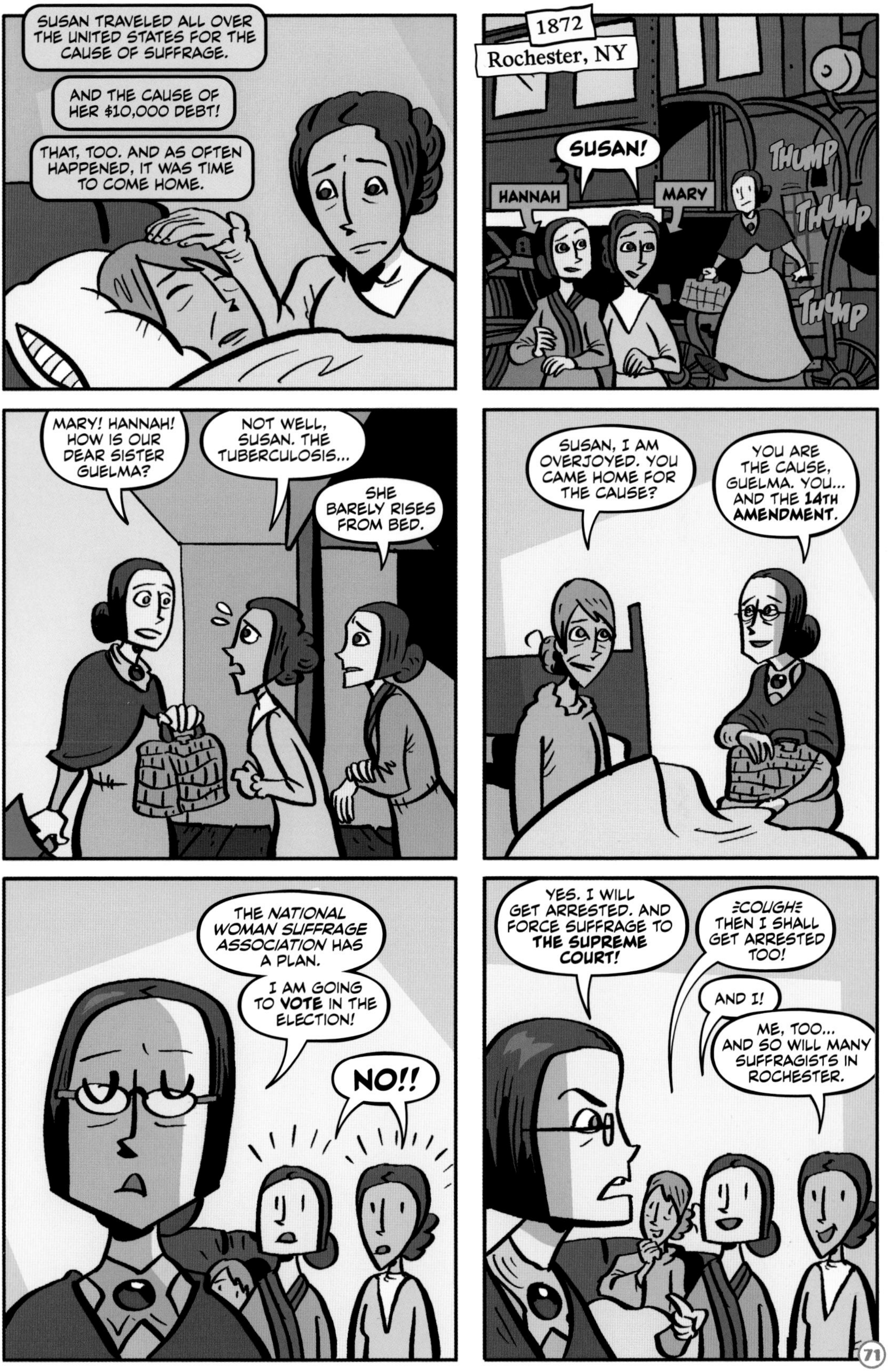
SUSAN TRAVELED ALL OVER THE UNITED STATES FOR THE CAUSE OF SUFFRAGE.
AND THE CAUSE OF HER $10,000 DEBT!
THAT, TOO. AND AS OFTEN HAPPENED, IT WAS TIME TO COME HOME.
1872
Rochester, NY
SUSAN!
HANNAH
MARY
THUMP
THUMP
THUMP
MARY! HANNAH! HOW IS OUR DEAR SISTER GUELMA?
NOT WELL, SUSAN. THE TUBERCULOSIS...
SHE BARELY RISES FROM BED.
SUSAN, I AM OVERJOYED. YOU CAME HOME FOR THE CAUSE?
YOU ARE THE CAUSE, GUELMA. YOU... AND THE 14TH AMENDMENT.
THE NATIONAL WOMAN SUFFRAGE ASSOCIATION HAS A PLAN.
I AM GOING TO VOTE IN THE ELECTION!
NO!!
YES. I WILL GET ARRESTED. AND FORCE SUFFRAGE TO THE SUPREME COURT!
COUGH THEN I SHALL GET ARRESTED TOO!
AND I!
ME, TOO... AND SO WILL MANY SUFFRAGISTS IN ROCHESTER.

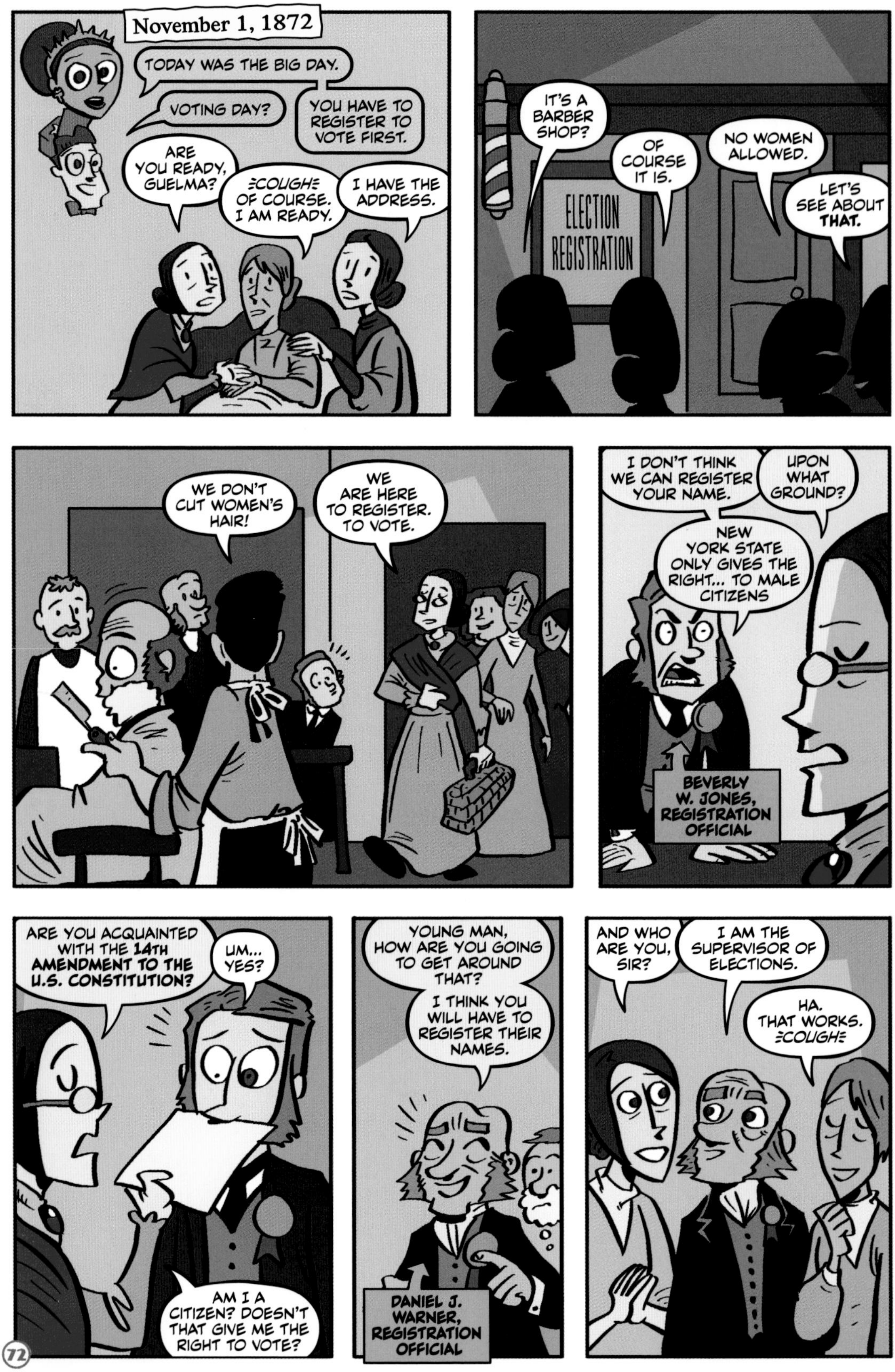
November 1, 1872
TODAY WAS THE BIG DAY.
VOTING DAY?
YOU HAVE TO REGISTER TO VOTE FIRST.
ARE YOU READY, GUELMA?
COUGH OF COURSE. I AM READY.
I HAVE THE ADDRESS.
IT'S A BARBER SHOP?
OF COURSE IT IS.
NO WOMEN ALLOWED.
LET'S SEE ABOUT THAT.
ELECTION REGISTRATION
WE DON'T CUT WOMEN'S HAIR!
WE ARE HERE TO REGISTER. TO VOTE.
I DON'T THINK WE CAN REGISTER YOUR NAME.
UPON WHAT GROUND?
NEW YORK STATE ONLY GIVES THE RIGHT... TO MALE CITIZENS
BEVERLY W. JONES, REGISTRATION OFFICIAL
ARE YOU ACQUAINTED WITH THE 14TH AMENDMENT TO THE U.S. CONSTITUTION?
UM... YES?
AM I A CITIZEN? DOESN'T THAT GIVE ME THE RIGHT TO VOTE?
YOUNG MAN, HOW ARE YOU GOING TO GET AROUND THAT?
I THINK YOU WILL HAVE TO REGISTER THEIR NAMES.
DANIEL J. WARNER, REGISTRATION OFFICIAL
AND WHO ARE YOU, SIR?
I AM THE SUPERVISOR OF ELECTIONS.
HA. THAT WORKS. COUGH

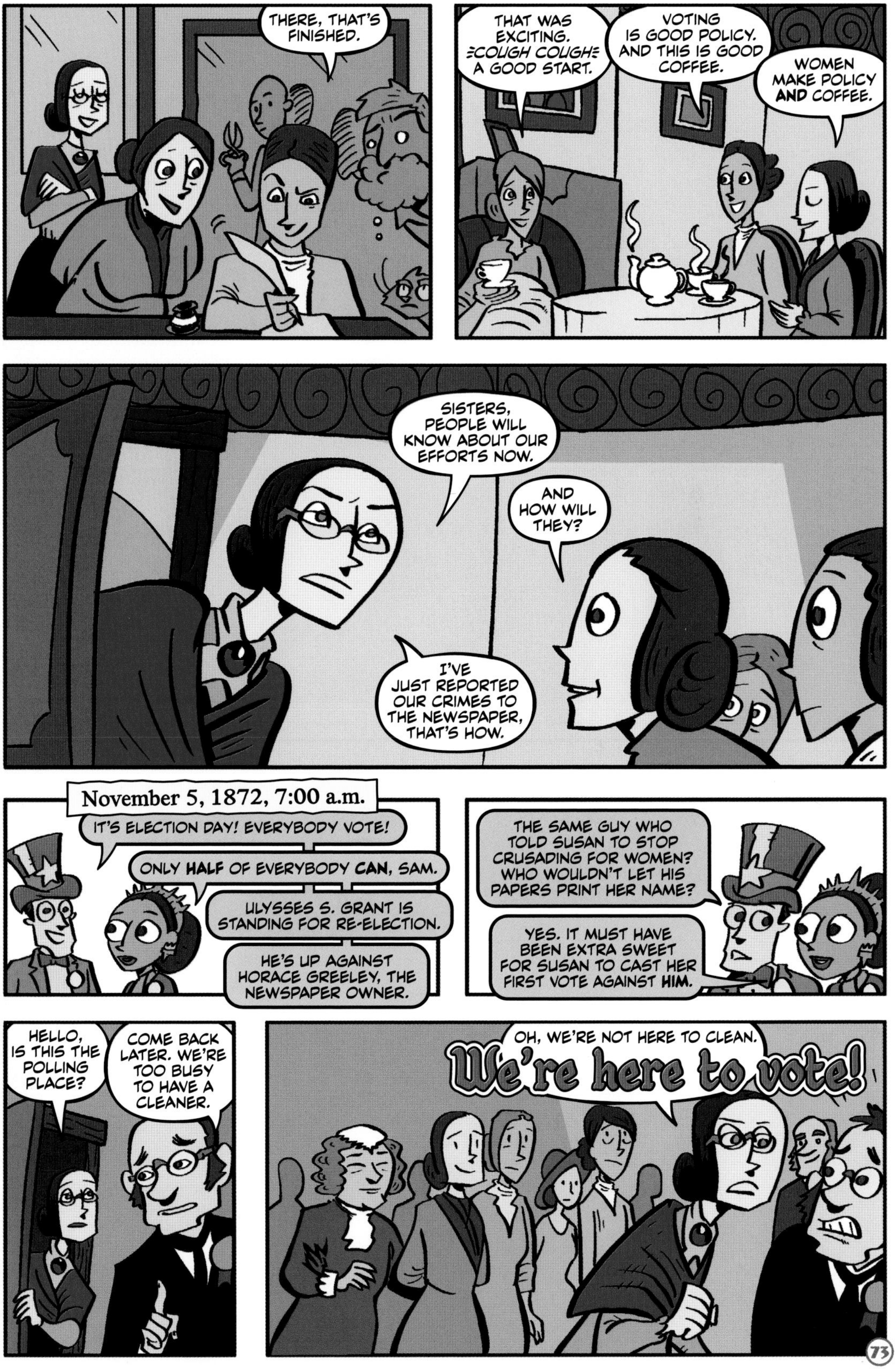
THERE, THAT'S FINISHED.
THAT WAS EXCITING. =COUGH COUGH= A GOOD START.
VOTING IS GOOD POLICY. AND THIS IS GOOD COFFEE.
WOMEN MAKE POLICY **AND** COFFEE.
SISTERS, PEOPLE WILL KNOW ABOUT OUR EFFORTS NOW.
AND HOW WILL THEY?
I'VE JUST REPORTED OUR CRIMES TO THE NEWSPAPER, THAT'S HOW.
November 5, 1872, 7:00 a.m.
IT'S ELECTION DAY! EVERYBODY VOTE!
ONLY **HALF** OF EVERYBODY **CAN**, SAM.
ULYSSES S. GRANT IS STANDING FOR RE-ELECTION.
HE'S UP AGAINST HORACE GREELEY, THE NEWSPAPER OWNER.
THE SAME GUY WHO TOLD SUSAN TO STOP CRUSADING FOR WOMEN? WHO WOULDN'T LET HIS PAPERS PRINT HER NAME?
YES. IT MUST HAVE BEEN EXTRA SWEET FOR SUSAN TO CAST HER FIRST VOTE AGAINST **HIM**.
HELLO, IS THIS THE POLLING PLACE?
COME BACK LATER. WE'RE TOO BUSY TO HAVE A CLEANER.
OH, WE'RE NOT HERE TO CLEAN.
We're here to vote!

ONLY REGISTERED VOTERS MA'AM.

OH, WE'RE REGISTERED.

I HAVE TO ASK YOU TO SWEAR AN OATH THAT YOU ARE QUALIFIED TO VOTE.

WE HAVE TO SWEAR?

NO, THIS IS GOOD. RAISE YOUR HANDS, LADIES.

I'D LOVE TO HEAR THAT OATH.

ONCE SOMEONE HAS SWORN AN OATH, THE LAW SAYS THEY MUST GET A BALLOT.

YES. GO AHEAD LADIES.

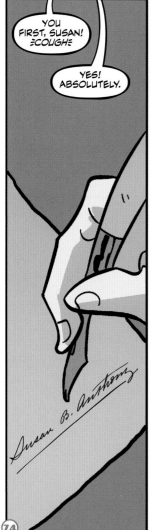

YOU FIRST, SUSAN! ≡COUGH≡

YES! ABSOLUTELY.

*Susan B. Anthony*

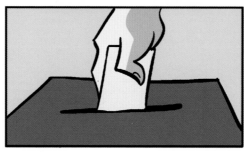

YOU SAID THEY WOULDN'T ≡COUGH≡ LET US VOTE.

WHO KNEW?

ON THE BOOK COVER, YOU'RE GETTING ARRESTED.

OH, THEY'RE JUST SELLING BOOKS. THAT DOESN'T LOOK LIKE ME AT ALL!

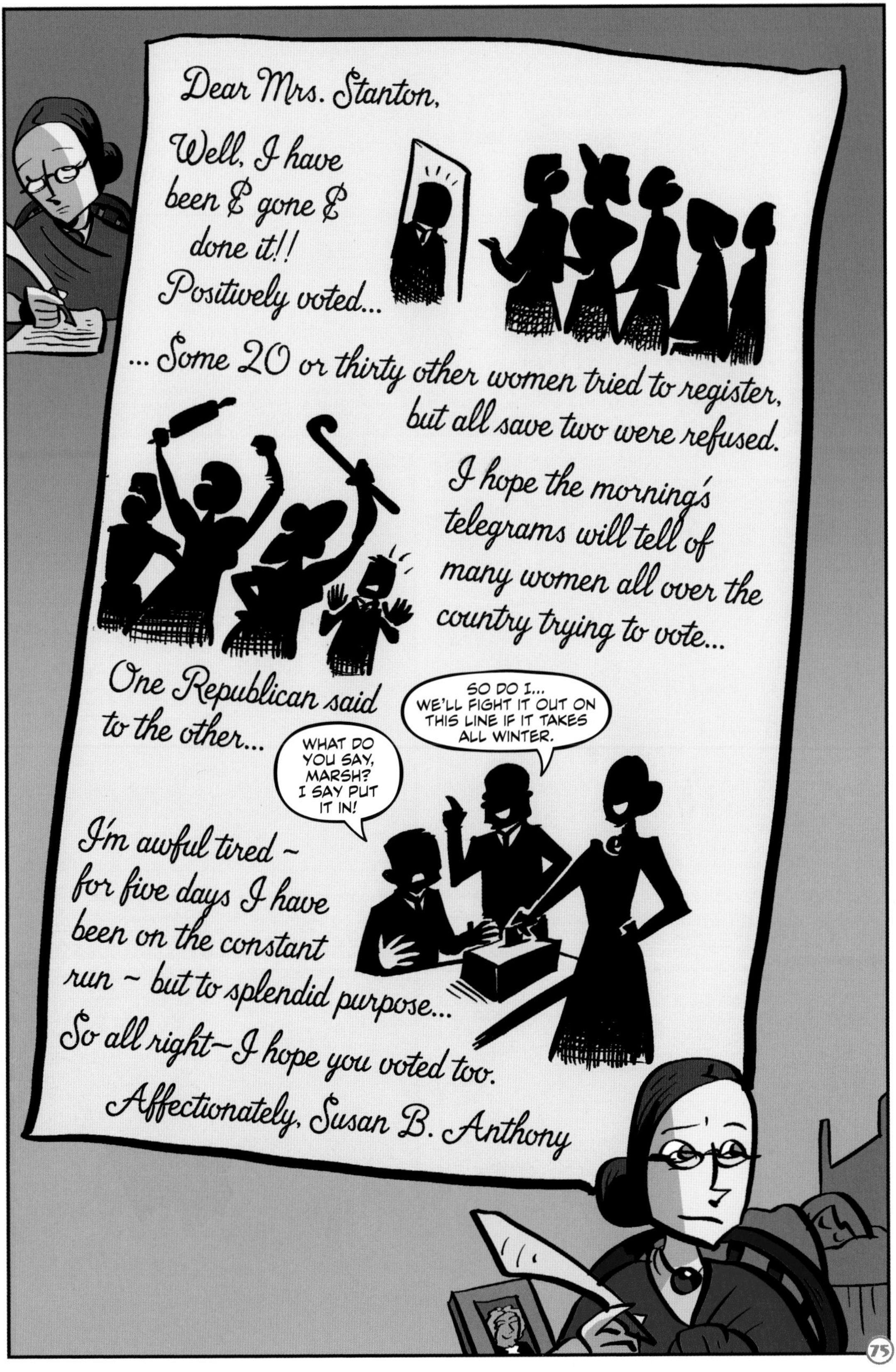
Dear Mrs. Stanton,
Well, I have been & gone & done it!! Positively voted...
... Some 20 or thirty other women tried to register, but all save two were refused.
I hope the morning's telegrams will tell of many women all over the country trying to vote...
One Republican said to the other...
WHAT DO YOU SAY, MARSH? I SAY PUT IT IN!
SO DO I... WE'LL FIGHT IT OUT ON THIS LINE IF IT TAKES ALL WINTER.
I'm awful tired ~ for five days I have been on the constant run ~ but to splendid purpose...
So all right ~ I hope you voted too.
Affectionately, Susan B. Anthony

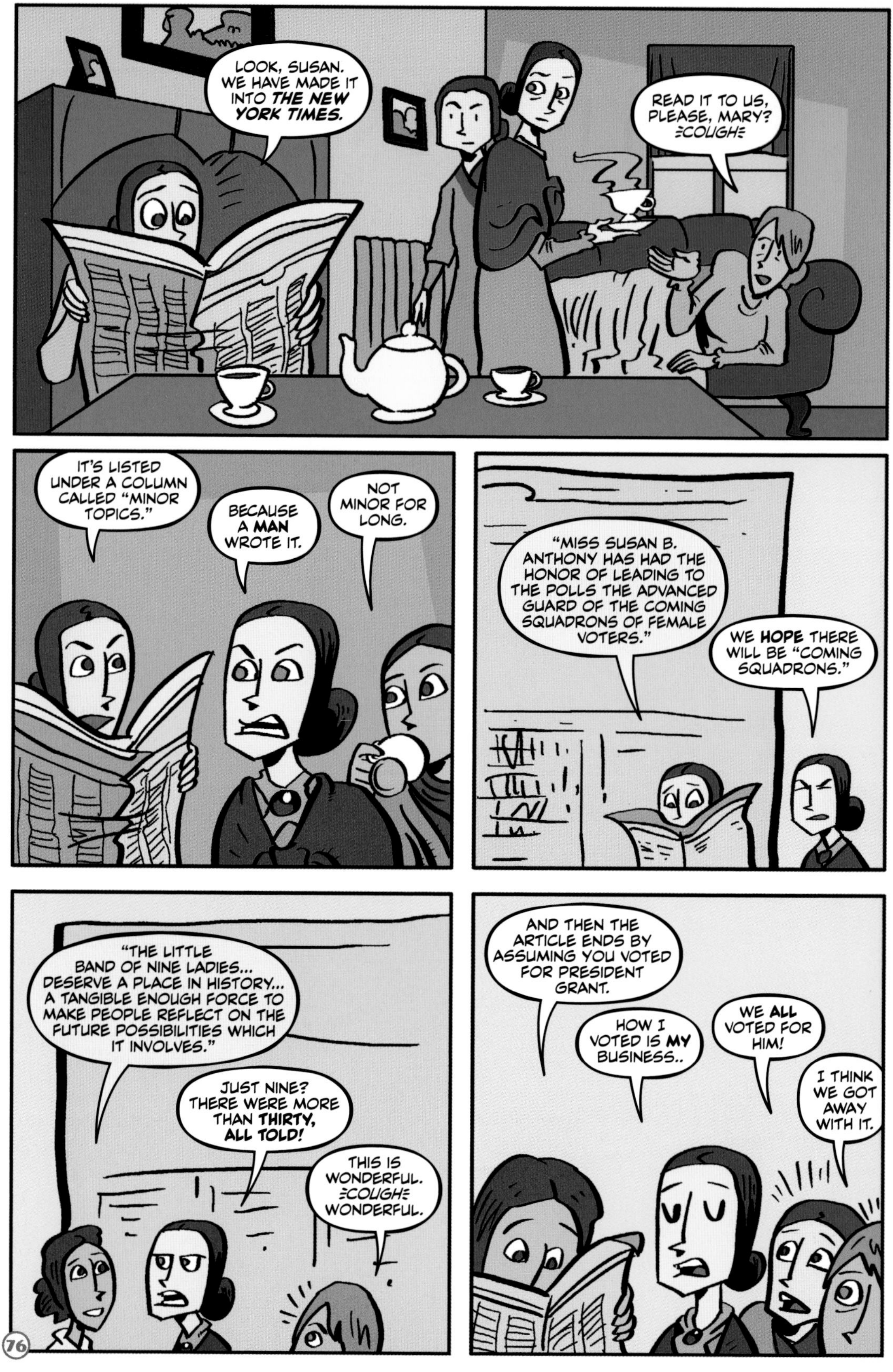
LOOK, SUSAN. WE HAVE MADE IT INTO THE NEW YORK TIMES.
READ IT TO US, PLEASE, MARY? COUGH
IT'S LISTED UNDER A COLUMN CALLED "MINOR TOPICS."
BECAUSE A MAN WROTE IT.
NOT MINOR FOR LONG.
"MISS SUSAN B. ANTHONY HAS HAD THE HONOR OF LEADING TO THE POLLS THE ADVANCED GUARD OF THE COMING SQUADRONS OF FEMALE VOTERS."
WE HOPE THERE WILL BE "COMING SQUADRONS."
"THE LITTLE BAND OF NINE LADIES... DESERVE A PLACE IN HISTORY... A TANGIBLE ENOUGH FORCE TO MAKE PEOPLE REFLECT ON THE FUTURE POSSIBILITIES WHICH IT INVOLVES."
JUST NINE? THERE WERE MORE THAN THIRTY, ALL TOLD!
THIS IS WONDERFUL. COUGH WONDERFUL.
AND THEN THE ARTICLE ENDS BY ASSUMING YOU VOTED FOR PRESIDENT GRANT.
HOW I VOTED IS MY BUSINESS..
WE ALL VOTED FOR HIM!
I THINK WE GOT AWAY WITH IT.

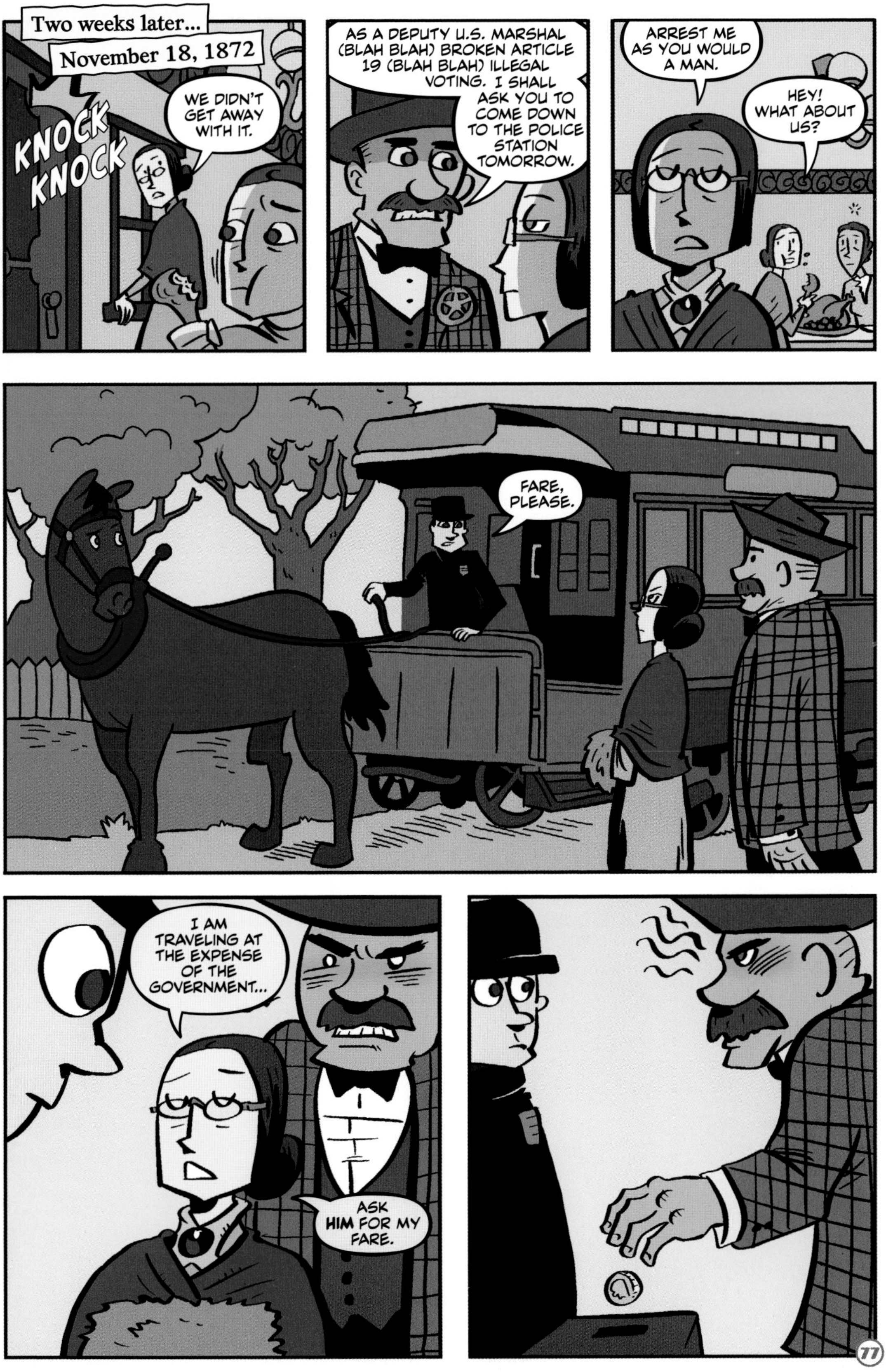
Two weeks later...
November 18, 1872
KNOCK KNOCK
WE DIDN'T GET AWAY WITH IT.
AS A DEPUTY U.S. MARSHAL (BLAH BLAH) BROKEN ARTICLE 19 (BLAH BLAH) ILLEGAL VOTING. I SHALL
ASK YOU TO COME DOWN TO THE POLICE STATION TOMORROW.
ARREST ME AS YOU WOULD A MAN.
HEY! WHAT ABOUT US?
FARE, PLEASE.
I AM TRAVELING AT THE EXPENSE OF THE GOVERNMENT...
ASK HIM FOR MY FARE.

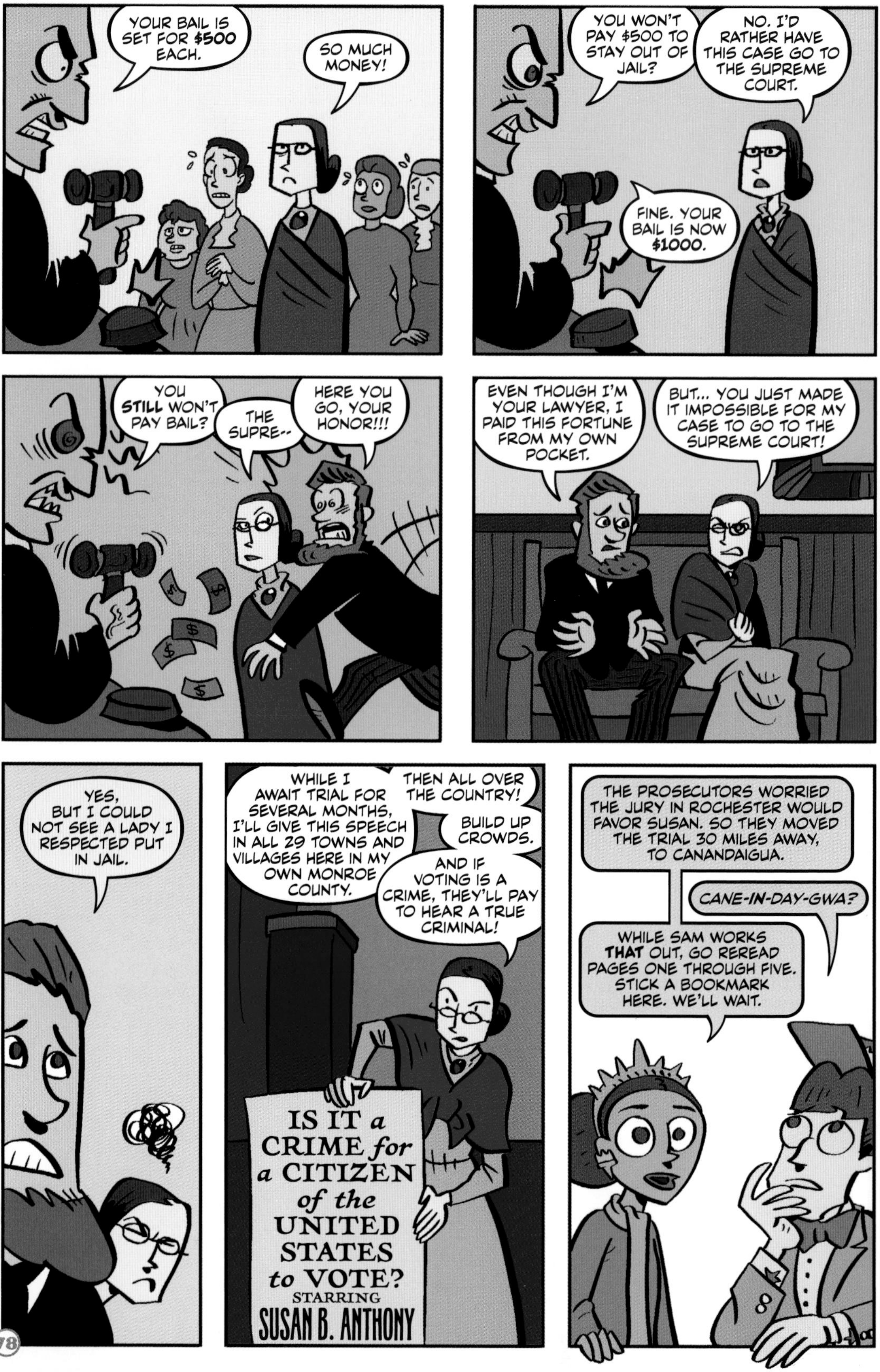
YOUR BAIL IS SET FOR **$500** EACH.
SO MUCH MONEY!
YOU WON'T PAY $500 TO STAY OUT OF JAIL?
NO. I'D RATHER HAVE THIS CASE GO TO THE SUPREME COURT.
FINE. YOUR BAIL IS NOW **$1000**.
YOU **STILL** WON'T PAY BAIL?
THE SUPRE--
HERE YOU GO, YOUR HONOR!!!
EVEN THOUGH I'M YOUR LAWYER, I PAID THIS FORTUNE FROM MY OWN POCKET.
BUT... YOU JUST MADE IT IMPOSSIBLE FOR MY CASE TO GO TO THE SUPREME COURT!
YES, BUT I COULD NOT SEE A LADY I RESPECTED PUT IN JAIL.
WHILE I AWAIT TRIAL FOR SEVERAL MONTHS, I'LL GIVE THIS SPEECH IN ALL 29 TOWNS AND VILLAGES HERE IN MY OWN MONROE COUNTY.
THEN ALL OVER THE COUNTRY!
BUILD UP CROWDS.
AND IF VOTING IS A CRIME, THEY'LL PAY TO HEAR A TRUE CRIMINAL!
IS IT *a* CRIME *for* *a* CITIZEN *of the* UNITED STATES *to* VOTE? STARRING SUSAN B. ANTHONY
THE PROSECUTORS WORRIED THE JURY IN ROCHESTER WOULD FAVOR SUSAN. SO THEY MOVED THE TRIAL 30 MILES AWAY, TO CANANDAIGUA.
*CANE-IN-DAY-GWA?*
WHILE SAM WORKS **THAT** OUT, GO REREAD PAGES ONE THROUGH FIVE. STICK A BOOKMARK HERE. WE'LL WAIT.

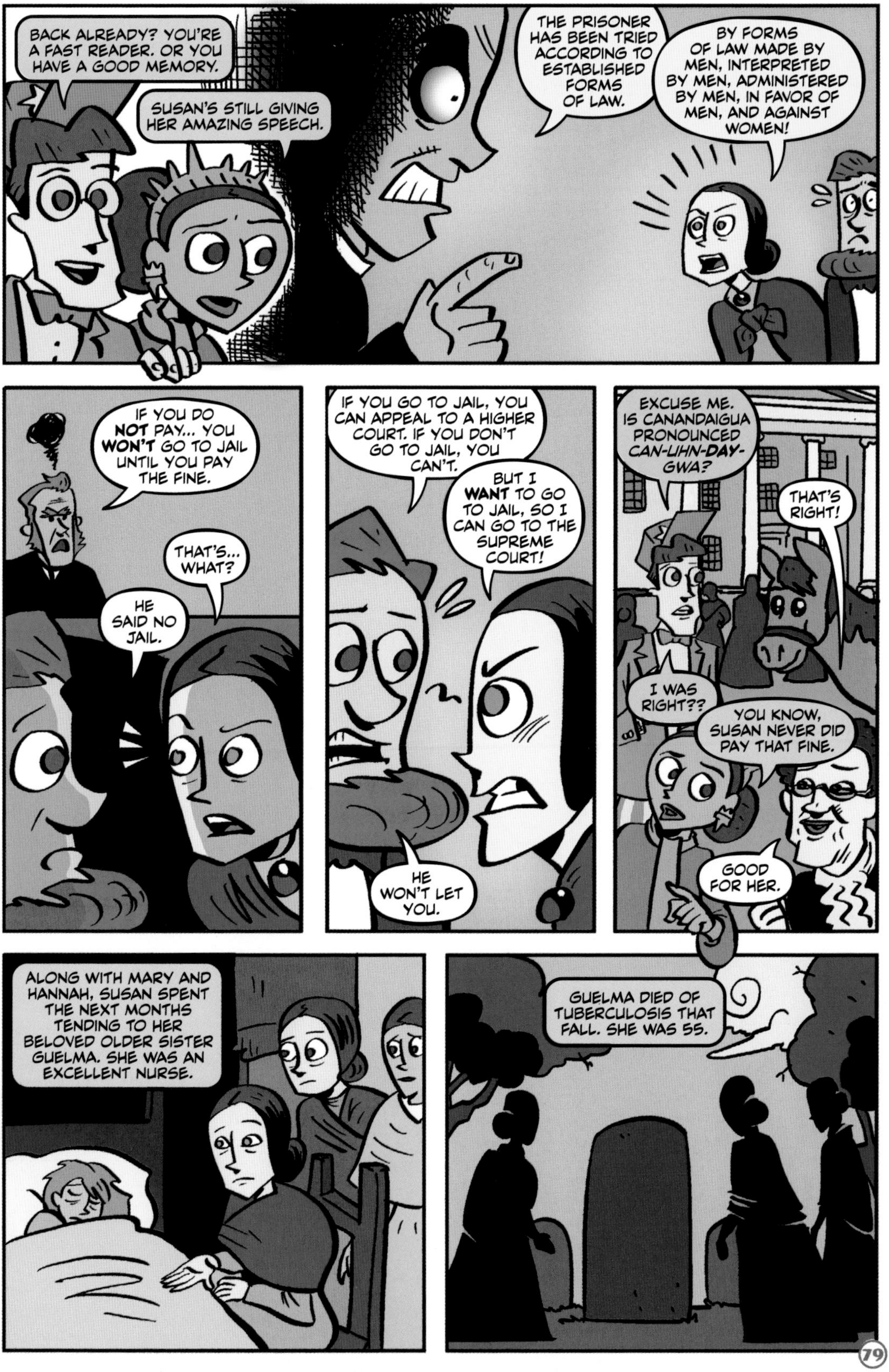
BACK ALREADY? YOU'RE A FAST READER. OR YOU HAVE A GOOD MEMORY.
SUSAN'S STILL GIVING HER AMAZING SPEECH.
THE PRISONER HAS BEEN TRIED ACCORDING TO ESTABLISHED FORMS OF LAW.
BY FORMS OF LAW MADE BY MEN, INTERPRETED BY MEN, ADMINISTERED BY MEN, IN FAVOR OF MEN, AND AGAINST WOMEN!
IF YOU DO **NOT** PAY... YOU **WON'T** GO TO JAIL UNTIL YOU PAY THE FINE.
THAT'S... WHAT?
HE SAID NO JAIL.
IF YOU GO TO JAIL, YOU CAN APPEAL TO A HIGHER COURT. IF YOU DON'T GO TO JAIL, YOU CAN'T.
BUT I **WANT** TO GO TO JAIL, SO I CAN GO TO THE SUPREME COURT!
HE WON'T LET YOU.
EXCUSE ME. IS CANANDAIGUA PRONOUNCED *CAN-UHN-**DAY**-GWA?*
THAT'S RIGHT!
I WAS RIGHT??
YOU KNOW, SUSAN NEVER DID PAY THAT FINE.
GOOD FOR HER.
ALONG WITH MARY AND HANNAH, SUSAN SPENT THE NEXT MONTHS TENDING TO HER BELOVED OLDER SISTER GUELMA. SHE WAS AN EXCELLENT NURSE.
GUELMA DIED OF TUBERCULOSIS THAT FALL. SHE WAS 55.

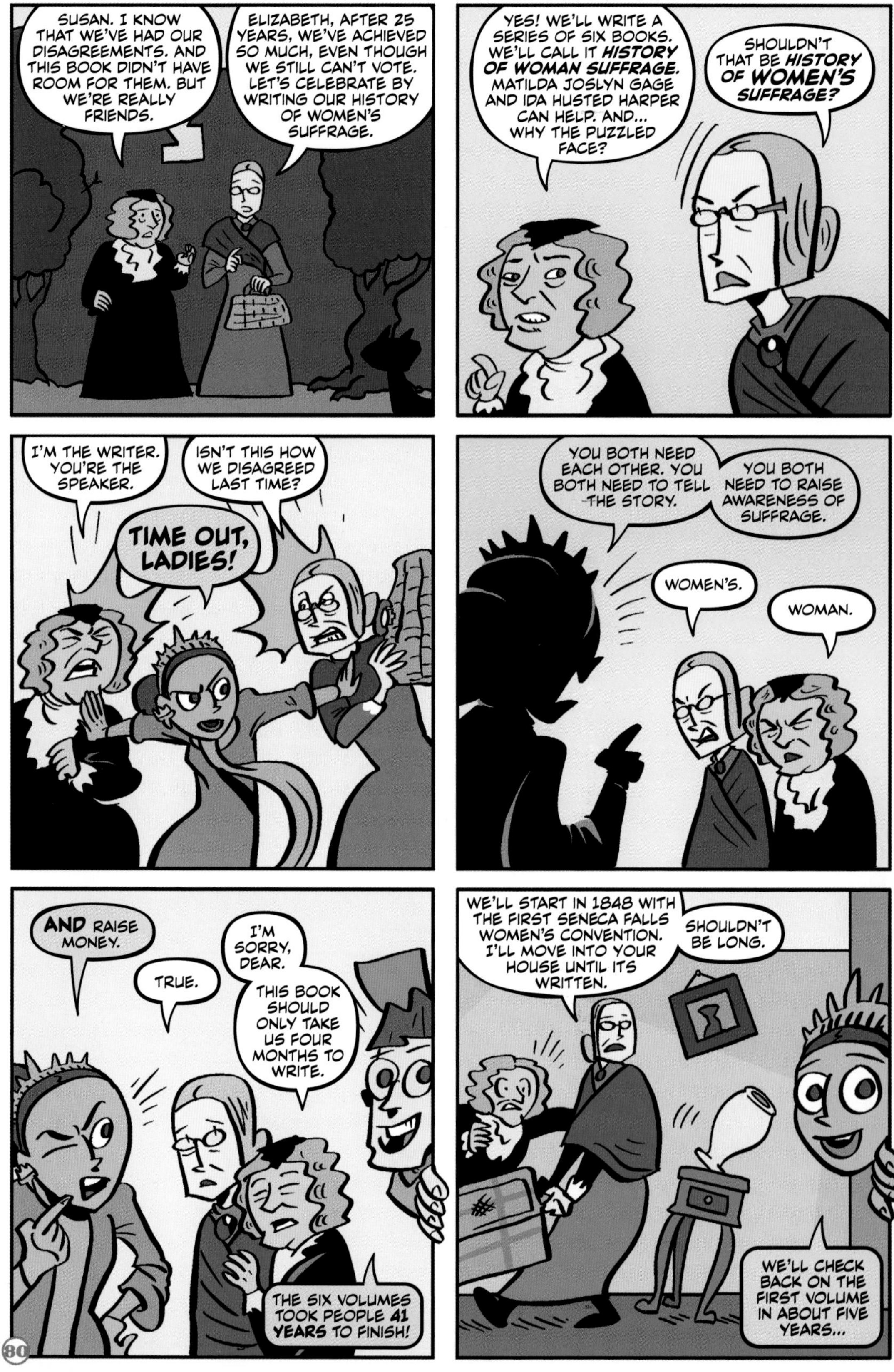
SUSAN. I KNOW THAT WE'VE HAD OUR DISAGREEMENTS. AND THIS BOOK DIDN'T HAVE ROOM FOR THEM. BUT WE'RE REALLY FRIENDS.
ELIZABETH, AFTER 25 YEARS, WE'VE ACHIEVED SO MUCH, EVEN THOUGH WE STILL CAN'T VOTE. LET'S CELEBRATE BY WRITING OUR HISTORY OF WOMEN'S SUFFRAGE.
YES! WE'LL WRITE A SERIES OF SIX BOOKS. WE'LL CALL IT ***HISTORY OF WOMAN SUFFRAGE.*** MATILDA JOSLYN GAGE AND IDA HUSTED HARPER CAN HELP. AND... WHY THE PUZZLED FACE?
SHOULDN'T THAT BE ***HISTORY OF WOMEN'S SUFFRAGE?***
I'M THE WRITER. YOU'RE THE SPEAKER.
ISN'T THIS HOW WE DISAGREED LAST TIME?
TIME OUT, LADIES!
YOU BOTH NEED EACH OTHER. YOU BOTH NEED TO TELL THE STORY.
YOU BOTH NEED TO RAISE AWARENESS OF SUFFRAGE.
WOMEN'S.
WOMAN.
**AND** RAISE MONEY.
TRUE.
I'M SORRY, DEAR.
THIS BOOK SHOULD ONLY TAKE US FOUR MONTHS TO WRITE.
THE SIX VOLUMES TOOK PEOPLE **41 YEARS** TO FINISH!
WE'LL START IN 1848 WITH THE FIRST SENECA FALLS WOMEN'S CONVENTION. I'LL MOVE INTO YOUR HOUSE UNTIL ITS WRITTEN.
SHOULDN'T BE LONG.
WE'LL CHECK BACK ON THE FIRST VOLUME IN ABOUT FIVE YEARS...

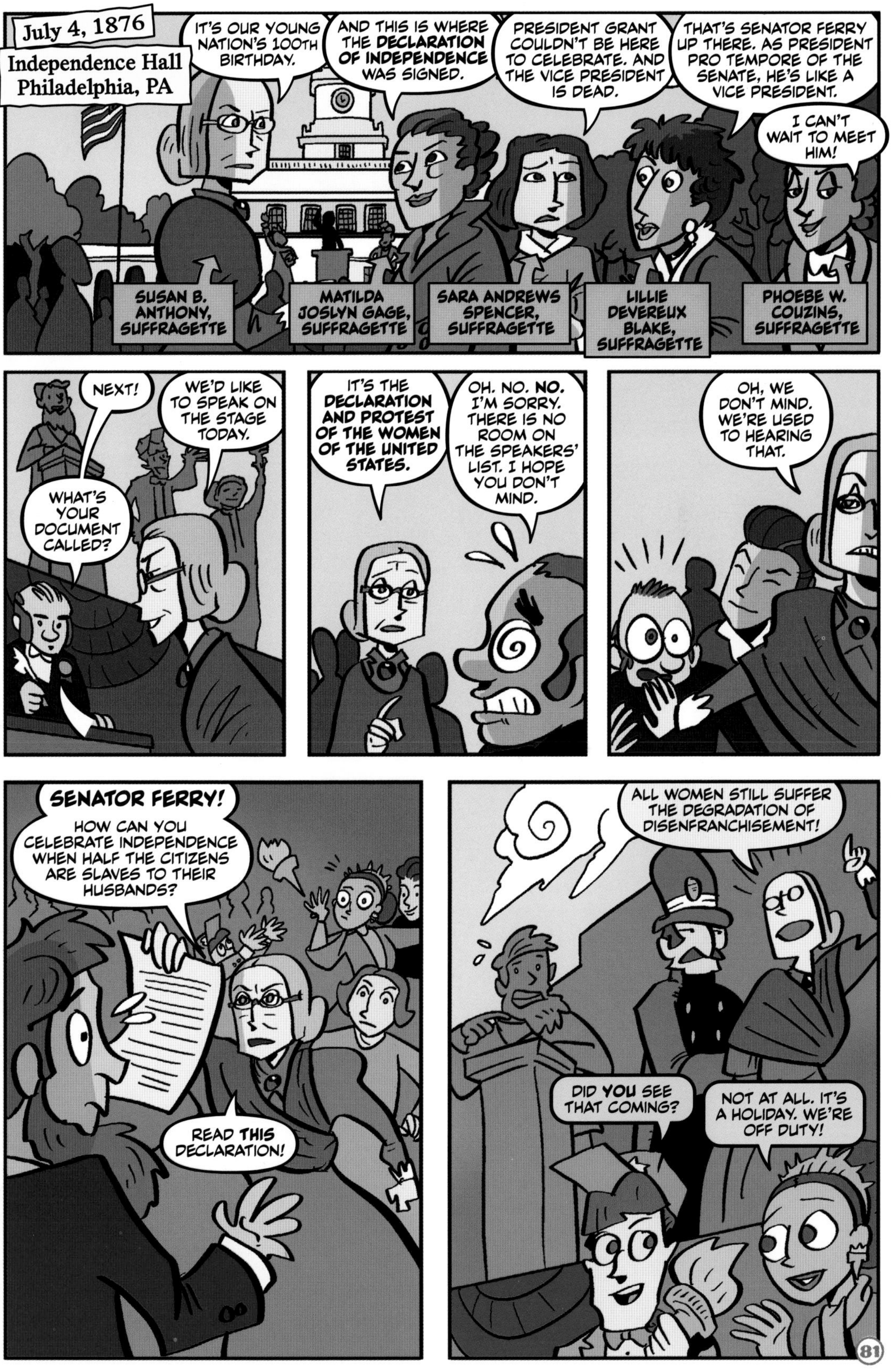
July 4, 1876
Independence Hall
Philadelphia, PA
IT'S OUR YOUNG NATION'S 100TH BIRTHDAY.
AND THIS IS WHERE THE DECLARATION OF INDEPENDENCE WAS SIGNED.
PRESIDENT GRANT COULDN'T BE HERE TO CELEBRATE. AND THE VICE PRESIDENT IS DEAD.
THAT'S SENATOR FERRY UP THERE. AS PRESIDENT PRO TEMPORE OF THE SENATE, HE'S LIKE A VICE PRESIDENT.
I CAN'T WAIT TO MEET HIM!
SUSAN B. ANTHONY, SUFFRAGETTE
MATILDA JOSLYN GAGE, SUFFRAGETTE
SARA ANDREWS SPENCER, SUFFRAGETTE
LILLIE DEVEREUX BLAKE, SUFFRAGETTE
PHOEBE W. COUZINS, SUFFRAGETTE
NEXT!
WE'D LIKE TO SPEAK ON THE STAGE TODAY.
WHAT'S YOUR DOCUMENT CALLED?
IT'S THE DECLARATION AND PROTEST OF THE WOMEN OF THE UNITED STATES.
OH. NO. NO. I'M SORRY. THERE IS NO ROOM ON THE SPEAKERS' LIST. I HOPE YOU DON'T MIND.
OH, WE DON'T MIND. WE'RE USED TO HEARING THAT.
SENATOR FERRY!
HOW CAN YOU CELEBRATE INDEPENDENCE WHEN HALF THE CITIZENS ARE SLAVES TO THEIR HUSBANDS?
READ THIS DECLARATION!
ALL WOMEN STILL SUFFER THE DEGRADATION OF DISENFRANCHISEMENT!
DID YOU SEE THAT COMING?
NOT AT ALL. IT'S A HOLIDAY. WE'RE OFF DUTY!

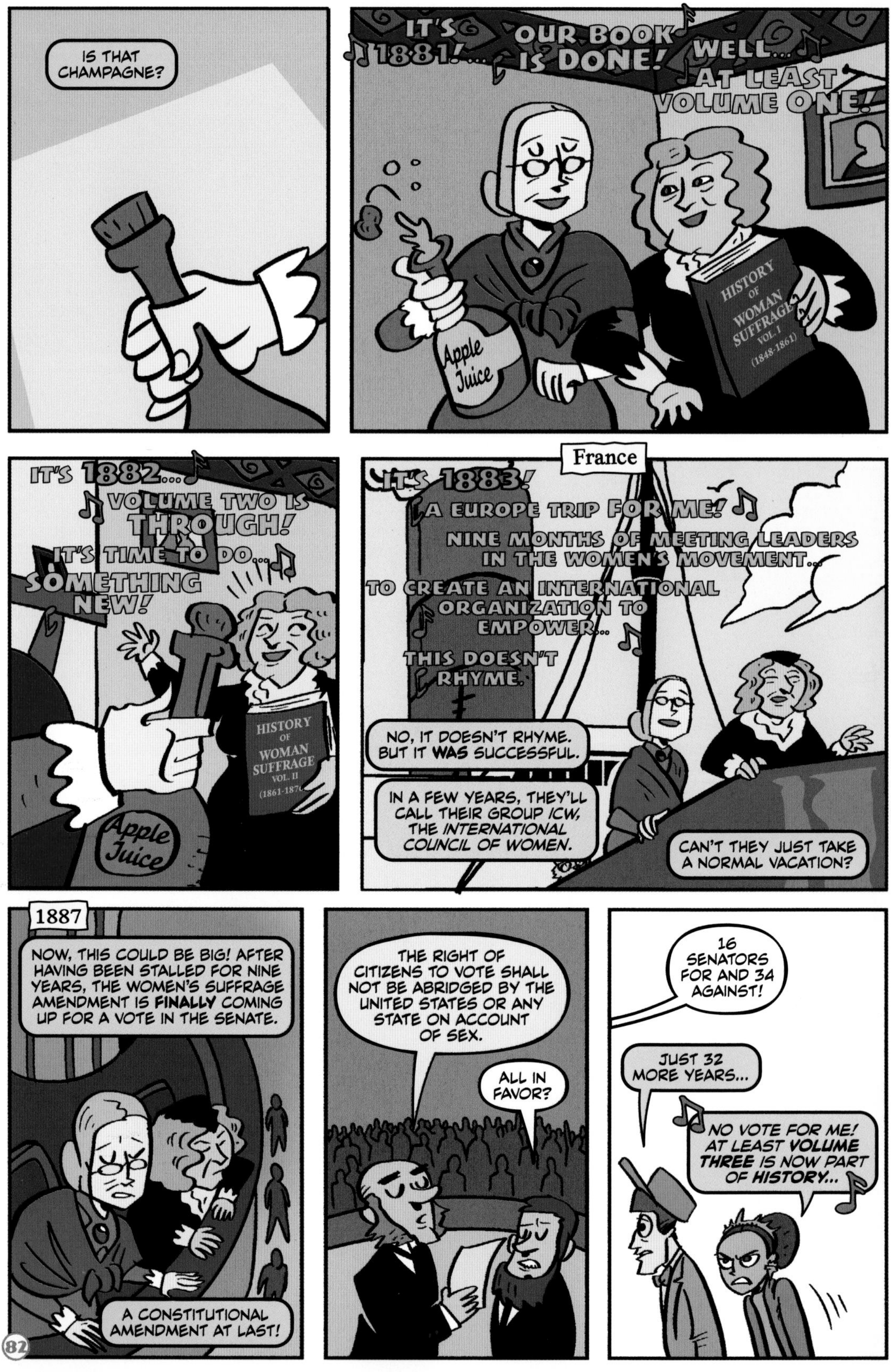
IS THAT CHAMPAGNE?
IT'S 1881!... OUR BOOK IS DONE! WELL... AT LEAST VOLUME ONE!
HISTORY OF WOMAN SUFFRAGE VOL. I (1848-1861)
Apple Juice
IT'S 1882... VOLUME TWO IS THROUGH! IT'S TIME TO DO... SOMETHING NEW!
HISTORY OF WOMAN SUFFRAGE VOL. II (1861-1876)
Apple Juice
France
IT'S 1883! A EUROPE TRIP FOR ME! NINE MONTHS OF MEETING LEADERS IN THE WOMEN'S MOVEMENT... TO CREATE AN INTERNATIONAL ORGANIZATION TO EMPOWER... THIS DOESN'T RHYME.
NO, IT DOESN'T RHYME. BUT IT WAS SUCCESSFUL.
IN A FEW YEARS, THEY'LL CALL THEIR GROUP ICW, THE INTERNATIONAL COUNCIL OF WOMEN.
CAN'T THEY JUST TAKE A NORMAL VACATION?
1887
NOW, THIS COULD BE BIG! AFTER HAVING BEEN STALLED FOR NINE YEARS, THE WOMEN'S SUFFRAGE AMENDMENT IS FINALLY COMING UP FOR A VOTE IN THE SENATE.
A CONSTITUTIONAL AMENDMENT AT LAST!
THE RIGHT OF CITIZENS TO VOTE SHALL NOT BE ABRIDGED BY THE UNITED STATES OR ANY STATE ON ACCOUNT OF SEX.
ALL IN FAVOR?
16 SENATORS FOR AND 34 AGAINST!
JUST 32 MORE YEARS...
NO VOTE FOR ME! AT LEAST VOLUME THREE IS NOW PART OF HISTORY...

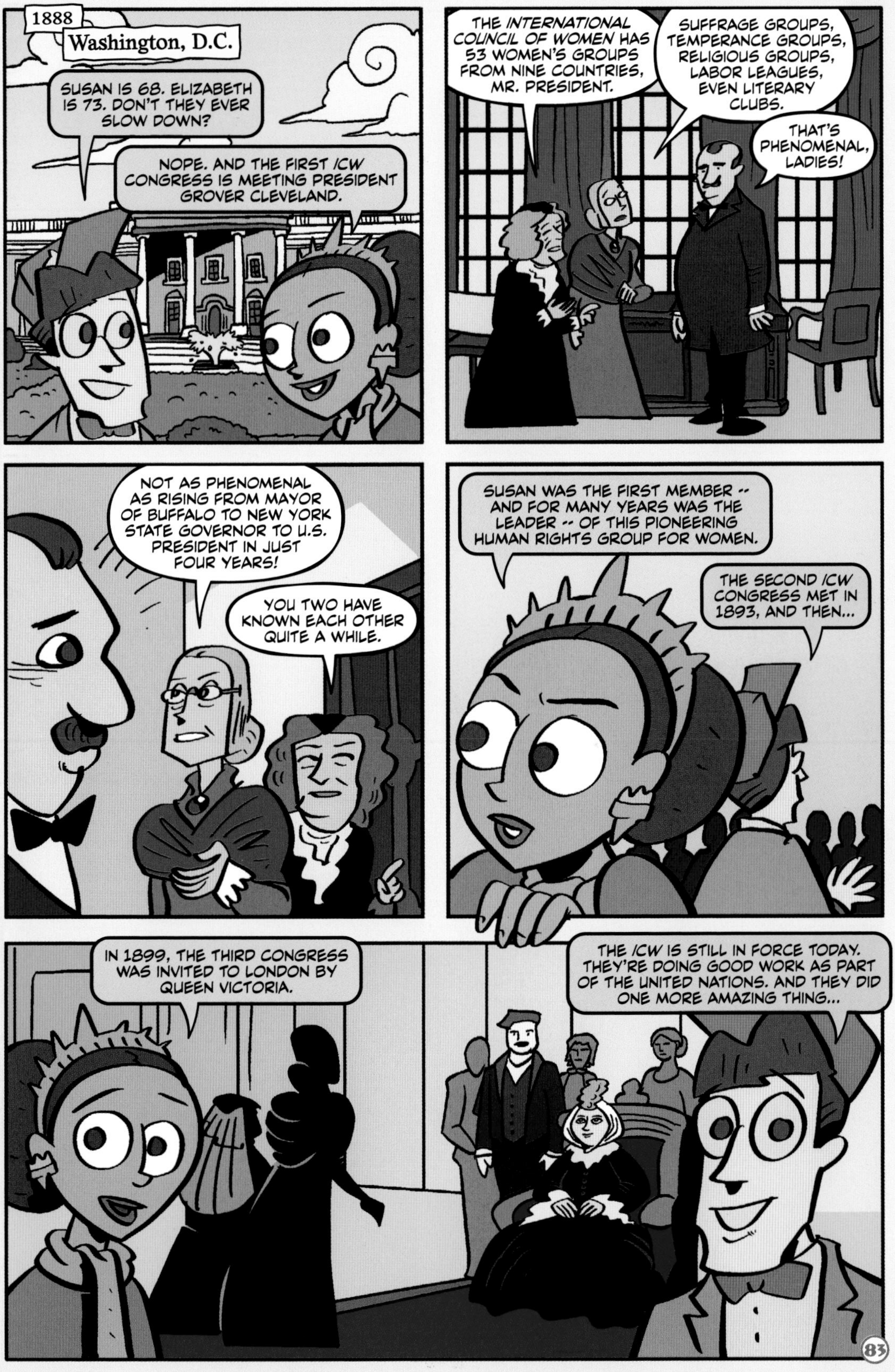
1888
Washington, D.C.
SUSAN IS 68. ELIZABETH IS 73. DON'T THEY EVER SLOW DOWN?
NOPE. AND THE FIRST ICW CONGRESS IS MEETING PRESIDENT GROVER CLEVELAND.
THE INTERNATIONAL COUNCIL OF WOMEN HAS 53 WOMEN'S GROUPS FROM NINE COUNTRIES, MR. PRESIDENT.
SUFFRAGE GROUPS, TEMPERANCE GROUPS, RELIGIOUS GROUPS, LABOR LEAGUES, EVEN LITERARY CLUBS.
THAT'S PHENOMENAL, LADIES!
NOT AS PHENOMENAL AS RISING FROM MAYOR OF BUFFALO TO NEW YORK STATE GOVERNOR TO U.S. PRESIDENT IN JUST FOUR YEARS!
YOU TWO HAVE KNOWN EACH OTHER QUITE A WHILE.
SUSAN WAS THE FIRST MEMBER -- AND FOR MANY YEARS WAS THE LEADER -- OF THIS PIONEERING HUMAN RIGHTS GROUP FOR WOMEN.
THE SECOND ICW CONGRESS MET IN 1893, AND THEN...
IN 1899, THE THIRD CONGRESS WAS INVITED TO LONDON BY QUEEN VICTORIA.
THE ICW IS STILL IN FORCE TODAY. THEY'RE DOING GOOD WORK AS PART OF THE UNITED NATIONS. AND THEY DID ONE MORE AMAZING THING...

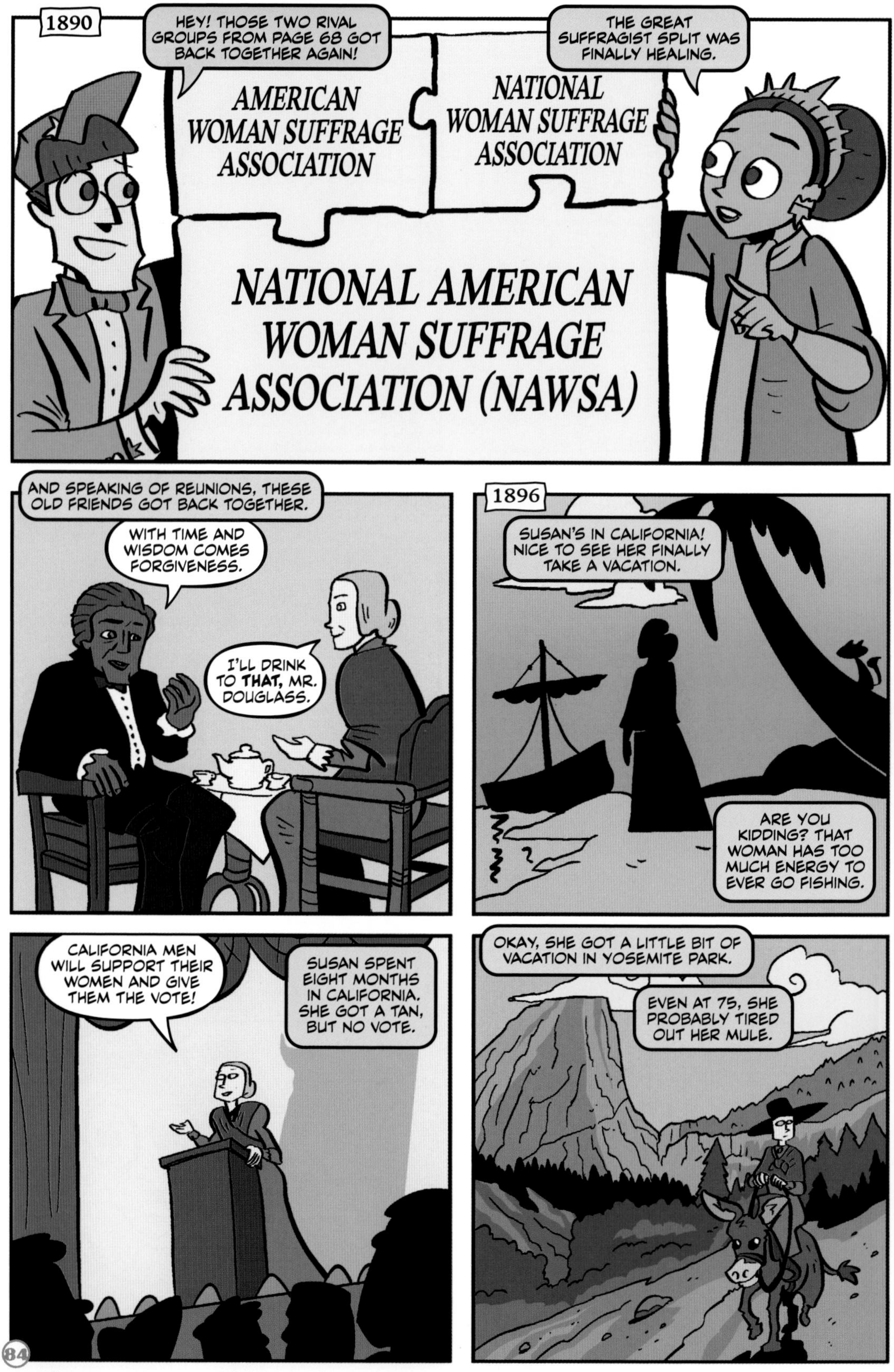
1890
HEY! THOSE TWO RIVAL GROUPS FROM PAGE 68 GOT BACK TOGETHER AGAIN!
THE GREAT SUFFRAGIST SPLIT WAS FINALLY HEALING.
AMERICAN WOMAN SUFFRAGE ASSOCIATION
NATIONAL WOMAN SUFFRAGE ASSOCIATION
NATIONAL AMERICAN WOMAN SUFFRAGE ASSOCIATION (NAWSA)
AND SPEAKING OF REUNIONS, THESE OLD FRIENDS GOT BACK TOGETHER.
WITH TIME AND WISDOM COMES FORGIVENESS.
I'LL DRINK TO THAT, MR. DOUGLASS.
1896
SUSAN'S IN CALIFORNIA! NICE TO SEE HER FINALLY TAKE A VACATION.
ARE YOU KIDDING? THAT WOMAN HAS TOO MUCH ENERGY TO EVER GO FISHING.
CALIFORNIA MEN WILL SUPPORT THEIR WOMEN AND GIVE THEM THE VOTE!
SUSAN SPENT EIGHT MONTHS IN CALIFORNIA. SHE GOT A TAN, BUT NO VOTE.
OKAY, SHE GOT A LITTLE BIT OF VACATION IN YOSEMITE PARK.
EVEN AT 75, SHE PROBABLY TIRED OUT HER MULE.

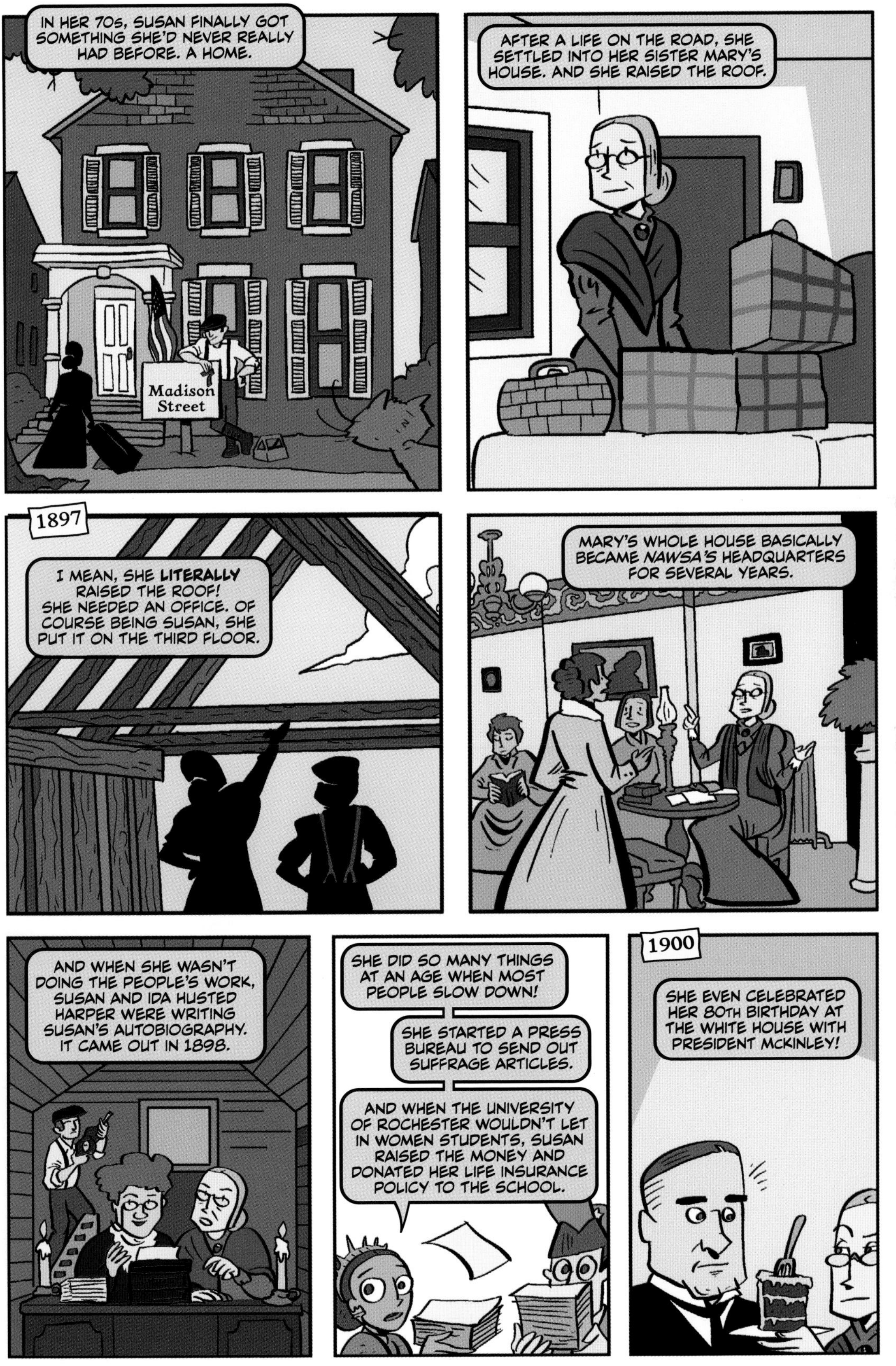
IN HER 70s, SUSAN FINALLY GOT SOMETHING SHE'D NEVER REALLY HAD BEFORE. A HOME.
Madison Street
AFTER A LIFE ON THE ROAD, SHE SETTLED INTO HER SISTER MARY'S HOUSE. AND SHE RAISED THE ROOF.
1897
I MEAN, SHE **LITERALLY** RAISED THE ROOF! SHE NEEDED AN OFFICE. OF COURSE BEING SUSAN, SHE PUT IT ON THE THIRD FLOOR.
MARY'S WHOLE HOUSE BASICALLY BECAME *NAWSA*'S HEADQUARTERS FOR SEVERAL YEARS.
AND WHEN SHE WASN'T DOING THE PEOPLE'S WORK, SUSAN AND IDA HUSTED HARPER WERE WRITING SUSAN'S AUTOBIOGRAPHY. IT CAME OUT IN 1898.
SHE DID SO MANY THINGS AT AN AGE WHEN MOST PEOPLE SLOW DOWN!
SHE STARTED A PRESS BUREAU TO SEND OUT SUFFRAGE ARTICLES.
AND WHEN THE UNIVERSITY OF ROCHESTER WOULDN'T LET IN WOMEN STUDENTS, SUSAN RAISED THE MONEY AND DONATED HER LIFE INSURANCE POLICY TO THE SCHOOL.
1900
SHE EVEN CELEBRATED HER 80TH BIRTHDAY AT THE WHITE HOUSE WITH PRESIDENT MCKINLEY!

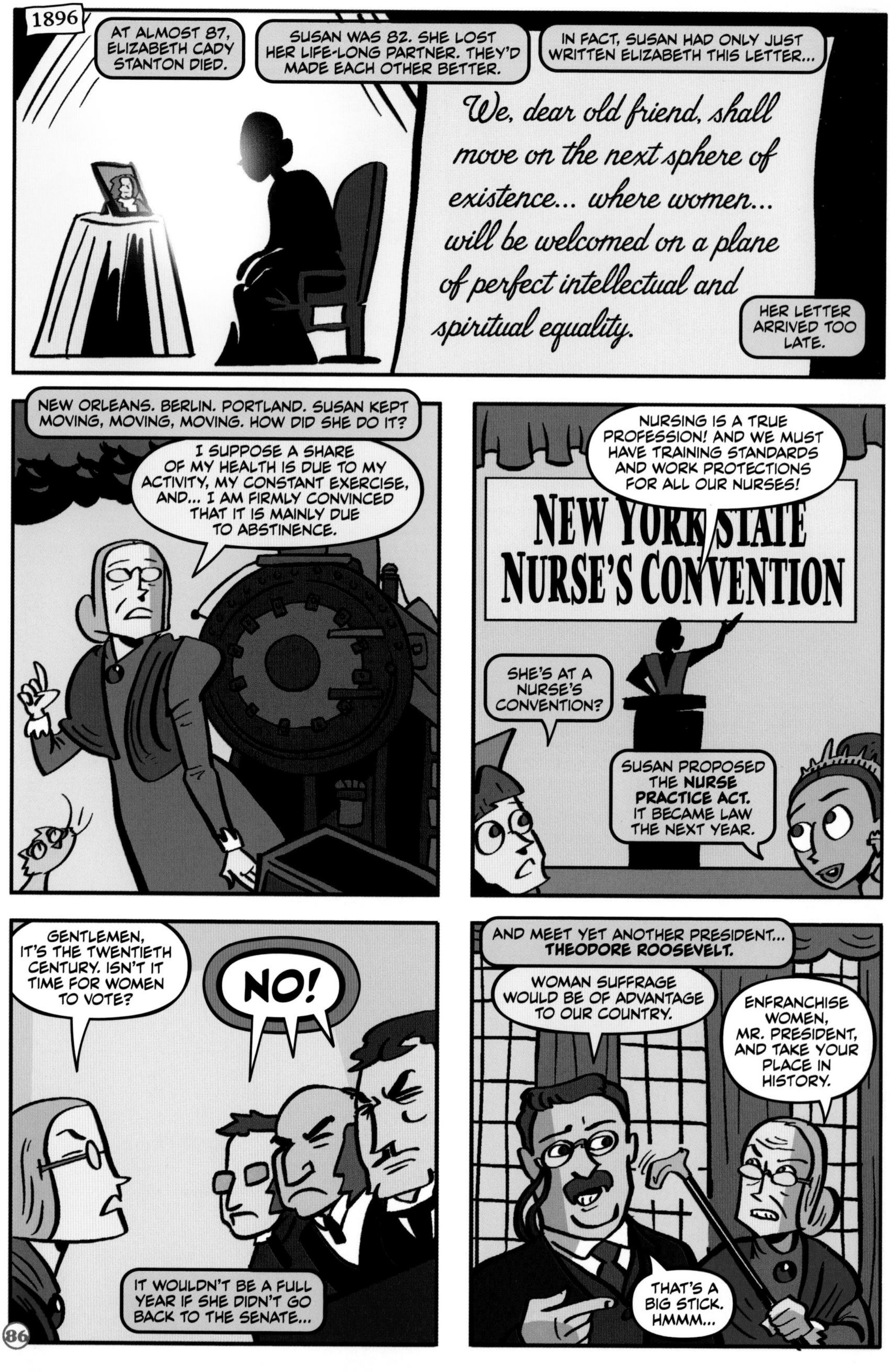
1896
AT ALMOST 87, ELIZABETH CADY STANTON DIED.
SUSAN WAS 82. SHE LOST HER LIFE-LONG PARTNER. THEY'D MADE EACH OTHER BETTER.
IN FACT, SUSAN HAD ONLY JUST WRITTEN ELIZABETH THIS LETTER...
We, dear old friend, shall move on the next sphere of existence... where women... will be welcomed on a plane of perfect intellectual and spiritual equality.
HER LETTER ARRIVED TOO LATE.
NEW ORLEANS. BERLIN. PORTLAND. SUSAN KEPT MOVING, MOVING, MOVING. HOW DID SHE DO IT?
I SUPPOSE A SHARE OF MY HEALTH IS DUE TO MY ACTIVITY, MY CONSTANT EXERCISE, AND... I AM FIRMLY CONVINCED THAT IT IS MAINLY DUE TO ABSTINENCE.
NURSING IS A TRUE PROFESSION! AND WE MUST HAVE TRAINING STANDARDS AND WORK PROTECTIONS FOR ALL OUR NURSES!
NEW YORK STATE NURSE'S CONVENTION
SHE'S AT A NURSE'S CONVENTION?
SUSAN PROPOSED THE **NURSE PRACTICE ACT.** IT BECAME LAW THE NEXT YEAR.
GENTLEMEN, IT'S THE TWENTIETH CENTURY. ISN'T IT TIME FOR WOMEN TO VOTE?
NO!
IT WOULDN'T BE A FULL YEAR IF SHE DIDN'T GO BACK TO THE SENATE...
AND MEET YET ANOTHER PRESIDENT... **THEODORE ROOSEVELT.**
WOMAN SUFFRAGE WOULD BE OF ADVANTAGE TO OUR COUNTRY.
ENFRANCHISE WOMEN, MR. PRESIDENT, AND TAKE YOUR PLACE IN HISTORY.
THAT'S A BIG STICK. HMMM...

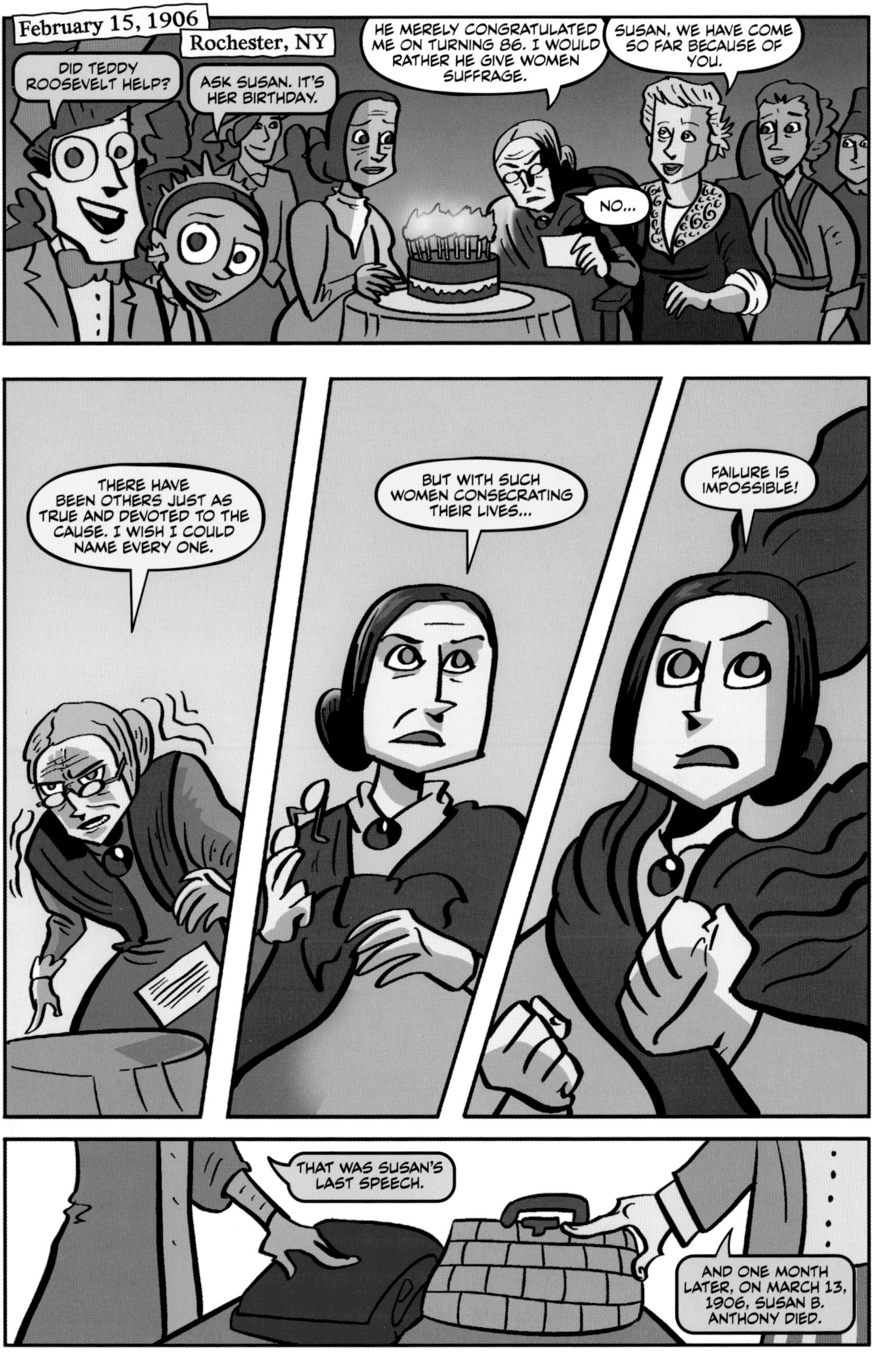
February 15, 1906
Rochester, NY
DID TEDDY ROOSEVELT HELP?
ASK SUSAN. IT'S HER BIRTHDAY.
HE MERELY CONGRATULATED ME ON TURNING 86. I WOULD RATHER HE GIVE WOMEN SUFFRAGE.
SUSAN, WE HAVE COME SO FAR BECAUSE OF YOU.
NO...
THERE HAVE BEEN OTHERS JUST AS TRUE AND DEVOTED TO THE CAUSE. I WISH I COULD NAME EVERY ONE.
BUT WITH SUCH WOMEN CONSECRATING THEIR LIVES...
FAILURE IS IMPOSSIBLE!
THAT WAS SUSAN'S LAST SPEECH.
AND ONE MONTH LATER, ON MARCH 13, 1906, SUSAN B. ANTHONY DIED.

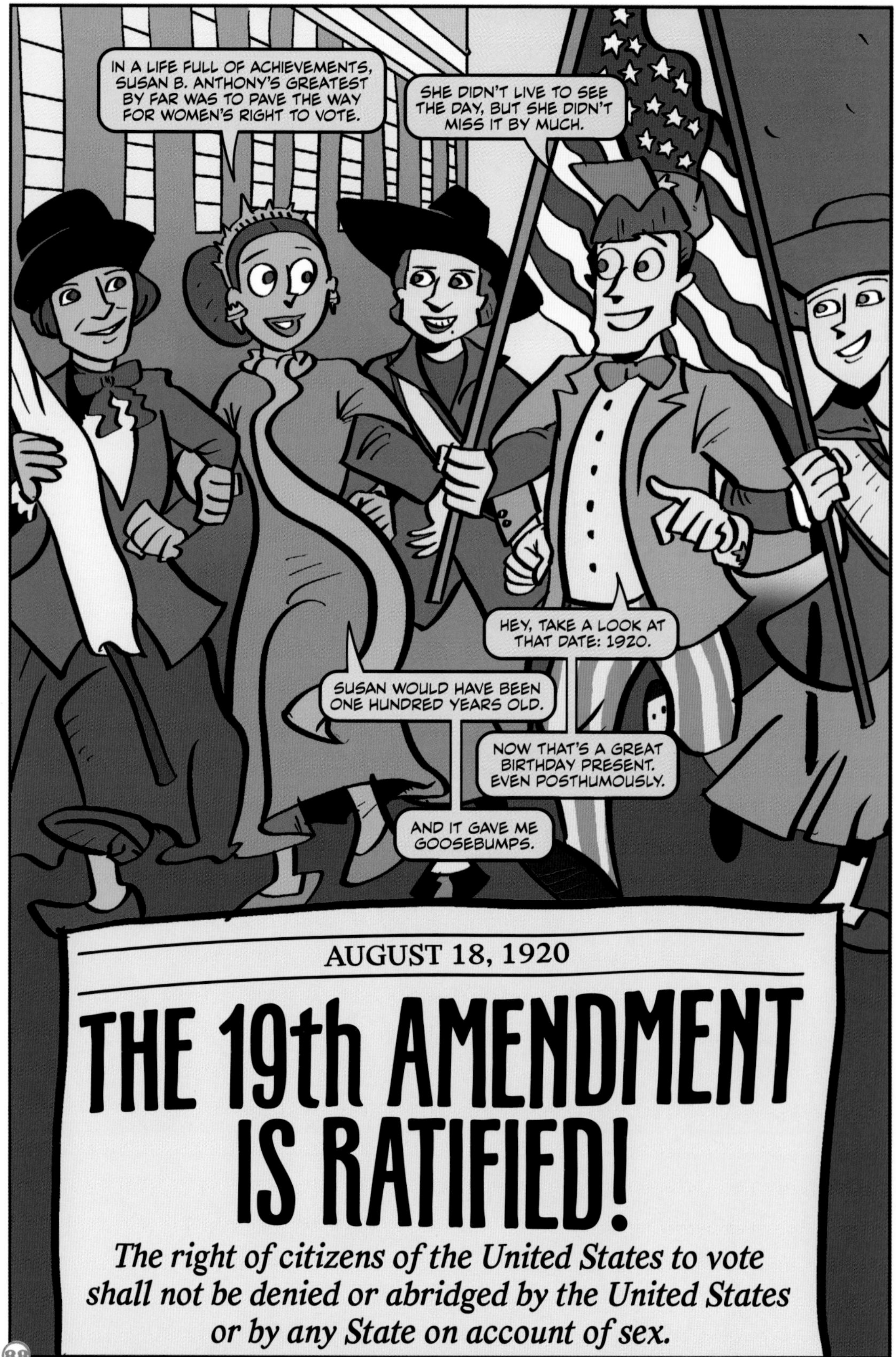
IN A LIFE FULL OF ACHIEVEMENTS, SUSAN B. ANTHONY'S GREATEST BY FAR WAS TO PAVE THE WAY FOR WOMEN'S RIGHT TO VOTE.
SHE DIDN'T LIVE TO SEE THE DAY, BUT SHE DIDN'T MISS IT BY MUCH.
HEY, TAKE A LOOK AT THAT DATE: 1920.
SUSAN WOULD HAVE BEEN ONE HUNDRED YEARS OLD.
NOW THAT'S A GREAT BIRTHDAY PRESENT. EVEN POSTHUMOUSLY.
AND IT GAVE ME GOOSEBUMPS.
AUGUST 18, 1920
THE 19th AMENDMENT IS RATIFIED!
The right of citizens of the United States to vote shall not be denied or abridged by the United States or by any State on account of sex.

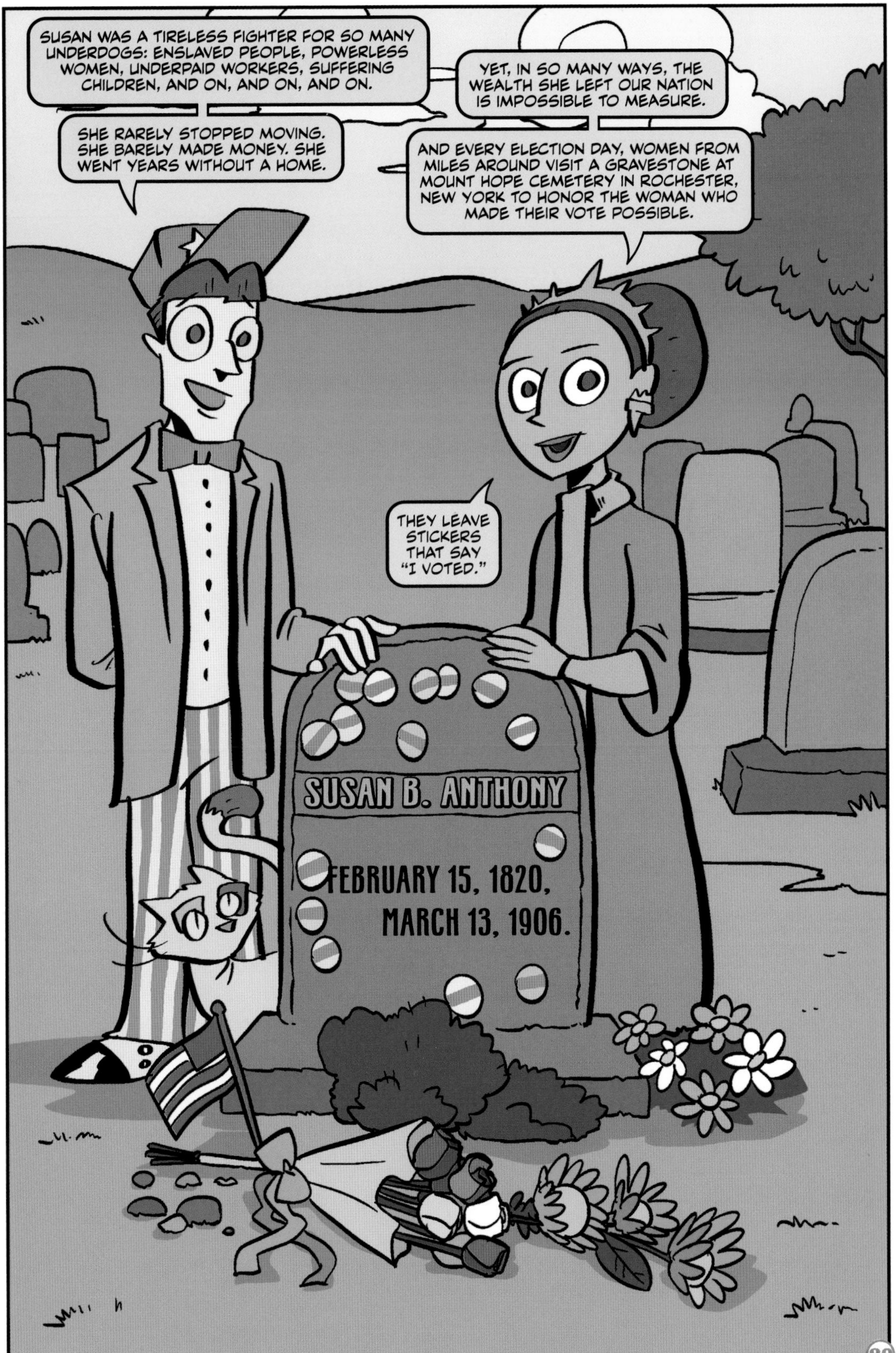
SUSAN WAS A TIRELESS FIGHTER FOR SO MANY UNDERDOGS: ENSLAVED PEOPLE, POWERLESS WOMEN, UNDERPAID WORKERS, SUFFERING CHILDREN, AND ON, AND ON, AND ON.
SHE RARELY STOPPED MOVING. SHE BARELY MADE MONEY. SHE WENT YEARS WITHOUT A HOME.
YET, IN SO MANY WAYS, THE WEALTH SHE LEFT OUR NATION IS IMPOSSIBLE TO MEASURE.
AND EVERY ELECTION DAY, WOMEN FROM MILES AROUND VISIT A GRAVESTONE AT MOUNT HOPE CEMETERY IN ROCHESTER, NEW YORK TO HONOR THE WOMAN WHO MADE THEIR VOTE POSSIBLE.
THEY LEAVE STICKERS THAT SAY "I VOTED."
SUSAN B. ANTHONY
FEBRUARY 15, 1820,
MARCH 13, 1906.

# GLOSSARY

**13TH AMENDMENT:** An addition to the **U.S. Constitution** primarily forbidding slavery.

**14TH AMENDMENT:** An addition to the **U.S. Constitution** primarily granting citizenship to anyone born in the United States, especially slaves.

**15TH AMENDMENT:** An addition to the **U.S. Constitution** primarily granting African American men the right to vote.

**ACTIVIST:** A person who agitates for a cause.

**AGITATE:** Seek the rights of a person or group by using campaigns, demonstrations, and protests.

**BLOOMERS:** Long loose-fitting women's underwear, worn in the 19th century.

**CANVASS:** To communicate with people in order to get them to vote a certain way.

**CONSORTIUM:** An association of several groups working together.

**DRED SCOTT DECISION:** A controversial 1850 Supreme Court decision that forbid the U.S. government from abolishing slavery.

**EMANCIPATION:** Freedom from slavery.

**ENFRANCHISE:** To give a group voting rights (To disenfranchise is to withhold voting rights).

**QUAKERS:** A humanist Christian group dedicated to peace, equality, and simplicity. Also known as the *Society of Friends.*

**SUFFRAGE:** The right to vote in elections.

**TEMPERANCE:** The act of not drinking alcohol.

**TUBERCULOSIS:** A possibly deadly lung disease caused by bacteria, which is curable today.

**UNDERGROUND RAILROAD:** A secret group of people who helped slaves escape to freedom.

# 19TH CENTURY U.S. WOMEN'S RIGHTS LEADERS

**LUCRETIA MOTT (1793-1880):** An abolitionist who became a mentor to Elizabeth Cady Stanton. Together they organized the pioneering 1848 Seneca Falls Women's Rights Convention which Susan missed, but her parents didn't.

**LUCY STONE (1818-1893):** The first woman to earn a college degree in Massachusetts, Lucy co-founded the *American Woman Suffrage Association*, the **Woman's Journal** newspaper, and was among the first women in the U.S. not to change her name after marriage.

**CARRIE CHAPMAN CATT (1860-1947):** Founder of the *League of Women Voters* and the *International Alliance of Women*, she led the final, successful charge by "an army of voteless women" for the **19th Amendment**.

**ANNA HOWARD SHAW (1847-1919):** She was both a physician and a Methodist minister at a time when women were rarely either. Anna worked alongside Susan B. for temperance, then was key in merging the *American* and *National Woman Suffrage Associations* in 1890.

**JULIA WARD HOWE (1819-1910):** Her "Battle Hymn of the Republic" was a popular Civil War tune. She co-founded the *AWSA* with Lucy Stone and edited the suffragist **Woman's Journal**. Howe also led the first efforts to establish Mother's Day.

**ALICE PAUL (1885-1977):** A primary strategist and activist for the **19th Amendment**, she organized rallies and marches; later, she led the *National Woman's Party*, a primary driver for the (still not ratified) **Equal Rights Amendment.**

**JEANETTE RANKIN (1880-1973):** The first woman elected to U.S. federal office, as a representative from Montana in 1916. Re-elected in 1940, the pacifist Rankin was the only House member to vote against war with Japan in December 1941.

**VICTORIA WOODHULL (1838-1927):** Ran for U.S. president in 1872, but lost. A sensationalist newspaper owner, and also a stockbroker; she was an advocate of a woman's right to marry, divorce, and bear children without restrictions.

# SUSAN B. ANTHONY TIMELINE

**1820** Susan B. Anthony is born to Daniel and Lucy Anthony on February 15 in Adams, Massachusetts.

**1826** The Anthony family moves to Battenville, New York; her father runs a cotton mill.

**1838** The mill goes bankrupt, she leaves her Quaker boarding school, they lose their home.

**1845** The family moves to a farm in Rochester, NY; they begin holding temperance and anti-slavery meetings which include Frederick Douglass.

**1846** At 26, hired as headmistress of a boarding school in Canajoharie, NY.

**1849** Gives her first speech, at a *Daughters of Temperance* supper in Rochester.

**1851** At an anti-slavery convention, she meets Elizabeth Cady Stanton, her lifelong friend.

**1852** Attends *Brothers of Temperance* convention, is forbidden from speaking, and so creates the parallel *Sisters of Temperance*.

**1856** Promotes married women's property rights and woman suffrage all across New York State. She becomes the New York State agent for the *American Anti-Slavery Society*.

**1861-1865** Spends the Civil War advocating for abolition.

**1866** At the *American Equal Rights Association* they founded, Anthony and Frederick Douglass debate whether suffrage for black men should occur before or along with women. This causes a rupture in their alliance, which lasts many years. She and Stanton begin the *National Woman Suffrage Association*.

**1868** With Stanton, begins publishing *The Revolution*, a suffragist newspaper.

**1872** Arrested for voting in the presidential election.

**1873** Tried and convicted of Voting While Female. She refuses to pay the $100 fine. The judge denies her a chance to appeal to a higher court by not imprisoning her.

**1881-1902** Anthony, Stanton, and others publish the *History of Woman Suffrage, Volumes I-IV*.

**1888** Co-founds the *International Council of Women*, a consortium of 50+ women's groups from nine countries, which is still in operation in conjunction with the United Nations.

| 1891 | Moves in with sister Mary in Rochester; Susan's first actual home in decades. The house becomes the unofficial headquarters of the national women's suffrage movement. |
| 1898-1900 | Publishes autobiography, meets President McKinley and Queen Victoria, and travels widely in pursuit of suffrage. |
| 1902 | Stanton dies; Anthony advocates for standardized nurse training, which becomes law. |
| 1905 | Meets with President Theodore Roosevelt in Washington, D.C., and the Senate yet again, to get the women's vote. |
| 1906 | Attends suffrage hearings in Washington, D.C. Gives her "Failure is Impossible" speech at her 86th birthday celebration. She dies at her Madison Street home on March 13. |
| 1920 | The **19th Amendment** gives U.S. women 21 and over the right to vote. Many call it the "Susan B. Anthony Amendment." |

# FIND OUT MORE

## BOOKS

Colman, Penny. *Elizabeth Cady Stanton and Susan B. Anthony: A Friendship That Changed the World.* New York: Henry Holt and Co., 2011.

Pollack, Pam & Belviso, Meg. *Who Was Susan B. Anthony?* Who Was? series. New York: Penguin Group, 2014.

Robbins, Dean. *Two Friends: Susan B. Anthony and Frederick Douglass.* New York: Orchard Books, 2016.

Sherr, Lynn. *Failure Is Impossible: Susan B. Anthony in Her Own Words.* New York: Times Books, 1996.

Stone, Tanya Lee. *Elizabeth Leads the Way: Elizabeth Cady Stanton and the Right to Vote.* New York: Henry Holt and Co., 2008.

## WEBSITES

The National Susan B. Anthony Museum and House, Rochester, New York
www.SusanB.org

The National Women's History Museum, Washington, D.C.
www.WomensHistory.org

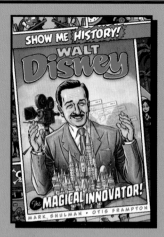

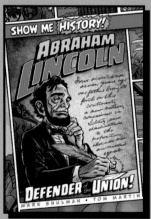

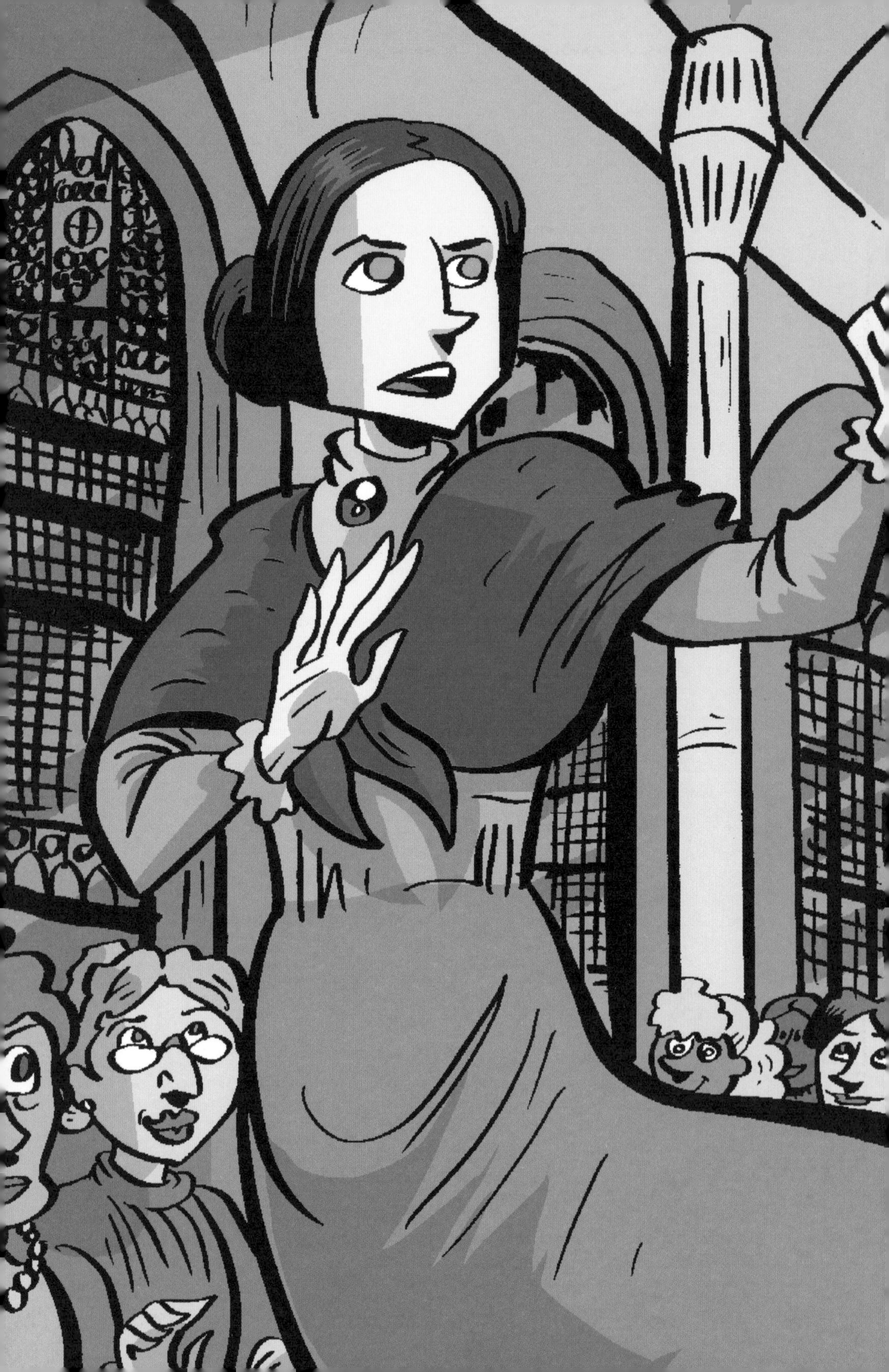